THE GREATEST SPECIAL OPS STORIES EVER TOLD

EDITED BY TOM MCCARTHY

Guilford, Connecticut

An imprint of Rowman & Littlefield

Distributed by NATIONAL BOOK NETWORK

British Library Cataloguing in Publication Information Available

Library of Congress Cataloging-in-Publication Data

The greatest special ops stories ever told / edited by Tom McCarthy.
   pages cm
  Includes bibliographical references.
  ISBN 978-1-4930-1859-8 (pbk.) — ISBN 978-1-4930-2207-6 (e-book)
  1. Special operations (Military science)—United States—History. 2. Battles—United States—History. I. McCarthy, Tom, editor.
  U262.G74 2016
  356'.160973—dc23

                                   2015034746

∞™ The paper used in this publication meets the minimum requirements of American National Standard for Information Sciences—Permanence of Paper for Printed Library Materials, ANSI/NISO Z39.48-1992.

Contents

Contents

INTRODUCTION

SURPRISE, SPEED, AND, MORE OFTEN THAN NOT, VIOLENCE.

It is not the long-term campaigns planned meticulously long ahead of time by armchair commandos in their safe, clean offices that win wars. More often, victory comes from catching the enemy off guard, wreaking havoc, and injecting a healthy dose of fear of the unknown.

That's been known for as long as people have been fighting. Goliath was not expecting the puny David to have a sling and a large rock, after all. He was caught off guard and paid the price for it.

Military theorists have been positing and championing special operations for thousands of years. Two well-known leaders who fought thousands of years apart and on widely different battlefields share many of the same thoughts.

Carl von Clausewitz, the Prussian general whose *On War* is still studied today, some three hundred years later, wrote, "The backbone of surprise is fusing speed with secrecy."

Take what he wrote about a battle won by his mentor, Frederick the Great:

> *It is the same with the battle of Liegnitz, 1760. Frederick the Great gained this fine victory through altering during the night a position which he had just before taken up. Laudon was through this completely surprised, and lost 70 pieces of artillery and 10,000 men. Although Frederick the Great had at this time adopted the principle of moving backwards and forwards in order to make a battle impossible, or at least to disconcert the enemy's plans, still the alteration of position on the night of the 14–15 was not made exactly with that intention, but as the King himself says, because the position of the 14th did not*

please him. Here, therefore, also chance was hard at work; without this happy conjunction of the attack and the change of position in the night, and the difficult nature of the country, the result would not have been the same.

Von Clausewitz, not a man who was penurious about sharing his thoughts, added this:

The moral effects which attend a surprise often convert the worst case into a good one for the side they favour, and do not allow the other to make any regular determination.

Sun Tzu, the Chinese strategist and philosopher who fought thousands of years before von Clausewitz, wrote, "Let your plans be dark and impenetrable as night, and when you move, fall like a thunderbolt."

In his influential *The Art of War,* Sun Tzu made his point in a way that is most apt for the stories in this collection:

All warfare is based on deception. Hence, when we are able to attack, we must seem unable; when using our forces, we must appear inactive; when we are near, we must make the enemy believe we are far away; when far away, we must make him believe we are near.

The stories here cover fighting and special operations from the French and Indian War to recent fights in Afghanistan. They show clearly that heroics and indifference to danger do not reside in only one special group of soldiers or in one war. The men in these stories, whether a new recruit marching with Rogers' Rangers in upstate New York or Navy SEALs on a lonely ridge in Afghanistan, have a great deal in common.

The dictionary definition, in many ways tepid in capturing what special operations are all about, says this:

Special operations (S.O.) are military operations that are considered "special" (that is, unconventional), usually carried out by dedicated special forces units. Special operations are performed independently or in conjunction with conventional military operations. The primary goal is to achieve a political or military objective where a conventional force requirement does not exist or might adversely affect the overall strategic outcome. Special operations are usually conducted in a low-profile manner that aims to achieve the advantages of speed and surprise of action against an unsuspecting target. Special ops are typically carried out with limited numbers of highly trained personnel that are able to operate in all environments, utilize self-reliance, easily adapt to and overcome obstacles, and use unconventional combat skills and equipment to complete objectives. Special operations are usually implemented through specific, tailored intelligence.

That's accurate, I suppose, but only to a degree. The definition fails to convey the grit and visceral energy and calm confidence that the men in these pages so ably illustrate. It's a book definition, but it's not a comprehensive definition.

For that you must read this book.

What is the common thread that draws together a team of snipers in Vietnam and a young Confederate naval officer who took it on himself to disrupt Union shipping and commerce along the Northeast coast? What compels a young man to say good-bye to the comforts of home and take up with rebel guerilla William Clarke Quantrill? What qualities do strategists look for when they are selecting a team to jump into hostile North Korea? Inner strength and unimpeachable belief in what they are doing might be two common elements. Disregard for life, their own and others, could be another thread.

Is there much difference in attitude between the two speakers below?

Here is what Cole Younger said of one raid he participated in with the notorious Quantrill:

We struck their camp at sunset. We were thirty-two; they eighty-four; but we were sure shots and one volley broke their ranks in utter confusion. Five fell at the first fire, and seven more died in the chase, the others regaining Independence, where the presence of the rest of the regiment saved them. That day my persistent pistol practice showed its worth when one of the militiamen fell, 71 yards away, actual measure.

Here is what heroic SEAL Marcus Luttrell wrote about the fight with the Taliban in the brutal and stark Hindu Kush more than 140 years later:

Neither of us saw him in time to return fire. I just said a quick prayer and stared back at him. Which was precisely when Axe banged two bullets right between his eyes, killed that tribesman stone dead instantly. I didn't have time to thank him, because the grenades were still coming in, and I just kept trying to drag Danny to safety. And like Axe, Danny kept firing.

The stories in this volume span more than 250 years. They celebrate men who walked through frozen forests on primitive snowshoes looking for the enemy and others who used modern communications to track down and kill an enemy, and report the result back to headquarters miles away.

Here you will read of a desperate crew of Confederate commerce raiders that literally threw everything but the kitchen sink at the approaching enemy and how a team trapped in North Korea found their way back to safety—and volunteered to go back again.

What drove these men? Civil War raiders and the SEALs who "walked small" and barefoot in the thick and steamy jungles of the Vietnam delta, miles from even the thinnest of hope that help was near if they failed? Was there anything different about US Marine snipers on a special mission and Civil War guerrillas who rode with the Gray Ghost?

No, I would say; just time and technology. The hearts and attitudes of the men you will read about here were the same.

These are special men, whose single passion led them to do extraordinary things under extraordinary and often lethal circumstances.

We all could learn from them.

Snipers, Brothers

Gina Cavallaro with Matt Larsen

THE DAY CPL. NEAL BRACE KILLED A MAN BECAME A PERSONAL TURN-
ing point for him and a source of amusement for the rest of his team,
Marine scout snipers who didn't think he had it in him.

It happened on a blazing hot morning in May 2008 in Afghanistan's
Helmand province a few days into the first major U.S. offensive in the
seven years since the Marines were first there. But it would be a fleeting
moment of levity for the team of scout snipers because no one knew that
only thirteen days later a tragedy would unfold against an enemy unlike
any they'd seen in Iraq.

Brace and the Marines from First Battalion, Sixth Marines, the battalion landing team for the Twenty-fourth Marine Expeditionary Unit,
were part of a force of more than three thousand Marines who streamed
into the Taliban stronghold to help NATO and Afghan forces take control of the lawless area.

The 1-6 Marines had deployed from their home at Camp Lejeune,
North Carolina, almost two months earlier and were deep inside Taliban
country with practically no training relevant to the Afghanistan mission.

In fact, they weren't even expecting to go to Afghanistan. They were
preparing for, perhaps dreaming of, a standard six-month Mediterranean
float, just as Marine units had done before the war, with glamorous ports
of call in places like Spain, Portugal, and Italy. The Marine Corps has
Marine expeditionary units around the world at any time in order to be
prepared wherever there is trouble. While they were at sea doing general
training, they got word that they'd be going to Afghanistan.

"We were all looking forward to it," said Brace, who had one deployment to Iraq under his belt when, in January 2008, Defense Secretary Robert Gates announced the March deployment of the Marines to Afghanistan for the first time since their 2001 trip there. "We were totally pumped up about going to Europe, but we realized it was absolutely insane to hope for that."

The region they went to in Afghanistan was dangerous and largely unchecked by coalition troops who were already stretched thin. Blanketed with poppy fields and crawling with fighters who were ready to take on the Americans and their coalition counterparts, the province belonged to the Taliban, which had had plenty of time to build up the battle space to its own advantage.

The Marines, many of whom were on their first deployment to Afghanistan, stumbled upon fighting positions that appeared to be old Russian outposts and random giant mounds of dirt in the middle of villages that had fighting holes on all sides. There were steel-reinforced bunkers, slits in the hillsides that ballooned into giant hiding spaces behind the outer earthen walls, and land mines. There were irrigation trenches with hollowed-out passages that led to underground bunkers in the middle of a field. When flooded with water, the trenches gave no clue of the bunkers' presence.

"The thing with Afghanistan was, they knew we were coming, they were fortified. Everything you can think of is made for warfare," said Cpl. Joel Alvarenga, a fellow sniper in the Weapons Company's surveillance and target acquisition, or STA (pronounced "stay"), platoon. Alvarenga had been to Iraq twice and wasn't sure he was ready or prepared for the rigors of the Afghan fight. "It's hot, you gotta hump everywhere. I'm pretty fit, but they told us we were going into mountains, too, so I thought it was going to be a lot of hiking. I lost thirty pounds in a month."

Their team, led by Sgt. Justin Cooper, was supporting A Company and was paired with another team for one of their first missions that the sniper team leaders developed to catch Taliban reinforcements traveling in from the west for the fight.

The twelve snipers and their Navy corpsman moved out from A Company's patrol base in the southernmost corner of Garmsir in a grueling overnight trek. They were loaded down with more than 150 pounds of equipment each, fighting heat and dehydration as they tried to find the quickest route to their destination west toward the Helmand River.

The route they took didn't end up being that quick, and at least one person fell out from exhaustion as they navigated through a swamp. They circled it twice and came across wadis and other rugged terrain that was infinitely more challenging on the ground than it looked on the map.

Their journey ended at a farming area, a cluster of individual walled compounds laid out in traditional Afghan style, an outgrowth of a war-torn land where every home is a fortress complete with fortified walls and gates. Each had several abandoned buildings that had a good number of windows and doors from which to get eyes on all approaches and shoot if they saw anything. The location was dangerously remote for the two teams, and a quick reaction force would have taken some time to arrive if the snipers were compromised. Still, they were imbued with the confidence and spirit of young men going out to prove themselves in combat—and they were heavily armed.

Each team had two M40A3 bolt-action sniper rifles—one of the best combat weapons ever devised and battle-proven in Iraq and Afghanistan—two MK11 semiautomatic sniper rifles, and a Barrett SASR .50-caliber rifle, plus two M249 squad automatic weapons, M4s, M16s, and M203 grenade launchers.

They settled into one of the mud brick compounds, splitting the two teams into separate buildings that each had five or six good shooting ports.

The landscape was a combination of fertile soil, tree orchards, and acres of poppy fields that fed the bulk of Afghanistan's lucrative opium trade and fueled the Taliban. The village was abandoned because its residents had moved out in anticipation of the arrival of the Marines, warned that there would surely be gun battles or worse.

It didn't seem possible to the teams that the area had truly been vacated, but emptiness was exactly what they found. "We were in this one-hundred-yard by one-hundred-yard compound in the middle of nowhere, and the closest compound to ours was four hundred yards away," Brace said. "There was no way anyone was going to see us or hear us."

It was desolate and quiet at 6 a.m. on May 6, and the temperature in the sunbaked Helmand Valley was creeping up toward one hundred degrees.

The unusually large group of snipers got as comfortable as they could in their spacious hide sites and tried to stay cool. The shooters sat on chairs or blocks with their weapons resting on the windowsills, scanning the vast open farmland for activity that never surfaced in the other empty compounds.

They placed canvas tarps overhead in the courtyards and doorways, but the tarps didn't do much to keep the heat at bay.

The first two guys on security in one building were Alvarenga, a battle-hardened sniper with a list of daring capers and kills he had racked up in Iraq, and Brace, an inexperienced sniper with one deployment to Iraq who was on the team more for his skills as a radio operator than as a reliable shooter.

After three years in the Marine Corps, Brace had only fired the .50-caliber rifle in training, and his reputation for having fired a warning shot at a pair of young, armed kids in Iraq instead of shooting to kill didn't help. He didn't fit the classic mold of a Marine, much less a killer, among his young and gritty enlisted teammates.

He didn't drink, spit, smoke, party, or curse, had no exploits with women to brag about, was careful with his money, reflective in thought, and while the other Marines were lifting weights at the gym in Afghanistan, Brace was off to the side doing calisthenics exercises.

Some Marines called him the church kid.

Physically, he was slender and fair-skinned, with smart blue eyes and a neat, steady way of carrying himself that screamed bookworm more than leatherneck. He could be unctuous, and he asked people questions that made them suspicious. "I honestly think they thought I was gay, and people actually asked me if I was in the criminal investigation division because of the way I interact with people," he said. "I just rubbed people the wrong way, and they didn't think I was a killer."

But Brace, who had joined the Marines with the intention of becoming an officer and later changed his mind for a host of reasons, held his own in his own way.

He regularly scored the maximum three hundred points on his physical fitness tests, led other Marines in physical training, and he knew his job exceptionally well, which put him beyond reproach as an asset for the team. Plus, he was better than anyone on the radio, and at least one Marine, a visionary platoon sergeant, saw Brace's value and potential, which would be revealed as he took on an important role in the days after the mission at the abandoned village.

Still, on that mission, in the middle of nowhere with eleven other snipers, Brace said, "nobody was expecting me to shoot."

From one vantage point in the house, the snipers could see about one hundred yards of what looked like a main path that intersected with a couple of other trails, and they began to spot men walking down those trails to the main path as well as those trying to be sneakier, who were crossing through a grove of trees before taking the main path. The men were dressed in robes and sometimes in uniform. They were all armed, and they had no idea that the Americans were watching them.

The first one came into view about an hour after the snipers set up in the house. Scanning the blindingly bright landscape with his 40-power scope, Cooper saw a lone man armed with an AK-47 assault rifle.

"Coop's like, 'I'd say that's a positive ID for enemy combatant,' and he shoots the guy with one shot, and the guy's dead," Brace said, recalling Cooper's words and his own reaction to the swift kill. "I was like, okay, this is our first mission. We've only been here an hour, and we've already killed a guy. This is interesting."

Another ninety minutes went by, and another armed man walked into the line of sight coming down the same trail in the opposite direction. He was bloodied and dazed for some reason, but his weapon made him a legitimate target so another Marine shot and killed him, too.

And on it went.

Less than an hour after the second armed man showed up on the trail, three men carrying AK-47s and RPK light machine guns came walking down the same trail. "Two rounds, two guys dead. One more round, one more guy's dead. So we've got five guys dead, and forty-five minutes later, Al and Coop kill another guy walking down the same trail," Brace said, referring to Alvarenga and Cooper by their nicknames.

"It was the total opposite of what we expected. There were just all these guys walking with guns. Every single one was a bona fide target, and they had no idea we were there," said Brace, who after five hours on the farm was now taking his turn on the .50-cal. It was dialed in for 760 yards when he and Cooper saw a man walking with a bicycle loaded down with weapons.

Coop fired, Brace fired, and the ball of dust from the .50 cal obscured Brace's view. Alvarenga saw the shot. "He looked right at me, and he's like 'Holy shit, Brace you just killed a guy!'" It was the first man he'd killed, and his reaction came from the gut.

"I started laughing, kind of like, I couldn't believe how easy it was, it was stupid. They told me to shut the hell up, but then they started laughing too," he recalled. "They're like, 'Brace, you're the guy we've been making fun of for two years now, and you just killed a guy with a .50-cal sniper rifle and you're laughing about it.' Then ten minutes later I killed another guy, and I guess it was just kind of overwhelming."

Over ten long hours in the heat of Afghanistan's southern plains, the team would kill twelve armed men who walked down that trail. Because of its isolation, the snipers' hide site, which they had now named the "reaper farm," would have been a haul for reinforcements to show up if things went south, but things had gone exceptionally well, and they were satisfied with the success of their dangerous mission. It proved to their commander that they could operate effectively for the company, and they got to plan more missions after that.

But the reaper farm mission would pale in comparison to a short, tragic battle some of them would witness on May 19.

Cooper was an influential man, a six-foot-tall people magnet from a small town in Mississippi with a natural way of bringing others along. His searching eyes, sensual good looks, and confidence were at once loathed and admired, and he inspired loyalty by being fair and keeping promises.

Nobody thought he was perfect, but he was perfect for them. He was capable and bold. His superb technical skills and personal instincts as a sniper were emulated and occasionally equaled by others on the team. He helped others get better by spending the time to share his knowledge, sitting and talking one-on-one. In the way he carried himself and showed faith in others, he taught simple, intangible things, like how to survive as a team in a life-and-death setting most Americans never see.

His acceptance of an unusual Marine like Brace was an example to everyone, though Brace never imagined himself hanging out with a guy like Cooper, whom Brace described as an "alpha dog" who did every rowdy, raunchy, rugged thing young men did to embody the image of a rock-hard Marine, pushing the limits and getting away with behavior that other Marines got in trouble for.

"He was a rascal, and I would call him somewhat of a pirate. He probably didn't like me as a person, but I couldn't tell because he would task me with things and I'd get them done and he was happy with that," said Brace, who also recalled Cooper's ability at the young age of twenty-two to understand and manage a group dynamic.

"He would not side with one group against another and say, 'You guys are all wrong, shut up, I'm the leader, you're done.' It was like the best possible form of mini-democracy I've ever had. Coop would listen to me. He'd listen to other people. He was just a good leader."

On May 19 Cooper was killed while deviating from his sniper mission to help a platoon that was pinned down in a fight. It was a dark day for the team.

His Marines hung their heads in sorrow, grief, and anger and forced themselves to move on without him for the five months they had left in their deployment. The faces of the Marines pictured around a shrine to him at his memorial service in the war zone show defiance, sadness, and regret, a hard resolve to accept the unacceptable.

Cooper's death was an especially heavy loss for Alvarenga, who saw their friendship as something beyond what he'd ever known. "He was like a brother. My brothers are my brothers," Alvarenga said, "but I've never been that close to anybody."

At boot camp on Parris Island in January 2005, Cooper and Alvarenga were in separate platoons, but they became fast friends during Infantry School at Camp Lejeune and deployed together almost immediately because their names began with letters at the top of the alphabet and that was how the Marine Corps chose the first thirty-seven in the class.

"They stopped at G," said Alvarenga, the son of Salvadoran immigrants who put three years of college aside and enlisted after learning of the death of a high school friend, a Marine he'd seen only weeks earlier whose descriptions of the war stirred something inside.

The friend, Cpl. Binh Le, was Vietnamese. He had been raised by an aunt and uncle in Virginia since the age of six and received his U.S. citizenship posthumously. A suicidal jihadist driving a car packed with explosives killed Le and another Marine, Cpl. Matthew Wyatt, on December 3, 2004. Three weeks later, Alvarenga drove to a Marine Corps recruiting station and signed up to honor his friend's sacrifice.

By August 2005, he and his new friend Cooper were on the streets of Ramadi, going on patrols and getting their feet wet on what would be the first of two deployments there. They became a pair to reckon with.

At home, the two were inseparable, protecting and defending one another, looking out for each other's girlfriends and forging such a trustful bond that they even anticipated one another's thoughts, decisions, and next moves.

"Coop was a badass, very confident. I'm the same way, but I know my limits. I don't think he knew his limits at times, and that's why he had me around. That's why we were on the same team because nobody could ever talk to him like I could talk to him," Alvarenga said. "I felt like if anybody messed with him, I was going to beat 'em up."

Cooper felt the same way about Alvarenga and actually did beat someone up outside a bar one time, another Marine who went to the bar management with a complaint about Alvarenga.

In the war zone, they honed their knowledge and got smart about sniping together.

Neither Marine was trained in the coveted courses at the prestigious Marine Corps Scout Sniper School, which is not uncommon for Marine snipers who often are chosen for abilities that look good on paper and then are trained by the team.

Alvarenga and Cooper learned their jobs on the go from their platoon sergeant, a Marine they considered a guru in the art of sniping.

"He's the best sniper I've ever met. He's a master, he's a teacher, and he taught us well. He passed on a lot of knowledge to Coop and me,"

Alvarenga said of his mentor, a staff sergeant who did not wish to be identified in print. The sergeant would also bring Brace into the fold of the team when Brace arrived for the team's second Iraq deployment in 2006.

The platoon sergeant, a thoughtful, measured man with a soft-spoken demeanor and a healthy suspicion of outsiders, taught his young Marines what to look for, how to spot the small things a sniper needs to detect the enemy, like a reflection on a little piece of glass, things that seem out of place, and shapes or materials that don't belong in the environment. He taught them how to conceal their outlines in a hide site, how to move at night, how to choose the right equipment for a mission, how to lighten their loads by learning to leave behind what they could live without.

They learned how to watch what the enemy was doing, and if it was something good, how to adopt it and enhance it. By the same token, they saw their own tactics used against them.

On a mission in northern Ramadi, Alvarenga saw such a tactic and couldn't really believe what he was seeing at first. It happened while his team and another sniper observer team were hiding out in the administration building of a medical college—a building they wrongly assumed was empty—to watch a highway for insurgent activity.

The snipers infiltrated at night, their faces streaked with black over a chalky white base, and settled into observation positions before dawn, taking for granted that the nice furniture and neat offices were normal for an abandoned building. Then the faculty who worked there started to arrive.

"We had no idea that the college was still running," Alvarenga said. "By 0600 we had detained like twenty people, and there were more people coming. We were running out of room to put these people in."

It wasn't the first time something like this had happened to a sniper team in Iraq. But it was the first time it had happened to them. They tried to deal with the wave of arriving workers like a batter dispatching flying baseballs in a batting cage. One by one.

They searched the men, left the women alone, and herded everyone into different rooms, soon concluding that the ratio of detainees to Marines was growing disproportionate.

"We ended up detaining like forty people, and there were only like eleven guys and more people were coming," Alvarenga said. "They would try to run when they saw our guys with their faces painted."

Everyone knew it was time to let the detainees go and suffer whatever consequences might arise from their release. But the snipers were surprised when, only thirty minutes after releasing the workers, their signal intelligence cell informed them that an attack was being planned on the building.

"The workers had contacted bad guys and told them there were a bunch of Americans in the building," Alvarenga said.

Trapped without an immediate escape plan, and told by their commanders to stay put in the two-story building for a while longer, the snipers blocked and covered all the windows, moved tables and chairs to the doors, fortified the entrances as best they could, and set up in additional areas where they could observe the building's perimeter.

Alvarenga slid his tactical periscope up into a window overlooking a building across the street. Almost immediately he saw a small flock of squawking birds surrounding one window and some kind of activity that looked unnatural.

"I see all these seeds flying, coming out of the window where the birds were. I was looking and zooming in closer, and I see this one bird sitting there with a little box right in the middle of his chest. So I was like, that can't be a bird, what the hell is that?" he said.

The bird seemed stiff, as if it moved mechanically. In one hair-raising moment, Alvarenga—and the sniper with the bird periscope across the street—realized they were staring at one another.

"He popped down, then slowly came back up to look at me, then popped down again, and I would do the same thing. Basically we're communicating that 'I see you and you see me,' but I also saw something in the periphery that's moving," he said.

Next to the window with the bird was a door with a hole the size of a small melon, and he could see the distinct outline of a machine gun barrel of some sort through the hole. No sooner had he seen it than it sent a burst of rounds, and so did the man from the window with the fake bird.

Alvarenga had wanted to call for a two-thousand-pound bomb to be dropped on the building because it was clear to everyone that, even though it was a school, which was off limits to shoot at according to the rules of engagement, insurgents were using it so it was fair game. Instead, he said, "When they popped their machine gun out and started shooting at us, I let them get their thirty rounds out, and then I popped up and started shooting back into that window, I shot two right through the window."

Alvarenga disintegrated the building's wooden frame with his M249 SAW machine gun, blowing away whatever sanctuary the bird shooter and doorway machine gunner thought they had.

During the three-hour gunfight, a car zoomed past the building and placed a stop-and-drop bomb in front of the only door, so the snipers breached a wall in the rear of the building that night and got away with no casualties.

Alvarenga never saw the bird again, but he was struck that the enemy was using the Americans' own tactics against them and then learned that other Marines had seen periscopes from time to time, homemade devices made with PVC pipe.

"The tactic with the bird periscope was the smartest thing I've seen over there. They learn from how we do things, and they get a lot off the Internet. People think these fighters aren't smart, but they are," he said.

Cooper and Alvarenga would go on hundreds of missions together and earn a reputation for being the kind of smash-and-bash Marines who weren't afraid to get the job done.

On their second deployment to Iraq, they were introduced to new team members, including Brace, who they thought was a joke.

"Al and Coop hated me. They had already been on one deployment, and they were really, really tough guys, like meat-and-potatoes, snake-eater types," Brace said. "They were pretty much the opposite of anybody I'd ever want to talk to or hang out with. And it wasn't just Al and Coop hating me, but everybody else hating me too, and I was like, this is bad."

During the seven-month deployment, the platoon sergeant was the one who took the time to get to know Brace, and he thrived as a Marine because of it.

More than an instructor, the platoon sergeant became a mentor with the credibility of someone who'd walked the walk and taken some bold action in battle that was never talked about outside the barracks. Approachable and easy to talk to, he was a sort of spiritual guide in terms of all things sniper related. He assigned Brace to a team in Iraq with an older, more mature leader who allowed him to become a radio operator, and he became a damn good one.

The platoon sergeant's relationship with Brace evolved into a different kind of mentorship, one that was based on their shared faith as Christians as well as a higher standard he demanded that Brace achieve.

"I didn't fit the mold as a Marine at all, and he realized that early on," Brace said. "He treated me a little bit differently. He was a little tougher on me than he was on the other guys, which was good because that finally got Cooper and Al to recognize that I was a pretty good radio operator."

After the deployment, back at Camp Lejeune, Brace stuck around and eventually Al and Coop asked him to be on their team, which stunned and pleased him because other guys were actively trying to kick him out.

"Coop had some grace and asked me, 'Will you follow me and my team and do the best you possibly can and will you protect me and the rest of the team if we get in trouble?' I said yes and remember thinking, Wow! Not what I expected from the beer-swilling, woman-hiding, rough-and-tumble, scream-in-everybody's-face kind of guy. I'd heard they were ruthless killing Marines, and if you wanted to survive, you would be on their team. I found out that was very true in Afghanistan, and I was very glad I was on their team," Brace said.

After the reaper farm mission in Afghanistan, the sniper team, led by Cooper, worked like dogs on back-to-back missions in the Helmand River valley against well-entrenched Taliban fighters who defended their territory with a vengeance and strong combat tactics. As intelligence about Taliban activity trickled in, the Marines responded by closing the distance with violence of action, and the snipers were an important part of that move.

In a village near A Company's patrol base on the southernmost reaches of Garmsir, it was learned that Taliban meetings were being held in a two-story building surrounded by dozens of other buildings occupied only by other Taliban, a perfect mission for the snipers.

On May 19, 2008, Cooper and another sniper team leader led their combined team of twelve snipers from the A Company patrol base on foot at 2 a.m. and headed toward the village to set up and watch the building.

The dark, early morning air was thick and hot, and each guy carried more than one hundred pounds of gear, enough essential equipment to stay mobile for at least four days: items like radios, batteries, C4 explosive, ammunition, food, water, and optics, plus their sniper rifles. The Barrett .50-cal rifle alone weighs about thirty pounds, and all the weight was in addition to the Marines' personal protective gear like body armor and helmets.

The walking infiltration as weighted down as pack mules was familiar to everyone; each man had done it repeatedly. And on this occasion a platoon of infantrymen was sent ahead to clear the village so the snipers could walk through to their predetermined hide site, passing the infantrymen after they had made it safe to move in.

As infantrymen themselves, the snipers were always ready to jump in and help if something happened, but it was understood that their mission was to reach their destination safely and begin eliminating targets of opportunity.

The sniper team's movement was about five kilometers and took more than an hour. Violence was expected, because the only people left in the village were fighters.

"We'd done this so many times I can't even count them all. We knew what we were doing. As soon as we walked out, we took fire outside the headquarters. We went right back in and planned another route," Alvarenga said.

The Taliban, they assumed, had night vision capability because they'd recently killed an entire squad of British soldiers and taken their equipment.

When the snipers got close to the infantry squads, Cooper found their commander and said they'd help clear the rest of the route, which the commander welcomed. But Alvarenga started to wonder why Cooper would bust out and offer help when they'd already had one setback and needed to get where they were going.

The idea became even more ominous as they walked up a pathway to the village, felt a rocket-propelled grenade fly over their heads, and saw the entire squad of infantrymen lying on their bellies on either side of the path, quietly aiming their rifles toward a three-foot wall leading into the village.

"I tell Coop, 'Hey, man, we are weighed down here, we have so much stuff. We don't do this, we're not here to do infantry work. It's not our job, and there's only a small amount of us who can do what we do,'" Alvarenga recalled telling his friend.

But Coop insisted, telling Al, "I know, man, but we gotta help these guys."

Not wanting to challenge his buddy, Alvarenga went along, following Cooper up to the low wall past the eerily quiet Marines on the ground, wishing later that one of them had spoken up.

"This is what really pissed me off. None of these guys along the path said anything to us, and we continued to walk along this path to the three-foot wall. There was a bunker they were taking fire from they could have told us about," Alvarenga said.

The infantrymen, in fact, had already fired on one bunker and possibly killed everyone inside. It was quiet, but as the snipers put their heavy loads on the ground and approached the wall, a tree behind a building just off to the right at about the two o'clock position burst into flames—a tactic by the enemy, they assumed, that was aimed at drowning out the Marines' night vision goggles.

Cooper found the lieutenant he'd spoken to earlier and told him to cover him and a four-man team that would go in and clear a small area to the left of the fire so the snipers could proceed.

They took a shot at the cleared bunker for good measure. The five of them—including the two sniper team leaders, Alvarenga, and two other snipers—lined up along the low wall, and then events happened quickly and went wrong even more quickly.

"Before I could tell the rest of the team, the other team leader had already jumped the wall, and I saw Coop jump the wall with them and two others jumped. I was like, 'He's not going by himself, forget that,'" Alvarenga said.

The five-man stack, with Cooper in the second position and Alvarenga in the fifth, and last, position, came under a sudden burst of fire from a bunker that was hidden between the burning tree and a building that was partially obscuring it. The only two Marines cut down by the fire were Cooper, who was mortally wounded, and Alvarenga, whose vest caught a bullet that exploded the attached M203 rounds and knocked him into an old bomb crater behind them.

No one else was shot.

As the rest of the stack scattered and began returning fire, some from back on the other side of the wall, Alvarenga came to at the bottom of the crater and heard someone shout that Coop was down. "I jumped up with nothing. I didn't have my gun and ran to Cooper and grabbed him and his gun. I was shooting with one hand and dragging him with the other, and the other team leader is firing and everybody's firing," Alvarenga said.

In the crater, Alvarenga desperately tried to wake Cooper while the Navy corpsman who jumped in after them desperately tried to figure out what was wrong with him. Cooper was unconscious. They started to undress him, and the whole time, Alvarenga said, "I was shooting back and freaking out. I told the guys to get him out of the hole and over the wall so they could get him out of there."

Alvarenga's world was spinning around the sight of his best friend, who was unresponsive, bleeding to death, slipping away right in front of him. With the casualty evacuation helicopter on its way, the infantry guys came with a stretcher to load Cooper up and get him to the landing zone back down the path.

Alvarenga was in charge of the team now so he couldn't go to the LZ. Ever protective of Cooper, "I told one of the infantry guys, 'Hey, take my friend to the LZ,' while I gathered the whole team. We continued to fire. The guys ran out of the bunker; we killed one, but by then a Predator was on station watching. All the guys were killed by a bomb that was dropped on the bunker."

As soon as he could, Alvarenga dragged both teams to a safer rear area to reorganize and then ran as fast as he could back around to the

LZ, carrying Cooper's guns and one hundred-pound pack. His inner panic made him run faster, and the speed felt as if it might help Cooper overcome the terrible thing that had just happened to him.

On the ground, hunched over his patient on the stretcher, the Navy corpsman applied a tourniquet, did a tracheotomy, and started CPR, none of which would save Cooper, who had been shot by a bullet that went through the tricep on his right arm, pierced his armpit, and ripped into his torso.

The corpsman saw the blood coming from Cooper's nose, but he couldn't figure out the source of the bleeding. Alvarenga watched with a tension he'd never known. Here was a problem for which he had no solution, a circumstance that was wildly out of his control.

"It was so in the moment," he said. "We were trying to do everything we could. We took all his crap off, but there was so much going on, he didn't see the bullet wound in his armpit. It wouldn't have mattered—the bullet went right through his chest and every vital organ. Even the doctors said even if it had been near a hospital in America, he wouldn't have made it."

Cooper hadn't uttered a word. He took his last breath before the helicopter arrived, as Alvarenga remembers it, and as the bird descended for a landing, Alvarenga told Cooper for the last time that he loved him.

Standing alone in the windy wake of the chopper, a sickening wave of guttural anguish possessed Alvarenga, a sucking grief so deep and overpowering that it nearly blinded him. He dropped his gun and stood there, weak-kneed, his hands covered with Cooper's blood, heaving heavy, dry sobs that took his breath away. His eyes watered and he cried, and cried, and cried. He was unable to stop crying.

He'd never had a cigarette in his life, but he smoked one that night and smoked the rest of a pack over the next two hours. Then he smoked a pack a day for the next two months. It was as if he couldn't get enough air, and the tobacco that filled his lungs let him know that he was at least breathing something.

And he thought about Cooper a lot. It was all he could think about. Of all the sniper missions they'd been on, it was hard to believe he would get cut down in a traditional small unit movement in an ambush they never saw coming. He and Coop had been invincible.

"I felt weird about this deployment, and I told him. I said, 'We've done a lot of crazy stuff already.' Our Ramadi deployment was pretty bad, and there were times we were scared a lot because bad guys were right next door. We put our life in danger all the time, but I told him there's something about this deployment. I didn't know why," said Alvarenga, who pondered another out-of-the-ordinary thing that happened that night.

"I have a hard time sometimes believing in God, but there's one thing I remember about that night," he said.

Before they went on the 2 a.m. mission, everyone was sleeping. That is, except Cooper and Alvarenga, who were talking quietly about home, their girlfriends, and what they were going to do with their lives. They considered trying out together for the Army Special Forces or going to school. They laughed about being neighbors when they got older.

Alvarenga saw Cooper reading his Bible, something he'd never seen him do.

"I said, 'You know, you gotta let me read that,' and he was like, 'Yeah, I'm working on it, too, on all this stuff.' There's something that happened that has to do with that moment we shared right there that night because I carried his Bible after that and I would read passages," Alvarenga said.

Cooper's death sent shock waves through the sniper platoon, and back at battalion headquarters, where Brace, the platoon sergeant, and their platoon leader, First Lt. Jason Mann, had gone the night before to resupply, his body was prepared for transport to Kandahar and then home to Mississippi.

Brace was sleeping when the news came in, and Mann went straight to his bunk and jostled him until he stirred.

"All I remember is that it was one of the most jarring moments of my life. It was shoving. Eyes wide open. 'Brace! Brace! You awake? Coop's dead, man.' I thought it was a nightmare," Brace said.

Mann, who was in shock himself, continued with his blunt bulletin of bad news, gruffly telling Brace: "Your team just got into an ambush and if you want to come see Coop before they take him back to Kandahar, you can come and see him."

In what Brace considers more than a coincidence to this day, Cooper had ordered him to go to battalion headquarters on the resupply with Mann and the platoon sergeant the night before the mission, even though they hadn't been given the mission before the threesome departed.

"He just said, 'You're the only one who's married so you're going back.' I probably would have been one of the guys in the stack, and as radio man I would have been next to Cooper," Brace speculated.

After the incident of May 19, Brace was tasked with interviewing everyone who was there and to write up a report. He, too, was baffled by the lack of action on the part of the infantrymen on the path to the ambush to stop the snipers from walking toward danger.

"What I heard is that this platoon couldn't operate. They had lost complete effectiveness; you could call them shell-shocked. They were lying down in a ditch, and the squad leader wasn't talking to anybody or doing anything, and our team walked past them," he said.

With Cooper gone, Alvarenga did his best to rally the team he was now in charge of. The team was benched for about five days before being tasked with another mission, and Alvarenga quietly pulled Brace close to him, even though the job of assistant team leader fell to another sniper.

The two men, once at odds and in opposite corners of their own idealistic worlds, now worked together, wrote stuff together, and attended meetings together. They handled Cooper's death differently.

"Al did the best he could to kill as many Taliban as he could possibly kill, and he killed dozens through a variety of means. I was more measured. I guess I realized that in a war you're expected to die. I didn't take it personally. I took it personally on the level that it was my team leader. But Al, it was his brother, they were as close as brothers," Brace said. "We didn't talk about Coop. I was just glad to be pulled face-to-face and being told, 'You're going to be my right-hand man now.'"

The pace of operations continued to be demanding, but dropped off during June, and on July 17, Mann, who was exceedingly well liked by the men, was killed when the building he was sleeping in collapsed in a non-hostile incident, crushing the team again and putting the platoon sergeant in charge of everyone.

In October, the Twenty-fourth Marine Expeditionary Unit packed up and left Afghanistan. Some of the snipers of 1-6 Marines stayed in and deployed again, but others, like Brace and Alvarenga, moved back into the civilian world.

Alvarenga got a job in Washington, D.C., working for a Vietnam veteran who counseled him on his grief for Cooper, telling him to use everything he'd done and seen to improve his own life and make himself stronger.

"He told me people like me are in a different category because of what we've seen and done. Not a lot of people have done what we've done," Alvarenga said, still lamenting the plans he and Cooper had for their Mediterranean float, pointing out that it's what young men join the Marine Corps to do.

"We were supposed to be in Spain," Alvarenga said, reflecting also on his acceptance of Brace.

"Neal was like a little brother. He proved himself on our first mission in Afghanistan. I think I helped him more than he helped me. After Coop died I put my feelings aside and stored it away until these guys were home and safe and then after that I fell apart," he said.

Alvarenga eventually returned Cooper's Bible to his family and has remained friends with Brace, who said he never thought he'd get to know, much less grow fond of, a man like Cooper.

"I trusted him," Brace said. "If he were around today, I'd follow him to the end of the world."

The Best-Laid Plans:
Mission to Tehran

Eric L. Haney

WHEN THE MISSION ALERT FOR TEHRAN HAD BEEN GIVEN, MY SQUADron was winter mountain training in the western United States. A Squadron had already deployed to a secret CIA site to begin planning. We returned immediately to Fort Bragg and quickly followed our mates to the seclusion of the isolation site. The most tense part of any mission is during the initial alert. That's when you're operating with half-assed information and surrounded by rumors.

This time was no exception. Most of the news we received at first was so ludicrous it didn't deserve the dignity of the term "intelligence." The CIA had no usable assets in place and was proving incapable of providing us with the type of information we needed, and they made it clear they would not take the risks entailed to get us what we needed. (This turned out to be a long-term problem for us that has never been resolved.) That's when Dick Meadows volunteered to lead a small undercover team into Tehran. Dick was a legend in Special Forces and the Rangers. He had been the ground commander on the 1970 Son Tay raid to liberate American POWs in North Vietnam. Now a retired major, he had been hired as a civilian consultant by Colonel Beckwith when we had formed the unit. Once Dick was on the ground inside Iran, a flow of usable information started to trickle in and we were able to start planning in earnest. Until Colonel Beckwith slammed his foot down, we had the all-too-common phenomenon of a mission being planned by men who wouldn't be taking part in it and putting their own lives at risk. Though SAS commandos had planned their own missions for years, it took Charlie Beckwith to sell the idea to the U.S. military. This was a sales job akin to administering a forced enema, and it didn't endear Charlie to any of the Pentagon armchair commandos who felt they should be running the operation.

But it became a Delta Force mandate: those who actually conduct the mission will be the ones to plan how to do it. It also prevents the Rambo syndrome from coming into play: nothing is impossible for those who don't actually have to do it. So, far away from Fort Bragg in the seclusion of our CIA hideaway, we dug in and started to figure out how to crack an egg without scrambling its insides. In effect, the embassy compound was now a prison complex. It was an egg we would have to break into, take, secure, hold, defend, evacuate hostages from, and last but not least, escape from ourselves. We soon had a basic plan we were confident would work. The plan was refined and rehearsed and refined and rehearsed and refined again as new intelligence came in. The changes felt endless, but no one ever despaired, because that is just the nature of this kind of beast. A combat plan is an animal in a constant state of metamorphosis and is under continual revision right up until the first shot is fired—at which time it usually ceases to have relevance. So each time we learned something new and important about the situation inside Iran and the captive embassy, we incorporated it into the developing plan. Eventually the parts started to come together until it felt smooth. At that point we finally knew exactly what to do when we got to the embassy.

The hard part was getting there. All during this time, the Air Force was playing a masterful shell game of gathering and staging aircraft from around the world, casually and randomly, so as not to alert the Soviets that we were up to something. Delta Force was playing a similar game. When the Soviet spy satellite window was open overhead, our rehearsal stage was dismantled and hidden and we slipped undercover. Back at Fort Bragg, the unit's support troops were working double duty to cover their own demanding functions while also going to the range, shooting, blowing off explosives, and in general making it look like the Sabre Squadrons were all still at home, their focus a million miles away from Iran.

Our biggest unresolved problem was how to get into Tehran. The Air Force could carry us into and out of Iran with their workhorse C-130s.

But we needed helicopters with long legs and a big lift capability to put us close to the city and later pluck us and the hostages back out again. And that's where some real problems started to show. At the Joint Chiefs level, the decision had been made that the rotary wing of the operation would be naval. On the surface, it seemed a sensible decision. After all, the helos would have to launch from a carrier, and we wanted things to look as normal as possible. But the helicopters were nothing but problems. They were maintenance nests at a time when maintenance and spare parts were a low priority—shortly after Vietnam and during the shoestring military budgets of the Carter administration.

To put it bluntly, the birds stunk. The crews weren't ready, and more important, I believe the pilots had convinced themselves the mission would never go. The question of the helicopters simply wouldn't go away. And this is where service parochialism reared its ugly head. Even as it became obvious that neither the naval air crews nor the Navy helicopters were capable of executing the mission, the edict came down: no change. The admirals would keep their piece of the pie no matter what the eventual cost.

My team was the last element scheduled to be lifted out of Tehran, and we were certain the helicopters would fail during the extraction phase. The plan called for us to lift out of a soccer stadium across the street from the embassy compound. While the stadium was a relatively defensible site (and a safe place for the hostages), it was a nightmare for helicopters—even the best of them. After some really bad experiences with those birds, we were convinced at least one of the choppers would crash in the stadium. Since a crash like that would leave us to our own devices in Tehran, my team prepared a plan for that contingency. We would clear out of the city in stolen cars, move north on foot into the remote Elburz Mountains, and then head across the border into Russia. Not an ideal situation but better, we thought, than taking the obvious route to Turkey, where Khomeini's henchmen would be waiting.

To assist in that eventuality, we took along our car theft kits, "escape and evasion" packets with maps, satellite signaling panels, ten thousand dollars in rials and U.S. currency, some "pointyyalky" phrase sheets, and a letter written in Farsi on Royal Saudi letterhead. The letter asked the

reader, as a good Muslim, to render assistance to us. We also had a pho-
netic English translation of the Farsi letter. The main problem we had
with this "help me" letter was that we figured anyone stupid enough to
believe what it said wouldn't be able to read!

By late January 1980, we felt confident in our plan. Given a little
luck, we could pull this thing off. But we needed a long, dark winter night
to cover us, and cold winter air to provide maximum lift for the aircraft.
As the diplomatic effort crawled nowhere, the nights became shorter
and warmer. If we were going, we needed to go soon. The concept of the
operation was this: Delta would infiltrate by teams to a staging base in
the United States. From there we would fly to a remote marshaling base
(REMAB) on a Soviet-built airfield in Egypt, where we would rendezvous
with other assets. The other assets for the mission included: A Ranger
company that was to seize an Iranian airfield at Masirah for use during
the extraction phase. A Ranger squad that would come with us to Desert
One with the mission of providing security for the helicopters during their
layup. A Special Forces team from Det-A, stationed in West Berlin, was to
retrieve the Americans holed up at the chancery of the Canadian embassy.
And a couple of former Iranian generals who were to provide some sort
of assistance (I've never known what kind) once we were in the country.

We were also supposed to take along a swaggering, loudmouthed,
smart-assed former member of SAVAK, the Iranian secret police. He
supposedly was a man who knew the underside of Tehran, but when
it came time to leave the United States, he developed what Colonel
Beckwith called "intestinal problems" (lack of) and refused to board the
plane. I guess he was fundamentally opposed to going into action against
anyone other than unarmed civilians.

From Egypt we would relocate to an island airfield off the coast of
Oman, lie low for a few hours, and then board the C-130 Combat Talon
aircraft for the flight into Iran. The helicopters, with several of our signal
squadron communicators aboard, would lift off from the carrier *Nimitz*
in the Persian Gulf and fly to a spot in the desert codenamed "Desert
One" to refuel from the C-130 tanker aircraft. From Desert One, we
planned to board the helos and spring forward to a hidden canyon where
the birds would be camouflaged and put to roost.

At sundown that day, Dick Meadows and his team would meet us with covered trucks to transport us to a side street adjacent to the embassy. Then we would slip over the walls of the embassy and execute the recovery of the hostages, while AC-130 gunships orbited overhead to address the expected hordes of armed militants, and Navy fighters controlled the skies to ward off the Iranian air force. My team's mission was to assault and clear the ambassador's residence and to recover the American women located there. I still have the door key to the kitchen entrance we planned to enter through. The cook brought the key out with him when he fled the country.

The other teams were tasked to assault and clear their respective areas of the embassy compound and recover the hostages in those locations. Two machine gun teams were assigned to fight off the inevitable visitors at the front gates; they were burdened like pack mules with more than one hundred pounds of ammo they carried. Then the extraction phase would begin. Fast Eddie, the demo man, would blow a hole in the walls of the embassy—right across the street from the stadium. We would take the hostages out and across the street to the stadium through a corridor held open by the machine gun teams. Then we'd load the hostages and their accompanying security teams onto the first helicopters and fly them out to the Iranian airfield the Rangers had seized. The rest of us would follow as the other helos staged in. From there we would load onto C-141s for the flight out of country with Navy fighters providing protective coverage. An ambitious plan, but certainly workable. It's a good thing we're not able to foretell our own future, otherwise most of us would never get out of bed in the morning.

While we were still in the CIA isolation camp during the planning phase, the only outsider we saw other than our handler was the cook. He was an old CIA employee who had seen all sorts of characters come and go over the years. One evening after supper he stood around with a few of us, smoking and joking as he waited for his truck to be loaded. Suddenly he became quiet and looked around the area as if he was seeing it for the first time. "Boys, I believe the last time we used this particular lodge was for the Bay of Pigs."

By the first of February, Delta was ready to give it a try. We weren't happy with the helos, but then again, we never would be. We were just going to trust that portion of the plan to luck and hope for the best. As February slid into March, we continued to rehearse and fine-tune the plan. Several times during the winter, we leaned forward in the foxhole and readied ourselves for imminent departure, only to be disappointed by another delay. March came and went. By the time April arrived, we were back home at Fort Bragg and more anxious than ever. The weather was warming and the nights were getting shorter.

When the execution order finally came we simply loaded our gear on the planes and slipped away quietly. By this time, no one paid the least attention to our movements. Our first stop was the remote marshaling base at Wadi Kena, Egypt. The fortified Soviet-built aircraft hangars were covered inside with human excrement. The Egyptians had used them as huge communal outhouses. The advance team spent several days before our arrival scrubbing the hangars with disinfectant just to make them habitable. When we arrived, what had been a deserted airstrip was throbbing with activity. We linked up with our other assets and waited a few days for the final word to go. Just prior to boarding the C-141 for the next phase of the journey, Colonel Beckwith asked us to pause for a prayer. Then, with the final amens still hanging in the air, we loaded up for the next stop on the journey—the airfield on the Omani island of Masirah. Arriving there in midmorning we found—wonder of wonders—tents set up for our shelter. Now, to most people that may seem like a small thing. But those who have ever been in the combat arms will recognize it for the true gift it was. Like any other band of nomads, we were accustomed to fending for ourselves. The idea that someone else would provide us with not just shelter from the sun but cold sodas was almost unthinkable. My comrades and I still thank the Air Force folks for that kind gesture.

If there is one thing that always sticks in my mind about how Delta Force goes about a mission, it is the utterly businesslike attitude of the men. There is none of that Hollywood crap. No posturing, no sloganeering, no high fivers, no posing, no bluster, and no bombast. Just a quiet determination to get on with the job. And in that fashion, late in the afternoon of 24 April 1980, we roused ourselves from siesta, made a final equipment check, test-fired our weapons, and climbed aboard the C-130s that would take us into Iran. My squadron was aboard the lead plane. For the course of the mission we—along with our attached Ranger squad, the two Iranian generals, and some Farsi-speaking drivers—would be known as "White Team." We would land at Desert One about ten minutes ahead of the others and provide security for the rest of the unit as they came in. I have been told that the command pilot of White Team's C-130 was an old lieutenant colonel with more C-130 flight hours than any living human being. That is probably true. And I have no doubts he sat in a specially constructed seat—one big enough to accommodate his huge brass balls. Twisting and squirming, hugging the ground, flying nap-of-the-earth, the Combat Talon aircraft threaded their way through gaps in the Iranian radar coverage. Flying low enough, to borrow a phrase from *Dr. Strangelove*, "to fry chickens in the barnyard." Even by Special Operations standards, that was a memorable flight.

On the way in I had been lying under the Ranger squad's jeep at the edge of the ramp. But when the three-minute warning sounded and the loadmaster yelled, "Grab something and hang on!" I reconsidered my position and wrapped myself around the diagonal brace just aft of the ramp hinge. We hit the ground hard—really hard—with no detectable change in speed or engine sound. The plane never bounced; the propellers just changed pitch, and we slowed so fast it felt like we had landed in a lake of molasses. I found out later that the pilot took her in at combat emergency landing speed so that if the plane broke through the desert crust, he would still have sufficient airspeed to wrestle her back into the air. Some pilot.

The ramp started to drop as soon as we had three wheels on the ground. Well before the plane had come to a halt, the Rangers had their motorcycles and the Jeep unchained, and were ready to leap out into the desert. My team was positioned to hit the ground first, followed by the Rangers and the rest of White Team. But as the back of the plane opened up and we could look outside, we saw headlights—right on top of us! We leaped off the plane like pouncing leopards. Three vehicles were almost on top of us. In the lead was a bus, followed by a gasoline tanker, and a small pickup truck that brought up the rear. My team went straight for the bus. We fired into the front of the vehicle, put a forty millimeter high-explosive round from a grenade launcher in front of the bumper, and fired a volley of rounds low into the step cavity where the passengers mount the bus. The fire was close enough to the driver that he immediately brought his vehicle to a halt. Bill shouldered the door open as our squadron commander, Major Logan Fitch, charged in and swept down the aisle as the lead man of the cheering team. Logan was never one to just stand back and give direction, he always led from the front—and this time he paid the price. As he barreled down the aisle to the rear of the bus, a young man in the back jumped up and punched Logan in the nose. A brave fellow. He was taken under control and Logan was the first to laugh about as he dabbed the blood off his lip.

In the meantime, other things were happening there on God's Little Acre. The Rangers had gone after the tanker truck that was now trying to maneuver away. I knew all those men well—they were the third squad of my old platoon. Young Ricky Magee was now a team leader and Allie Jones was the squad leader. I also distinctly remember hearing someone shout, "Shoot that truck!" to a Ranger carrying an M-72 antitank rocket. "Ba-woom!" The rocket launched, followed immediately by another, infinitely more spectacular "Ba-woom!" as the warhead missed low under the front bumper, hit the ground, skipped forward, and detonated in the belly of the tanker, setting off the gasoline it contained. The driver and his partner hurled themselves out of the cab and dove into the pickup following them. In a cloud of dust, the little truck then rocketed out of the area so fast the Ranger motorcycle couldn't catch up and was recalled before he got too far out.

While this was happening, we dismounted the bus passengers and searched them. For the most part, they were old men and women, with a few children and several young men thrown in for good measure. About forty very frightened people in all. And they had good reason to be frightened, for it looked like World War Three had erupted around them. There are few armies in the world that would not have killed them outright, but our feelings for those people were, but for the grace of God, they could be our own families or friends. By the time we had them searched and seated on the side of the road, the other planes were slashing in out of the darkness, and soon there were people all over the place. We decided to kidnap the bus passengers. We would load them on one of the C-130s for backhaul out of the country that night and fly them back in for release after the mission was completed. Major Fitch detailed my team to stand guard over the passengers since we were the ones who had initially taken control of them. I finished searching the prisoners by the light of the burning tanker. After we seated them on a low ridge of dirt edging the track, Bill Oswalt and I stepped to the end of the line to take a quick breather and compare notes. We stood mesmerized in the desert night watching the flaming tanker in this remote part of an ancient world. The column of fire soaring some three hundred feet into the sky was absolutely biblical. I was certain the glow could be seen for a hundred miles across the Iranian desert.

"Bill, do you think this mission is compromised?" I asked.

Bill nodded toward the tanker.

"Eric, I'll bet Ray Charles could see that damned thing."

And then, glancing at the seated passengers-cum-prisoners, he said, "Just think of it, Eric. For a year, we worked like dogs to become America's counterterrorist outfit, and what do we do on our very first mission? We hijack a fucking bus."

Every group of human beings has a few members who stand out, and our guests were no exception. One was a little boy about five years old. He sat right next to his grandmother, and even though it was obvious he was scared, he put on a stern face and made it clear he was ready to defend his grandma if anyone threatened her. Another was the brave guy, now flex-cuffed, who had punched Logan in the nose. And last, but certainly not least, was the one we quickly dubbed the "Village Idiot."

In our very limited Farsi (we had learned about twenty phrases), we told the people to sit still and shut up. But there's always one person who doesn't get the message. Ours was a poor guy in his mid-twenties who was slightly, but obviously, limited in his mental faculties. He would lean over to talk to his neighbor in a loud whisper, and his cringing neighbor would lean away, gesturing him to shut up—and surely telling the guy between gritted teeth that he would get them all killed. Twice I had

33

walked over to the young man to tell him to be quiet. The second time, I stuck the muzzle of my CAR-15 under his nose to emphasize the point.

He was silent for at least a minute and then went at it again. This time as I charged over to him, his neighbors on either side rolled away in self-protection. He looked up with horror on his face when I jammed my weapon's muzzle under his left ear, heaved him up on tiptoes, and frog-marched him up the road away from the group. He was convinced he was being taken away for execution, and I'm sure his comrades thought the same. As I led him away from the group of prisoners, he set up a kind of pitiable wailing it seems only Middle Easterners are capable of. He squalled and slobbered and begged and beseeched, all with upraised hands clasped in prayer as I marched him twenty meters away, turned him so his back was to his friends, pushed him to the ground and left him to sit alone. I could hear him snuffling and mumbling what were probably prayers of thanksgiving (or curses) for his deliverance from certain death as I walked back to my position near the rest of his comrades.

In the glow of the fire, the faces of the passengers all looked relieved. Whether from the fact that their fellow traveler had not been killed or that he could no longer get the rest of them in trouble, I wasn't sure. So there we all were. A nice fire to keep off the chill, some new friends to keep us company—but no helicopters. The tanker C-130s were arriving now and the birds that had brought us in needed to leave. But Colonel Kyle, the air commander, would keep them with us until the helos arrived. Just in case. Hours ticked by. We were burning precious darkness, and still no choppers. Several times we thought we detected them, but it was just our wishful thinking. Then suddenly, high in the sky—too high, in fact—we saw one. He had his lights on and was making his way to the flaming beacon we had lit. Close behind him came the rest, but it turned out we were short one bird. One had developed some sort of engine trouble as soon as it crossed the shoreline of the Persian Gulf and had turned back for the carrier. The rest of the flight had forged ahead, straight into a nabob—a storm of very fine dust particles that can tower thousands of feet into the sky. This was the undoing of the helicopter force.

The commander of the naval aviators was a badly shaken man when he arrived. He was obviously rattled, and I heard him say that he had never been through anything like that in his life. His demeanor was that of a man looking for a way out. He was led away to a conference with Colonels Kyle and Beckwith. While the powwow was going on, another pilot ran up to report that his bird was showing transmission warning lights and was not flyable. The plan called for six helos to go forward from Desert One. We expected that at least one would fail to crank at the hide site because they were notoriously difficult to start on their own power. We were now down to five helicopters, with the expectation of losing at least one more. Things seemed to be steadily disintegrating, but we had come so far and Tehran was now so close.

A radio call was placed to Major General James Vaught, the task force commander, to advise him of the situation. He wisely left the decision-making to the commanders on the ground. Even under the best of circumstances, Charlie Beckwith was not known for his patience, but he had controlled himself pretty well up till now. But as he listened to the pilots talking themselves out of going forward, he had enough.

"Awright, goddamn it! Let's get the hell out! Scrub the mission for tonight. We'll return to Masirah and the *Nimitz* while we still have darkness. Reconfigure and come back tomorrow night. Radio Dick Meadows about the situation and load up on the tanker planes for the trip out. Okay, do it!"

The tanker we boarded was refueling three of the helicopters as we climbed inside. A C-130 tanker carries the fuel in huge flat rubber bladders that completely cover the floor of the aircraft, and these are what we sprawled out on. Think of it as sitting on a carpet made of twenty thousand pounds of jet fuel. But at least the outsides of the fuel bladders were dry. The interiors of the helicopters always ran with dripping fuel and hydraulic fluid, making it hard to even walk in them. The Air Force put up with no such sloppiness. We scattered throughout the plane by teams. Our four-man team (Bill, Chris, Mike, and myself) settled against the fuselage just forward of the left wheel-well and relaxed a little. It was hot inside the plane, so we shucked off our black field jackets and put them behind our backs as padding between ourselves and the metal points and edges sticking out of the inner wall of the plane. We also wedged our CAR-15s between the edge of the bladders and the skin of the aircraft so they wouldn't rattle all over the place during takeoff. We would need both hands to hang on with. Getting off the ground was going to be a lot rougher than the landing. Finally the helicopters were refueled and the plane was closed up and readied for takeoff. The whole time the C-130s were on the ground, their engines ran at full RPM but with the props feathered. So to those of us inside, there was really no difference in sound between a plane in flight and one on the ground. A number of my mates were already asleep when we felt the plane start to move forward. But then something went terribly wrong.

Just as we lurched forward, as if the brakes had been released, a storm of blue sparks exploded over head and up front. My first thought was that the bank of electronics between the flight deck and the cargo hold had shorted out—and here we were sitting on all this jet fuel. My initial frantic thought was—where's the nearest fire extinguisher? I glanced about for its location. Then things started happening in fragments of seconds. The universe switched to slow motion, as it often appears to me when my life is in dire jeopardy. While the sparks were still flying, the crew door of the plane blew in with an explosion and a wave of fire. Willy Corman was sitting in the hole of the stairwell to the flight deck, just in front of the crew door when it blew. But the flames turned upward instead of down, and he shot out of the hole like he'd been fired from a cannon. My teammate Chris jumped to his feet and yelled, "Haul ass!" At that instant, the flight deck erupted with a blast of fire and the ceiling over our heads in the forward part of the cabin was engulfed in roaring flames. My first thought was that it was useless to even try to move. I was sitting on ten tons of jet fuel, I was a lifetime forward of the aft jump doors, and there was no way I'd ever make it out. My next thought was—to hell with that! I've got to try! So I took and held a deep breath I fully expected would be my last, and started moving. It seems ironic now, but during the extensive psychological testing we underwent during selection, I remember being asked the question, "What are you afraid of?"

I didn't hesitate to answer: Fire. I fear it above anything else.

A quick glance aft showed that most of the squadron was already jammed up near the right rear jump door forty feet away. It wasn't open yet, but even if it were, I'd never get there before flames poured over me.

In the split second it had taken for me to get to my feet, the flames had burned through the top of the fuselage and were cascading down the walls. I turned and ripped the blackout cover off a porthole midway down the left side. Nothing but the fire outside! I continued down the left side of the plane just ahead of the cataract of flame. I was in a race for my life, and the fire matched me step for step. I made it to the back of the plane, just ahead of the flames, to the left jump door. I grabbed the handle and gave it a heave.

When it cracked loose from the floor, a wide, flat sheet of flame gushed inside and Don Feeney yelled at me, "Close that fucking door!" I slammed it shut and momentarily denied entry to that torrent of fire. While I was hurtling down the left side of the plane, our squadron sergeant major, Dell Rainey, quenched the initial confusion with a short command: "Fall in, boys, and get the door like a jump."

That's what everyone did, and that's what saved us. The logjam at the door cleared immediately and the line moved with fire-hose urgency— just like we were jumping on a short drop zone. Dell's calmness and presence of mind saved many of us. I know it saved me. When I turned from slamming the left door shut, the line on the other side had only three or four men in it, and they disappeared as I plunged straight across the plane and followed them through the hope of that open door. By the time I got there, it was ringed with fire down to the level of the floor.

Fire was just starting to eat at the rubber fuel bladders, and I could see a frenzied hurricane of fire blowing outside that I still had to leap through. But I was out. I hit the ground on top of someone who had fallen (it was "lucky" Willie) and together we scrambled away from that hellish inferno. Bounding to my feet, I released the breath I had been holding and sucked down a lungful of hot air. But I had to keep moving. I was being showered with burning fragments from the rapidly disintegrating C-130.

I sprinted out about fifty meters, turned to face the plane, and flung myself down on the sand to view the catastrophe. It had probably only been thirty seconds since the initial explosion. A lifetime. I saw a body lying in the jump door of the furiously burning plane. Just at the moment I saw him, the bird seemed to hiccup. It looked like the flames took a short, deep breath and then spat the man out onto the desert sand. Two other men ran up and dragged him away. That man was Air Force Sergeant Joe Byers. He had fallen down from the burning flight deck, so terribly burned he was barely able to call for help. Jeff Houser and Paul Lowry heard Byer's faint cry. They threw their field jackets across their faces and ran back into the flames to drag him out. They had gotten him to the door, but he was deadweight and they had to drop him to save themselves.

But it seemed the fire didn't like Joe's flavor and spit him out. What incredible luck. One of our mates, Frank MacAlyster was sound asleep when the plane detonated. He woke up to a furiously burning aircraft and people diving out the jump door. In his confusion, Frank thought we had taken off while he was asleep and had been hit by something in flight. His first thought had been "Where are the parachutes?" And his next thought, "Where are those fools going?" But he couldn't stay in the furnace of the plane so he launched himself out the door in a hard-arched skydiving position and, after a half-second of free fall, slammed into the ground. Several days later, I asked him what he'd thought he was going to do once he was out of the plane without a parachute.

He answered, "One problem at a time, Sarge. One problem at a time."

By now the plane was almost consumed. The munitions inside were cooking off and the two Redeye antiaircraft missiles we carried had launched themselves out into the night sky. I thought we were under ground attack and that the plane had been hit by rocket-propelled grenades. Trying my best to look dead, I was lying with the right side of my face in the dirt, watching with my left eye, with my right arm and .45-caliber pistol tucked underneath my body. I figured I'd wait like this for the ground assault force to come sweeping around the tail of the remains, let the first wave of troops go past me hoping they weren't shooting the dead, then kill the last one and take his rifle. With a bit of luck I might get a machine gunner.

While I was running this through my mind, out of the corner of my eye I saw my close friend, J. T. Robards, come running over. He dropped to the ground and threw an arm over me.

"You all right?" he asked. "I thought you were dead."

"Yeah, J.T., I'm fine. Just playin' possum," and I told him my intention.

"Wrong answer, Bubba," he replied. "We aren't under attack. The damn chopper hit us. Look."

He pointed to the wreckage. That's when I finally noticed what was left of the helicopter on top of the plane, just as the whole flaming mass started to collapse. We got to our feet and started moving away. Other survivors of the collision were moving back toward where the other planes had been, calling, "Get aboard, the planes are taking off."

It was no joke. They were taking off.

"Should we destroy the helicopters?"

The crews had abandoned them and were nowhere to be seen.

"No, they're going to call in an air strike to take care of them, just get on the planes!"

By now, a half-dozen of us had linked up and were chasing after a taxiing C-130. But as we drew nearer, it closed its ramp and picked up speed, blinding us in its dust as it rolled for takeoff.

J.T. yelled and pointed, "That's the last one. We have to catch it!"

And then I could see it through the dust. Someone was shining a light off the back of the ramp, searching back and forth across the desert. We ran to that light as hard as we could. The plane was picking up speed for takeoff. As we got close to the ramp of the moving plane, I saw Rodney Headman hanging off the back, held at the knees by Logan Fitch. He was sweeping the desert with his headlamp, looking for strays. I was the last man dragged aboard just as the ramp closed and the plane moved into takeoff position.

Damn. I was back aboard another fuel tanker! But anything was better than being left behind. On the takeoff run, we plowed straight across the dirt berm running along the roadway, bounced five feet into the air, smashed back down, but continued to gather speed until finally we were airborne. But where were all our teammates?

Bill and I were together.

"When did you last see Mike and Chris? Did they make it out?"

"I think so. They were both in front of me but I didn't see them outside."

"Did anyone see them?"

Everyone was looking for missing teammates. The plane had been consumed in less than a minute and it had been impossible to know where everyone went. We got a list of those aboard our plane and gave it to the crew chief, asking that it be relayed to the other planes and that they do the same. He said he would do it when things settled down a bit.

Don Geeney and Keith Parsons were taking care of the injured air crewman. His hands had been burnt to claws and his face and head were charred and in pretty bad shape. To cool him down they poured canteens of water over his flight suit, which was so hot it steamed when the water hit it. But he survived. His worst injuries were to his lungs. Thanks to reconstructive surgery, a year later his hands looked fairly normal.

Jesus Hotel Christ! This had been some night. Things had come apart like a two-dollar shirt. Daylight was coming on rapidly and we were still a long way from friendly territory. How much worse was it going to get? Well, there was nothing I could do about any of it right now. I was just a passenger again, so like any good soldier, I curled up on top of the bladder and went to sleep. I came awake to shouting.

"What the hell's going on now?" I asked.

"The loadmaster said we're low on fuel and may not make it back. We're going to lower the ramp and throw out pumps, hoses, and anything else we can shove out of the plane. Maybe we can at least make it to the Persian Gulf and ditch her near a Navy ship!"

That's just great. Really what we needed to top off this extravaganza. I couldn't remember anyone ever surviving a C-130 ditching. This last act was going to be a real crowd pleaser. We threw out everything we didn't need to keep the plane in the air and hoped it would be enough. It was. We made it back to Masirah Island. I heard later that when the engines finally shut down, there was no measurable fuel in the tanks. Once on the ground, we took stock. Everyone in the squadron was still alive—a real gift after what had happened. Most of us were scorched—Jeff and Paul more than anyone else—but none of us were terribly burned.

But what about the air crews? Three Marines dead in the chopper. The pilot and the copilot had escaped unharmed. Five killed on the flight deck of the C-130. Only two had escaped from up front, both badly burned.

What the hell happened?

That's when we found out that as the last chopper finished refueling, she had lifted off to move away. But the pilot became disoriented in the dust cloud and drifted too far to the right, so the blades of the helicopter had slashed through the top of the C-130. This pulled the chopper on top of the plane at its left wing root. At the impact, the huge auxiliary fuel tank in the cargo bay of the chopper exploded, bathing the plane in burning fuel. The plane's spinning props spread fuel all over itself, assisting in its own immolation.

Beckwith gave the order to go aboard a C-141 that was waiting to carry us back to Egypt. From there we would make it back to the States and think of something else. It was a sad, quiet, introspective flight. When we arrived in the States, we transloaded to a couple of C-130s for the short hop to our CIA site. All of B Squadron sat in the aft part of our plane for takeoff. The loadmaster waved his arms and yelled that half of us had to move forward, but we told him to go to hell. No one was about to budge from a seat near those lifesaving jump doors. Back at camp, we lounged in our hideaways while the controversy of the failed attempt raged on outside. This was the beginning of the frenetically dramatized news coverage that is now so much a part of our national being.

And as we watched and listened to the television commentators endlessly chewing the event, I remarked to J.T., "Man, we were the ones who caused all this." One Sunday morning, President Carter came to visit us. Up until then, he had been a remote figure, but following his visit, we became very fond of him and had a lot of respect and affection for the man. He told us he accepted full responsibility for what had happened and that there would be no witch-hunts as far as we were concerned. But there was a funny little side note to the President's visit. Carter was accompanied on his trip by Zbigniew Brzezinski, the President's national security adviser. The President walked through our assembled ranks, speaking with us individually, and Brzezinski followed along in his wake. That's when we noticed that Brzezinski, though dressed in a business suit, was wearing a pair of bright green, high rubber boots, the kind you wear for mucking out stables or slopping hogs.

My mate, Branislav Urbanski, was on my immediate right, and as Carter stopped to speak with me I could hear Brzezinski and Branislav chatting in Polish. After the politicos had departed, I asked Brani what he had said to his compatriot. He replied with delight, "I asked Brzezinski why he was wearing those stupid-looking boots, and he told me, 'The President called me just a few minutes before we left Washington and said, "I want you to come with me, we're going to the farm." And I thought . . .'" (The CIA site we were using is nicknamed "The Farm.")

When we finally returned to Fort Bragg, we were told to go away—to disappear for two weeks—and then call in for instructions. Until then, we were to lie low, avoid the press, and relax. And that's just what I did. With a fishing pole, a small boat, and nineteen fat Georgia bass the first day.

Riding with Quantrell

Cole Younger

(Editor's note: The accepted spelling for the "Chief of the Guerrillas" is "Quan-trill." We will use the author's "Quantrell" throughout.)

MANY CAUSES UNITED IN EMBITTERING THE PEOPLE ON BOTH SIDES OF the border between Missouri and Kansas.

Those Missourians who were for slavery wanted Kansas admitted as a slave state, and sought to accomplish it by the most strenuous efforts. Abolitionists on the other hand determined that Kansas should be free, and one of the plans for inviting immigration from the Eastern Northern states where slavery was in disrepute, was the organization of an Immigrant Aid Society, in which many of the leading men were interested. Neither the earnestness of their purpose nor the enthusiasm of their fight for liberty is for me to question now.

But many of those who came to Kansas under the auspices of this society were undesirable neighbors, looked at from any standpoint. Their ideas on property rights were very hazy, in many cases. Some of them were let out of Eastern prisons to live down a "past" in a new country. They looked upon a slave owner as legitimate prey, and later when lines became more closely drawn a secessionist was fit game, whether he had owned slaves or not.

These new neighbors ran off with the horses of Missouri people without compunctions of conscience and some Missourians grew to have similarly lax notions about the property rights of Kansans. These raiders on both sides, if interfered with, would kill, and ultimately they developed into what was known during the war as "Freebooters," who, when they found a stable of horses or anything easily transportable, would take it whether the owner be abolitionist or secessionist in sympathy.

It was a robbery and murder by one of these bands of Kansas Jayhawkers, that gave to the Civil war Quantrell, the Chief of the Guerrillas.

A boy of 20, William Clarke Quantrell, had joined his brother in Kansas in 1855 and they were on their way to California overland when a band of Jayhawkers in command of Capt. Pickens, as was afterwards learned, raided their camp near the Cottonwood river; killed the older boy, left the younger one for dead, and carried off their valuables.

But under the care of friendly Indians, Charles Quantrell lived.

Changing his name to Charley Hart, he sought the Jayhawkers, joined Pickens' company, and confided in no one.

Quantrell and three others were sent out to meet an "underground railroad" train of negroes from Missouri. One of the party did not come back.

Between October, 1857, and March, 1858, Pickens' company lost 13 men. Promotion was rapid. Charley "Hart" was made a lieutenant.

No one had recognized in him the boy who had been left for dead two summers before, else Capt. Pickens had been more careful in his confidences. One night he told the young lieutenant the story of a raid on an emigrant camp on the Cottonwood river; how the dead man had been left no shroud; the wounded one no blanket; how the mules were sold and the proceeds gambled for.

But Lieut. "Hart's" mask revealed nothing.

Three days later Pickens and two of his friends were found dead on Bull Creek.

Col. Jim Lane's orderly boasted of the Cottonwood affair in his cups at a banquet one night.

The orderly was found dead soon after.

Quantrell told a friend that of the 32 who were concerned in the killing of his brother, only two remained alive, and they had moved to California.

The fight at Carthage in July 1861, found Quantrell in Capt. Stewart's company of cavalry. I was there as a private in the state guard, fighting under Price. Then came Gen. Lyon's fatal charge at Wilson's creek, and Gen. Price's march on Lexington to dislodge Col. Mulligan and his command.

Here Quantrell came into the public eye for the first time. His red shirt stood out in the first rank in every advance; he was one of the last when the men fell back.

After Lexington, Quantrell went with the command as far as the Osage river, and then, with the consent of his officers, came up the Kansas line again to settle some old scores with the Jayhawkers.

—◦—

I was only seventeen when Col. Mockbee gave a dancing party for his daughter at his home in Harrisonville which was to terminate seriously for some of us who were there.

The colonel was a Southerner, and his daughter had the Southern spirit, too. Probably this was the reason that inspired the young Missouri militiamen who were stationed at Harrisonville to intrude on the colonel's party. Among them was Captain Irvin Walley, who, even though a married man, was particularly obnoxious in forcing his attentions on the young women. My sister refused to dance with him, and he picked a quarrel with me.

"Where is Quantrell?" he asked me, with a sneer.

"I don't know," I answered.

"You are a liar," he continued, and as he went down in a heap on the floor, he drew his pistol, but friends came between us, and at their solicitation I went home and informed my father of what had taken place. He told me to go down to the farm in Jackson county, and to keep away from the conflict that Walley was evidently determined to force. Next morning I started. That night Walley and a band of his scouts came to my father's house and demanded that he surrender me, on the ground that I was a spy, and in communication with Quantrell. Father denounced it as a lie.

Though a slave-owner, father had never been in sympathy with secession, believing, as it turned out, that it meant the death of slavery. He was for the Union, in spite of his natural inclinations to sympathy with the South.

A demand that I surrender was conveyed to my father by Col. Neugent, who was in charge of the militia at Harrisonville, again charging that I was a spy. I never doubted that his action was due to the enmity of Walley. My parents wanted me to go away to school. I would have liked to have stayed and fought it out, and although I consented to go away, it was too late, and I was left no choice as to fighting it out. Watch was being kept for me at every railroad station, and the only school I could reach was the school of war close at home.

Armed with a shot-gun and revolver, I went out into the night and was a wanderer.

Instant death to all persons bearing arms in Missouri was the edict that went forth Aug. 30 of that year from Gen. John C. Fremont's headquarters at St. Louis, and he declared that all slaves belonging to persons in arms against the United States were free. President Lincoln promptly overruled this, but it had added to the bitterness in Missouri where many men who owned slaves were as yet opposed to secession.

It was "hide and run for it" with me after that. That winter my brother-in-law, John Jarrette, and myself, joined Capt. Quantrell's company. Jarrette was orderly sergeant. He never knew fear, and the forty that then made up the company were as brave men as ever drew breath.

We were not long quiet. Burris had a detachment raiding in the neighborhood of Independence. We struck their camp at sunset. We were thirty-two; they eighty-four; but we were sure shots and one volley broke their ranks in utter confusion. Five fell at the first fire, and seven more died in the chase, the others regaining Independence, where the presence of the rest of the regiment saved them. That day my persistent pistol practice showed its worth when one of the militiamen fell, 71 yards away, actual measure. That was Nov. 10, 1861.

All that winter Independence was the scene of a bloody warfare. One day early in February Capt. Quantrell and David Pool, Bill Gregg and George Shepherd, George Todd and myself, charged in pairs down three of the streets to the court house, other members of the company coming through other streets. We had eleven hurt, but we got away with ammunition and other supplies that were badly needed. Seven militiamen died that day.

Another charge, at daybreak of Feb. 21, resulted badly. Instead of the one company we expected to find, there were four. Although we killed seventeen, we lost one, young George, who fell so close to the guns of the foe that we had considerable difficulty in getting him away for burial. Then we disbanded for a time. Capt. Quantrell believed that it was harder to trail one man than a company, and every little while the company would break up, to rally again at a moment's notice.

In March Quantrell planned to attack Independence. We met at David George's and went from there toward Independence as far as Little Blue church, where Allen Parmer, who afterward married Susie James, the sister of Frank and Jesse, told the captain that instead of there being 300 Jayhawkers in Independence, there were 600. The odds were too strong, and we swung around to the southwest.

Thirteen soldiers who guarded the bridge at the Big Blue found their number unlucky. The bridge was burned and we dined that day at the home of Alex. Majors, of Russell, Majors and Waddell, the freighters, and rested for the night at Maj. Tale's house, near New Santa Fe, where there was fighting for sure before morning.

A militia command, 300 strong, came out to capture us, but they did not risk an attack until nearly midnight.

Capt. Quantrell, John Jarrette, and I were sleeping together when the alarm was given, the sentry's challenge, "Who are you?" followed by a pistol shot.

We were up on the instant.

So stealthy had been their approach that they had cut the sentry off from us before alarming him, and he fled into the timber in a shower of lead.

There was a heavy knock on the outer door, and a deep voice shouted: "Make a light."

Quantrell, listening within, fired through the panel. The visitor fell.

While we barricaded the windows with bedding, the captain polled his men. "Boys," he said, "we're in a tight place. We can't stay here and I do not mean to surrender. All who want to follow me out can say so; all who prefer to give up without a rush can also say so. I will do the best I can for them."

Four voted to surrender, and went out to the besieging party, leaving seventeen.

Quantrell, James Little, Hoy, Stephen Shores and myself held the upper story, Jarrette, George Shepherd, Toler and others the lower.

Anxious to see who their prisoners were, the militiamen exposed themselves imprudently, and it cost them six.

Would they permit Major Tate's family to escape? Yes. They were only too glad, for with the family out, the ell, which was not commanded by our fire, offered a tempting mark for the incendiary.

Hardly had the Tates left than the flames began to climb the ell.

There was another parley. Could we have twenty minutes? Ten? Five? Back came the answer:

"You have one minute. If at its expiration you have not surrendered, not a single man among you shall escape alive."

"Thank you," said I; "catching comes before hanging."

"Count six then and be damned to you!" shouted back George Shepherd, who was doing the dickering, and Quantrell said quietly, "Shotguns to the front."

There were six of these, and behind them came those with revolvers only. Then Quantrell opened the door and leaped out. Close behind him were Jarrette, Shepherd, Toler, Little, Hoy and myself, and behind us the revolvers.

In less time than it takes to tell it, the rush was over. We had lost five, Hoy being knocked down with a musket and taken prisoner, while they had eighteen killed and twenty-nine wounded. We did not stop till we got to the timber, but there was really no pursuit. The audacity of the thing had given the troops a taste of something new.

They kept Hoy at Leavenworth for several months and then hanged him. This was the inevitable end of a "guerrilla" when taken prisoner.

———

Among the Jackson county folks who insisted on their right to shelter their friends was an old man named Blythe.

Col. Peabody at Independence had sent out a scouting party to find me or anyone else of the company they could "beat up." Blythe was not at home when they came but his son, aged twelve, was. They took him to the barn and tried to find out where we were, but the little fellow baffled them until he thought he saw a chance to break through the guard, and started for the house.

He reached it safely, seized a pistol, and made for the woods followed by a hail of bullets. They dropped him in his tracks, but, game to the last, he rolled over as he fell, shot one of his pursuers dead, mortally wounded a second, and badly hurt a third.

They put seventeen bullets in him before he could shoot a fourth time.

A servant who had witnessed the seizure of his young master, had fled for the timber, and came upon a party of a dozen of us, including Quantrell and myself. As he quickly told us the story, we made our plans, and ambushed at the "Blue Cut," a deep pass on the road the soldiers must take back to Independence. The banks are about thirty feet high, and the cut about fifty yards wide.

Not a shot was to be fired until the entire command was in the cut.

Thirty-eight had started to "round up" Cole Younger that morning; seventeen of them lay dead in the cut that night and the rest of them had a lively chase into Independence.

To this day old residents know the Blue Cut as "the slaughter-pen."

Early in May, 1862, Quantrell's men were disbanded for a month. Horses were needed, and ammunition. There were plenty of horses in Missouri, but the ammunition presented more of a problem.

Capt. Quantrell, George Todd and myself, attired as Union officers, went to Hamilton, a small town on the Hannibal and St. Joseph Railroad, undetected by the company of the Seventh United States Cavalry in camp there, although we put up at the principal hotel. Todd passed as a major in the Sixth Missouri Cavalry, Quantrell a major in the Ninth, and I a captain in an Illinois regiment. At Hannibal there was a regiment of Federal soldiers. The commander talked very freely with us about Quantrell, Todd, Haller, Younger, Blunt, Pool and other guerrillas of whom he had heard.

While in Hannibal we bought 50,000 revolver caps and such other ammunition as we needed. From there we went to St. Joseph, which was under command of Col. Harrison B. Branch.

"Too many majors traveling together are like too many roses in a bouquet," suggested Todd. "The other flowers have no show."

He reduced himself to captain and I to lieutenant.

Our disguise was undiscovered. Col. Branch entertained us at his headquarters most hospitably.

"I hope you may kill a guerrilla with every bullet I have sold you," said one merchant to me. "I think if ever there was a set of devils let loose, it is Quantrell, Todd, Cole Younger and Dave Pool."

From St. Joseph we went to Kansas City in a hack, sending Todd into Jackson county with the ammunition. When within three miles of Kansas City the hack was halted by a picket on outpost duty, and while the driver argued with the guard, Quantrell and I slipped out on the other side of the hack and made our way to William Bledsoe's farm, where we were in friendly hands.

—~·~—

Col. Buell, whose garrison of 600 held Independence, had ordered that every male citizen of Jackson county between 18 and 45 years of age should fight against the South.

Col. Upton Hays, who was in Jackson county in July and August, 1862, recruiting a regiment for the Confederate army, decided that it was the time to strike a decisive blow for the dislodging of Buell. In reconnoitering the vicinity he took with him Dick Yager, Boone Muir and myself, all of whom had seen service with Capt. Quantrell.

It was finally decided to make the attack August 11th. Colonel Hays wanted accurate information about the state of things inside town.

"Leave that to me," said I.

Three days remained before the battle.

Next morning there rode up to the picket line at Independence an old apple-woman, whose gray hair and much of her face was nearly hidden by an old-fashioned and faded sun-bonnet. Spectacles half hid her eyes and a basket on her arm was laden with beets, beans and apples.

The left rein was leather but a rope replaced the right.

"Good morning, grandmother," bantered the first picket. "Does the rebel crop need any rain out in your country?"

The sergeant at the reserve post seized her bridle, and looking up said:

"Were you younger and prettier, I might kiss you."

"Were I younger and prettier, I might box your ears for your impudence."

"Oh, ho! You old she-wolf, what claws you have for scratching!" he retorted, and reached for her hand.

The quick move she made started the horse suddenly, or he might have been surprised to feel that hand.

But the horse was better than apple-women usually ride, and that aroused some suspicion at Col. Buell's headquarters, so that the ride out was interrupted by a mounted picket who galloped alongside and again her bridle was seized.

The sergeant and eight men of the guard were perhaps thirty paces back.

"What will you have?" asked the apple-woman. "I am but a poor lone woman going peaceably to my home."

"Didn't you hear the sergeant call for you, damn you?" answered the sentinel.

A spurred boot under the ragged skirt pierced the horse's flank; the hand that came from the apple basket fired the cocked pistol almost before the sentry knew it, and the picket fell dead.

The reserve stood as if stupefied.

That night I gave Quantrell, for Col. Hays, a plan showing the condition of affairs in Independence.

The morning of the 11th the attack was made and Col. Buell, his force shot to pieces, surrendered.

The apple-woman's expedition had been a success.

It was in August, 1862, nearly a year after the party at Col. Mockbee's, that I was formally enrolled in the army of the Confederate States of

America by Col. Gideon W. Thompson. I was eighteen, and for some little time had been assisting Col. Hays in recruiting a regiment around my old home.

It was within a day or two after the surrender of Buell at Independence that I was elected as first lieutenant in Capt. Jarrette's company in Col. Upton B. Hays' regiment, which was a part of the brigade of Gen. Joseph O. Shelby.

We took the oath, perhaps 300 of us, down on Luther Mason's farm, a few miles from where I now write, where Col. Hays had encamped after Independence.

Millions of boys and men have read with rising hair the terrible "black oath" which was supposed to have been taken by these brave fighters, but of which they never heard, nor I, until I read it in books published long after the war.

When Col. Hays camped on the Cowherd, White, Howard and Younger farms, Quantrell had been left to guard the approaches to Kansas City, and to prevent the escape to that point of news from the scattered Confederate commands which were recruiting in western Missouri. At the same time he was obtaining from the Chicago and St. Louis papers and other sources, information about the northern armies, which was conveyed by couriers to Confederate officers in the south, and he kept concealed along the Missouri river skiffs and ferry boats to enable the Confederate officers, recruiting north of the river, to have free access to the south.

The night that I was enlisted, I was sent by Col. Hays to meet Cols. Cockrell, Coffee, Tracy, Jackman and Hunter, who, with the remnants of regiments that had been shattered in various battles through the south, were headed toward Col. Hays' command.

It was Col. Hays' plan for them to join him the fifteenth, and after a day's rest, the entire command would attack Kansas City, and, among other advantages resulting from victory there, secure possession of Weller's steam ferry.

Boone Muir and myself met Coffee and the rest below Rose Hill, on Grand river. Col. Cockrell, whose home was in Johnson county, had gone by a different route, hoping to secure new recruits among his neighbors, and, as senior colonel, had directed the rest of the command to encamp the next evening at Lone Jack, a little village in the southeastern portion of Jackson county, so called from a solitary big black jack tree that rose from an open field nearly a mile from any other timber.

At noon of Aug. 15, Muir and I had been in the saddle twenty-four to thirty hours, and I threw myself on the blue grass to sleep.

Col. Hays, however, was still anxious to have the other command join him, he having plenty of forage, and being well equipped with ammunition as the result of the capture of Independence a few days before. Accordingly I was shortly awakened to accompany him to Lone Jack, where he would personally make known the situation to the other colonels.

Meantime, however, Major Emory L. Foster, in command at Lexington, had hurried out to find Quantrell, if possible, and avenge Independence. Foster had nearly 1,000 cavalrymen, and two pieces of Rabb's Indiana battery that had already made for itself a name for hard fighting. He did not dream of the presence of Cockrell and his command until he stumbled upon them in Lone Jack.

At nightfall, the Indiana battery opened on Lone Jack, and the Confederate commands were cut in two, Coffee retreating to the south, while Cockrell withdrew to the west, and when Col. Hays and I arrived, had his men drawn up in line of battle, while the officers were holding a council in his quarters.

"Come in, Colonel Hays," exclaimed Col. Cockrell. "We just sent a runner out to look you up. We want to attack Foster and beat him in the morning. He will just be a nice breakfast spell."

Col. Hays sent me back to bring up his command, but on second thought said:

"No, Lieutenant, I'll go, too."

On the way back he asked me what I thought about Foster being a "breakfast spell."

"I think he'll be rather tough meat for breakfast," I replied. "He might be all right for dinner."

But Cockrell and Foster were neighbors in Johnson county, and Cockrell did not have as good an idea of Foster's fighting qualities that night as he did twenty-four hours later.

The fight started at daybreak, hit or miss, an accidental gunshot giving Foster's men the alarm. For five hours it waged, most of the time across the village street, not more than sixty feet wide, and during those five hours every recruit there felt the force of Gen. Sherman's characterization—"War is hell."

Jackman, with a party of thirty seasoned men, charged the Indiana guns, and captured them, but Major Foster led a gallant charge against the invaders, and recaptured the pieces. We were out of ammunition, and were helpless, had the fight been pressed.

Riding to the still house where we had left the wagon munitions we had taken a few days before at Independence, I obtained a fresh supply and started for the action on the gallop.

Of that mad ride into the camp I remember little except that I had my horse going at full tilt before I came into the line of fire. Although the enemy was within 150 yards, I was not wounded. They did mark my clothes in one or two places, however.

Major Foster, in a letter to Judge George M. Bennett of Minneapolis, said:

"During the progress of the fight my attention was called to a young Confederate riding in front of the Confederate line, distributing ammunition to the men from what seemed to be a 'splint basket.' He rode along under a most galling fire from our side the entire length of the Confederate lines, and when he had at last disappeared, our boys recognized his gallantry in ringing cheers. I was told by some of our men from the western border of the state that they recognized the daring young rider as Cole Younger. About 9:30 a.m., I was shot down. The wounded of both forces were gathered up and were placed in houses. My brother and I, both supposed to be mortally wounded, were in the same bed. About an hour after the Confederates left the field, the ranking officer who took command when I became unconscious, gathered his men together and returned to Lexington. Soon after the Confederates returned. The first man who entered my room was a guerrilla, followed by a dozen or more men who seemed to obey him. He was personally known to me and had been my enemy from before the war. He said he and his men had just shot a lieutenant of a Cass county company whom they found wounded and that he would shoot me and my brother. While he was standing over us, threatening us with his drawn pistol, the young man I had seen distributing ammunition along in front of the Confederate line rushed into the room from the west door and seizing the fellow, thrust him out of the room. Several Confederates followed the young Confederate into the room, and I heard them call him Cole Younger. He (Younger) sent for Col. Cockrell (in command of the Confederate forces) and stated the case to him. He also called the young man Cole Younger and directed him to guard the house, which he did. My brother had with him about $300, and I had about $700. This money and our revolvers were, with the knowledge and approval of Cole Younger, placed in safe hands, and were finally delivered to my mother in Warrensburg, Mo. Cole Younger was then certainly a high type of manhood, and every inch a soldier, who risked his own life to protect that of wounded and disabled enemies. I believe he still retains those qualities and would prove himself as good a citizen as we have among us if set free, and would fight for the Stars and Stripes as fearlessly as he did for the Southern flag. I have never seen him since the battle of Lone Jack. I know much of the conditions and circumstances under which the Youngers were placed after the war, and knowing this, I have great sympathy for them. Many men, now prominent and useful citizens of Missouri, were, like the Youngers, unable to return to their homes until some fortunate accident threw them with men they had known before the war, who had influence enough to make easy their return to peace and usefulness. If this had occurred to the Youngers, they would have had good homes in Missouri."

It is to Major Foster's surprise of the command at Lone Jack that Kansas City owes its escape from being the scene of a hard battle August 17, 1862.

Quantrell was not in the fight at Lone Jack at all, but Jarrette and Gregg did come up with some of Quantrell's men just at the end and were in the chase back toward Lexington.

In proportion to the number of men engaged, Lone Jack was one of the hardest fights of the war. That night there were 136 dead and 550 wounded on the battlefield.

With two big farms in Jackson county, besides money-making stores and a livery stable at Harrisonville, my father at the outbreak of the war was wealthy beyond the average of the people in northwestern Missouri. As a mail contractor, his stables were filled with good horses, and his property was easily worth $100,000, which was much more in those days, in the public esteem, than it is now.

This, perhaps, as much as Walley's enmity for me, made him the target for the freebooters who infested the Kansas line. In one of Jennison's first raids, the Younger stable at Harrisonville was raided and $20,000 worth of horses and vehicles taken. The experiment became a habit with the Jayhawkers, and such visits were frequent until the following fall, when the worst of all the indignities heaped upon my family was to be charged against them—the murder of my father.

When the body was discovered, it was taken in charge by Capt. Peabody, who was in command of the militia forces in Kansas City, and when he found $2,000, which father had taken the precaution to conceal in a belt which he wore about him, it was sent home to our family.

It has been charged that my father tried to draw his pistol on a party of soldiers, who suspected me of the murder of one of their comrades and wanted to know my whereabouts. This is false. My father never carried a pistol, to my knowledge, and I have never had any doubt that the band that killed him was led by that same Capt. Walley. Indeed he was suspected at the time, accused of murder, and placed under arrest, but his comrades furnished an alibi, to the satisfaction of the court, and he was released.

He is dead now, and probably he rests more comfortably than he ever did after that night in '62, for whether he had a conscience or not, he knew that Missouri people had memories, and good ones, too.

But the freebooters were not through.

My sisters were taken prisoners, as were the girls of other families whose sons had gone to join the Confederate army, their captors hoping by this means to frighten the Southern boys into surrender.

After my mother's home was burned, she took her children and went to Lafayette county. Militiamen followed her, shot at Jim, the oldest of the boys at home, fourteen, and drove him into the brush. Small wonder that he followed his brother as a soldier when he became old enough in 1864!

Despairing of peace south of the Missouri, mother crossed into Clay county, remaining until the War between the States had ended. But not so the war on her. A mob, among whom she recognized some of the men who were pretty definitely known to have murdered my father, broke in on her after she had returned to Jackson county, searched the house for Jim and me, hung John, aged fourteen, to a beam and told him to say his prayers, for he had but a little time to live unless he told where his older brothers were. He defied them and was strung up four times. The fourth time the rope cut deep into the flesh. The boy was unconscious. Brutally hacking his body with knives, they left him for dead.

June 2 of that year, before John had recovered from his injuries, mother died.

———

It was along about the first week in October, 1862, that I stopped with a dozen men at the home of Judge Hamilton, on Big Creek, in Cass county. We spent the afternoon there, and just before leaving John Hays, of my command, dashed up with the news that Quantrell was camped only two miles west. He also gave the more important information to me, that some of Captain Parker's men had arrested Steve Elkins on the charge of being a Union spy, and were taking him to Quantrell's camp to hang him.

I lost no time in saddling up, and followed by my little detachment, rode hastily away to Quantrell's camp, for red tape occupied little space in those days, and quick action was necessary if anything was to be done.

I knew Quantrell and his men well and was also aware that there were several Confederate officers in the camp. The moment we reached our destination, I went at once to Captain Charles Harrison, one of the officers, and my warm personal friend, and told him openly of my friendship and esteem for Elkins. He promised to lend me all his aid and influence, and I started out to see Quantrell, after first telling my men to keep their horses saddled, ready for a rescue and retreat in case I failed of a peaceable deliverance.

Quantrell received me courteously and kindly, as he always did, and after a little desultory chat, I carelessly remarked, "I am surprised to find that you have my old friend and teacher, Steve Elkins, in camp as a prisoner."

"What! Do you know him?" asked Quantrell in astonishment.

I told him that I did, and that he was my school teacher when the war broke out, also that some half a hundred other pupils of Elkins were now fighting in the Southern army.

"We all care for him very deeply," I told Quantrell, and then asked what charges were preferred against him. He explained that Elkins had not been arrested on his orders, but by some of Parker's men, who were in vicious humor because of their leader's recent death. They had told Quantrell that Elkins had joined the Union forces at Kansas City, and was now in Cass county as a spy.

I jumped to my feet, and said that the men that made the charges lied, and that I stood ready to ram the lie down their throats with a pistol point. Quantrell laughed, and chided me about letting my hot blood get the better of cold judgment. I insisted, however, and told him further that Elkins' father and brother were Southern soldiers, and that Steve was a non-combatant, staying at home to care for his mother, but that I was in no sense a non-combatant, and would stand as his champion in any fight.

Quantrell finally looked at his watch, and then remarked: "I will be on the move in fifteen minutes. I will release Elkins, since you seem so excited about it, and will leave him in your hands. Be careful, for Parker's men are rather bitter against him."

Happy at heart, I dashed away to see Elkins, with whom I had only passed a few words and a hand-shake to cheer him up. He knew me, however, and realized that I would save him or die in the attempt, for from a boy it was my reputation that I never deserted a friend.

When I joined him again, several of Parker's men were standing around in the crowd, and as I shook hands with Elkins and told him of his freedom, I added, "If any damned hound makes further false charges against you, it's me he's got to settle with, and that at the pistol point."

I made that talk as a sort of bluff, for a bluff is often as good as a fight if it's properly backed up. As Quantrell and his men rode away in the direction of Dave Daily's neighborhood, I told Elkins to hit out West until he came to the Kansas City and Harrisonville road, and then, under cover of night, he could go either way. I shook his hand goodbye, slapped him on the shoulder, and have never seen him since.

I followed Quantrell's men for half a mile, fearing that some stragglers might return to take a quiet shot at Elkins, and then stopped for something to eat, and fed our horses.

At the time that I defended Elkins before Quantrell, I knew that Steve's sympathies were with the North, and had heard that he had joined the Federal army. But it mattered nothing to me—he was my friend.

When Col. Hays went south in the fall to join Shelby, Capt. Jarrette went with as many of his company as were able to travel and the wounded were left with me in Jackson county.

Missouri militia recognized no red cross, and we were unable for that reason to shelter our men in farm-houses, but built dug-outs in the hills, the roofs covered with earth for concealment.

All that winter we lay in the hollows of Jackson county, while the militia sought to locate the improvised hospitals.

It was a winter of battles too numerous to be told here, and it was a winter, too, that laid a price upon my head.

Capt. Quantrell and his men had raided Olathe and Shawnee-town, and among the killed at Paola on the way out from Olathe was a man named Judy, whose father had formerly lived in Cass county, but had gone to Kansas as a refugee. Judy, the father, returned to Cass county after the war as the appointive sheriff.

It was a matter of common knowledge to the guerillas, at least that young Judy had been killed by Dick Maddox and Joe Hall, and that as a matter of fact at the time of the fight I was miles away at Austin, Mo. But Judy had secured my indictment in Kansas on the charge of killing his son, and threatened me with arrest by a posse so that from 1863 to 1903 I was never in Cass county except as a hunted man. Years afterward this killing of Judy turned up to shut me out of Missouri.

Frequent meetings with the militia were unavoidable during the winter and there was fight after fight. Clashes were almost daily, but few of them involved any large number of men.

George Todd and Albert Cunningham, who were also caring for squads of soldiers in our neighborhood, and I made an expedition early in the winter across the Kansas line near New Santa Fe, where our party of 30 met 62 militiamen. Todd led the charge. With a yell and a rush, every man with a revolver in each hand, they gave the militia a volley at a hundred yards, which was returned, but no men could stand in the face of a rush like that and the militia fell back. In their retreat they were reinforced by 150 more and returned to the attack, driving Todd and his comrades before them. With six men I was holding the rear in the timber when a detachment of 52 ran down upon us. It was a desperate fight, and every man in it was wounded more or less. John McDowell's horse was killed under him and he, wounded, called to me for help.

Packing him up behind me, we returned to our camp in safety.

This was the McDowell who less than three months later betrayed one of our camps to the militia in Independence and brought down upon us a midwinter raid.

Todd had his camp at Red Grenshaw's, Cunningham was on the Little Blue, and mine was near Martin O. Jones' farm, eight miles south of Independence.

Todd's spirit of adventure, with my hope to avenge my father's murder, combined in a Christmas adventure which has been misrepresented by other writers.

Todd said he knew some of the band who had killed father were in Kansas City, and Christmas day six of us went in to look them up.

Leaving Zach Traber with our horses just beyond the outposts, the rest of us hunted them until it must have been nearly midnight. We were in a saloon on Main street. I had called for a cigar, and glancing around, saw that we had been recognized by a trooper who had been playing cards. He reached for his pistol, but he never pulled it.

I do not know how many were killed that night. They chased us well out of town and there was a fight at the picket post on the Independence road.

Col. Penick, in command at Independence, hearing of the Kansas City adventure, put a price of $1,000 on my head and other figures on those of my comrades.

It was to get this blood money that six weeks later, Feb. 9, the militia drove my mother out of her house and made her burn it before their eyes.

I was a hunted man.

Kicking Charlie's Ass

John J. Culbertson

JANUARY 1967 HAD BROUGHT FOUR NEW REPLACEMENTS TO THE 5TH Marine Snipers and assurance to Sergeant Tom Casey that the informal training of his shooters was being noticed at 1st Marine Division in Da Nang. Casey had taken his three sniper teams to An Hoa to accompany the increased combat patrols in the deadly Arizona Territory when the new sniper candidates settled into the old sniper billets at Hill 35 outside Chu Lai. He was informed of the arrival of his new charges, but what with the preparations for Operation Tuscaloosa in their final phase, he was consumed with his operational orders.

Tuscaloosa jumped off with little enemy contact, but the river crossing presented the Leathernecks of 2/5 with one of their greatest battlefield challenges in the Vietnam War. Casey had to give hard-earned credit to his three sniper teams. They had eliminated over a dozen Viet Cong and North Viets while removing enemy snipers and heavy weapons that threatened the grunts trapped on the sandbar and later along the jungle trails to La Bac 1 and La Bac 2.

By now, the 5th Marine Sniper Platoon had racked up over sixty confirmed enemy kills. Generally, it was assumed that ten to twenty percent of all wounded Communist combatants would eventually die of their wounds due to lack of proper medical aid and the high incidence of infection. The actual contribution to the official "body count" figures amassed by the 1st Marine Division after each patrol skirmish or battle probably would have more accurately shown over a hundred kills by the snipers. During 1967 in particular, the high number of large-scale battles made tally of official enemy battle deaths very sketchy indeed. The Communist forces always removed any dead or badly wounded soldiers during chaotic battles, often dumping their bodies into previously dug holes or tunnels to deceive American officials.

The grunts and sniper teams both expressed little concern about the body count figures. They knew when they were kicking Charlie's ass. They also knew when the enemy got an ambush to click just right and chewed up an American patrol. The distinct advantage in surprise and stealth went to the Viet Cong, who never tried to competently annihilate the Marine forces, but instead settled on giving the Americans a good bloody nose now and then, which was sure to make headlines with the anti-war press back home in the United States. Tom Casey thought his Marines would win the war if they could make the Viet Cong and the recent North Vietnamese infiltrators stand and fight.

The average American military thinker could not accurately fathom the planning and political objective of their Communist counterparts. This period of large-scale, relatively static conventional battles would eventually convince more flexible Communist high command that it was impossible for them to win against the powerful American military's vast advantages in firepower, mobility, airpower and fighting spirit. The early years of the war pitted the Marine's finest all-volunteer units, with extremely high morale, against Viet Cong soldiers who were growing weary of dying and living like sightless moles inside the tunnels that undercut the countryside.

The only major obstacle that the Marines had to get a handle on was the Viet Cong's absolute mastery of the terrain. During the river crossing on Tuscaloosa, the Viet Cong set up and executed a masterful U-shaped ambush of startling proportions. If the Communists had possessed the same level of offensive firepower as the American Marines, they might well have won the battle.

The Marine generals in Da Nang knew they had Charlie on the ropes, and they pressed their battalions ever more aggressively into the hostile paddies, praying for another decisive fixed engagement. Meanwhile, Sergeant Casey represented the ideal aggressive warrior spirit that had made the Marines masters of every battlefield and foe for over two hundred years.

Casey constantly worked on increasing his snipers' proficiency by providing ambush firepower and highly accurate supporting fire for the large number of squad platoon-size patrols now crisscrossing the Arizona Territory daily. The success of the snipers' supporting efforts on Tuscaloosa also reached the ears of other Marine battalions in the regiment.

The 1st battalion, 5th Marines, at Hill 51 just south of Tam Ky requested the services of Casey's sniper teams to run ambushes and night patrols in their TAOR in the rice fields twenty-five miles south of Da Nang. Casey was starting to chafe at the bit to get back to Hill 35 while his new snipers had been going out on patrols, but the youngsters had not received any of his personal attention. The late December group of newly arriving sniper candidates included Ramon Mendoza, Martin Berry, Charles Monroe, Dennis Bolton, Calvin Brown, and Jimmy Hudson. The monsoon rains were falling in increasingly heavier torrents, and most patrols experienced scant success in cornering the enemy, who was consumed with hit-and-run ambushes and the nightly mining of the major roads, thwarting Marine supply efforts.

Casey was finally relieved and ordered back to Chu Lai. His three sniper teams based in An Hoa were left in the capable hands of Corporal Ron Willoughby, who'd distinguished himself on Operation Tuscaloosa along with his young, heroic partner, Vaughn Nickell. The two men had made a name for the sniper platoon as fearless and deadly marksmen. All the platoon leaders in 2/5 started requesting the services of the Grim Reaper's younger brothers from the 5th Marine Sniper Platoon. Ulysses S. Black and Loren Kleppe also put in their share of night patrols and ambushes.

The Marines of 2/5 were commanded by Lieutenant Colonel William E. Earhart, who had seen the benefits of night patrolling in providing security to the home base by interdicting enemy patrols. The Viet Cong were especially effective during the winter season when long dark nights prevailed over the An Hoa Basin. The Viet Cong had never been timid about probing Marine lines at night.

Once the veteran VC commanders found a weak spot in the perimeter defenses, suicide teams of sappers would be sent in to infiltrate by surprise and set off high-explosive chargers. The explosives carried by practically naked VC suicide soldiers were borne in knapsack-like satchels and were either time or command detonated. The Viet Cong targeted Marine ammunition dumps, artillery emplacement, helicopter parks, and any command communication centers. They would often soften up An Hoa with short mortar attacks and then employ infantry small-arms-probing fire before running their sappers through a breech in the Marines' defenses. An Hoa had never been successfully penetrated before, although the Viet Cong had mortared and probed the security guards' bunkers along the airstrip on many occasions. The giant Marine base at Da Nang had been successfully attacked, and the ammunition and aviation fueled dumps blown up.

Chu Lai had been attacked on several occasions in late 1966, and the snipers provided the ambush deterrent and the vigilant observation missions that had saved the 11th Marines artillery batteries from total destruction.

Sergeant Tom Casey had devised a regular schedule of night ambushes, daylight patrols, and defensive bunker placements that had made the vital artillery positions safe from continued sapper infiltration. He had finally received the credit he was due for planning and executing a solid defense strategy protecting artillerymen on Hill 35. The commanding officer of the 11th Marines, Maj. I. L. Carver, in a memorandum dated December 21, 1966, recommended Casey for the Bronze Star for outstanding combat performance in keeping with the highest traditions of the U.S. Naval Service.

Casey was courageous, skillful, and completely devoted to his men, but naturally, since he was only a sergeant, he never received his medal. As Captain Doherty, perhaps the most honest and forthcoming officer I ever served under, said: "If the Marines gave medals to every man who performed a courageous act on the battlefield or risked his life for his buddies—well, I'd need an army of clerks to type out all the awards. I can tell you this one fact, though—on Operation Tuscaloosa during the fight on the sandbar, all my boys were *men* that day!"

Sergeant Thomas G. Casey can forever be remembered here, at least, as a true and proud combat leader whose snipers would follow him anywhere. There was perhaps no finer combat leader serving in the Marines during 1966 and 1967 than Sergeant Tom Casey. With or without his Bronze Star, he will forever serve as an example of strength, honor, and leadership to his snipers.

In keeping with his excursion into the realm of battlefield glory, let me also say that Luther Humiton, John Lafley, John Jessmore, and the big redhead Benny Burns, and I would also have followed Captain Jerry Doherty in to the flames of hell. And we felt more confident when battle-proven NCOs Gunny Huzak, Gunny Hones, and Gunny Gutierrez, or the battlefield's premier combat NCO, Sergeant Harold Wadley, were present to back up the officers with experienced counsel and a steady hand.

The first major operation scheduled after Tuscaloosa was Independence. Sergeant Casey selected Dennis Toncar and Fred Sanders to accompany the Golf Company warriors of the 2nd Battalion, 5th Marines. The Golf Company Marines were raring to see some combat after providing a platoon-blocking force on Tuscaloosa that finally halted the Viet Cong's escape and forced their fleeing commander and his remaining troops into La Bac 1 and La Bac 2. The Golf Company Marines had proved their toughness and resiliency by patrolling the An Hoa Basin month in and month out. Now the razor-sharp Marines were gung-ho as they boarded choppers to commence their assault on Viet Cong strongholds to the south in the Que Son Valley.

On February 1st, 1967, Sanders and Toncar heaved their fear up the slanting ramp of a CH-46 Sea Knight helicopter. The entire assemblage of Golf Company was transported in four helicopters over the Que Son Mountains directly south of An Hoa. The rice fields swam like sunfish under the helicopter's belly as the double-propped troop transport cleared the mountains. The paddies ran into a series of small, jungle-infested hills that grew smaller until they disappeared under the lazy blue ribbon of the Thu Bon River as it wound past An Hoa in the extreme west.

The green bug-like choppers came in low in single file, and the rear cargo ramps hydraulically lowered as swarms of green-clad Marines jumped off into the dirt pastures of the valley. The Marines deployed without incident and formed up into platoons marching in columns abreast and fanning out across the flat landscape. The officers and NCOs moved their troops about a thousand meters through light brush toward a shallow series of dark hills.

Almost at once, small arms fire cracked into the Golf point unit, and the Marines went to ground, seeking a clear direction to return fire. Sanders and Toncar, in the middle of the column, tugged at their equipment, trying to break out their binoculars to get a fix on the enemy fire team. The first shots were followed by a long burst of automatic fire while more Viet Cong reinforced their ambush team and directed heavy, accurate, plunging fire onto the Marine point. Fred Sanders shouldered his M1-D and peered through the scope, trying desperately to pick out the muzzle flashes of the enemy gunners.

Just as he and Toncar located the dust kicking up from the enemy muzzle blasts, an accurate burst of fire tore into the point man's chest and he fell dead on the spot. Two other point fire-team members took glancing hits that were not fatal, but the effect of having three point scouts down in the first minutes of the firefight was unnerving as hell. Fortunately, the Viet Cong were satisfied with their initial success and immediately broke off the encounter.

Golf Company got its composure back and hurriedly formed a loose perimeter while the skipper radioed An Hoa for medevac. After ten minutes elapsed, the trusty old UH-34 slid out of the sun and bounced to a rest in a cloud of dust and turbulence. The Golf corpsman had raced to tie off the wounds of the two surviving grunts with battle dressings. One man was a serious bleeder, and the corpsman tied a tourniquet around his upper thigh to slow the bleeding. The Marines were tagged, and the KIA (Killed In Action) was lifted by his shoulders and boots by four other survivors and shoved into the helicopter's cargo bay. The chopper lifted off and headed north toward the battalion aid station at An Hoa, fifteen miles away.

The Golf Company commander gave the order to saddle up, the new point scout broke trail, heading deeper into the Que Son Valley. Within ten minutes the Marine column was snaking over an incline of paddy dikes that rose toward treelines that shaded another of the many hamlets in the area.

Suddenly, another flight of incoming bullets ripped through the humid midday air and slammed into the point scout and his lead fire-team members. The deadly rounds cut clean through the protective Kevlar flack vests, then flesh and bone, killing the fourth replacement scout where he stood. He never knew what had lanced his tender body and ended his young life. Two more line grunts were hit along with the point scout and went down screaming in fear as the 7.62mm short, Chinese 123-grain full-metal-jacketed bullets with steel cores broke through bone and sinew, sending the rest of the point squad diving for cover.

The Golf Company gunnery sergeant glanced at Sanders and Toncar. They were still scoping the field, looking for enemy shooters. The Company gunny was another Korean War veteran, and he knew he had to get some accurate return fire on the Viet Cong position right away or there would be hell to pay. The Viet Cong gunfire picked up rhythm, and the deadly missiles from their SKS rifles and AK-47 assault rifles poured into the Marine lines.

The gunny waved a massive hand toward the point and yelled at Fred Sanders, "You two snipers, get your weapons and take the point. We got to shoot our way out of here. There ain't enough fuckin' cover here to hide a damn rabbit."

Fred Sanders was a Tennessee boy. All "Sons of the Confederacy" take a certain pride in battlefield heroics, which no doubt emanates from the bygone fields of glory at Bull Run and the bitter defeats at Shiloh and Gettysburg. However, there was one thing Fred Sanders was not, and that was a dumb shit. Sanders looked at Toncar, who looked back at him in mortal dread of taking the point with a scoped sniper rifle that had no fields of vision for close-quarter shooting. Sanders got up his nerve and explained to the gunny that he couldn't see the enemy well enough close up to keep on target. Every shot from the heavy recoiling M1-D Garand would throw the scope completely off target. By the time Fred Sanders could ride the recoil back to his natural point of aim and fire again, he might as well be "dead right there."

"Gunny, I can't see shit through this here scope up close like that," Sanders said. "We ain't been taught to take the point! We're supposed to cover your troops when they move, or shoot somebody way off yonder!"

The gunny looked around as the enemy fire stopped for a second time that afternoon. He rubbed sweat off his face and looked into Sanders's eyes. "Well, dammit, if you two boys can't walk point or shoot that fuckin' rifle up close," he said, "what the hell are you snipers good for?"

The Golf Company gunny was expressing the same doubts that many old combat hands felt about the proper employment of Marine sniper teams. The infantry commanders and staff NCOs knew that their veteran point scouts and riflemen could shoot better than any soldiers on earth. The average Marine combat leader relied on company artillery, such as mortars and recoilless rifles, heavy artillery and air support, when their units got hit hard and couldn't advance. Most combat leaders considered snipers to be a pain in the butt. Many officers simply told the sniper teams to get in the column and become regular infantry.

On Tuscaloosa, of course, 5th Marine Snipers had made a decisive contribution to the survival of the trapped Marines on the sandbar. Later in the battle, the snipers eliminated enemy mortar positions and machine gun nests, allowing the infantry to advance and destroy the enemy. Carefully and wisely employed, the snipers of Tom Casey's growing detachment would prove that an accurate long-range weapons team could take out enemy leaders, crew-served weapons, medics, signalmen, and opposing menacing snipers.

Another medevac chopper was called into remove the second group of dead and wounded. The Golf Company commander got on the radio to the 11th Marines artillery batters at An Hoa and gave his company's position and azimuth of march. Artillery would stay on call with 8-inch howitzers that could reach the Marines' position if they were ambushed again.

The column got to its feet and moved more warily towards the string of hamlets nestled along a grove of banana and date trees some five hundred meters to the southeast. The Marines were being sucked deeper into the Que Son Valley and were rapidly extending the limits of the protective artillery fan. Finally, the third Golf point scout broke through light brush that skirted the second village. The point fire team went to ground as the gunny called Fred Sanders and Dennis Toncar forward to scope out the ville with their binoculars.

Toncar observed about a dozen small hooches and as many men grouped around a fire in the middle of a small clearing. One Vietnamese was holding a Chi-Com automatic rifle as he stood watch at the front of a hut. The others bullshitted and smoked long Vietnamese pipes. Another two Viet Cong porters strode past and gathered soldiers, hefting large bundles of rice or some other foodstuff over their shoulders.

The gunny got on the radio and made a Situation Report (SITREP) to battalion headquarters in An Hoa. The artillery battery at the 11th Marine Headquarters looked over their plotting boards and realized that the Golf Company patrol was at the far limit of the big guns' range—out almost 17,000 meters. Finally realizing that his company was getting into some deep shit, the gunny ordered Sanders to take out the Viet Cong sentry. Two squads of Golf Company grunts edged forward, low-crawling with M-14 rifles cradled in their elbows.

Fred Sanders spread his legs into a comfortable prone position and pulled his left wrist back, tightening up the slack in his hasty sling. The M1-D was heavy but the weight steadied the shot. The side-mounted, 2.5-power scope came up into his eye, and the focus was bright as the crosshairs centered on the sentry's chest. Sanders had time, and watched his sights bore into the Viet Cong. The air filled his chest, and he slowly exhaled most of it until the rifle's sights fell back on the sentry, who looked bored and relaxed. The trigger slack took up until the two-stage pull stopped. Sanders squeezed ever so gently until the trigger broke, sending the heavy .30-06 match bullet smashing cleanly through the Viet Cong's sternum—exploding his heart as if it had been cleaved with an axe. The sentry was lifted off his feet and flung against a nearby hut, where he lay limp.

Never underestimate the Marine Corps' ability to achieve the proper degree of destruction when there are villages to be burned and Viet Cong to be violently dispatched.

As Fred Sanders took his sniper rifle down from his shoulder and gave a self-assured smile to his buddy Dennis Toncar, the two squads of the Golf Company grunts opened fire with everything they had in the general direction of the unlucky Viet Cong village. M-12s blasted away, tearing the thatch in chunks from the walls of previously pristine huts. M-79s lobbed 40mm high explosive grenades by the dozen through the roofing and interiors of now burning hooches. A young Golf Company grunt stood stiffly aiming his M-72 Light Antitank Assault Weapon into the center of the ville's main street, where the prostrate bodies of Viet Cong who had not escaped into spider holes or tunnels under the huts still lay. The rocket-propelled warhead sped behind a stream of propellant gasses into a large outbuilding, blowing the thatch and lodge poles high into the gray sky in a fiery orange ball of death. M-60 machine gun crews traversed their weapons from one side of the village to the other. Their bullets lifted thatch and hundreds of wood splinters that brewed up into a storm of chaos spreading across the village.

The grunts finally got their fill of death and disaster, and their adrenal glands could finally rest for another tortured day. A perimeter was set up around the village, and the fallen Viet Cong were left where they had died. Some lucky few Viet Cong soldiers had escaped to the nearest tunnel complex, which would lead outside the village into the jungle—and safety. The Golf Company grunts figured that they would eventually run across the lucky bastards who escaped and finally put them out of their misery. Fred Sanders had just begun to relax, and he spoke quietly to Dennis Toncar about having lined up the Viet Cong sentry for the first kill of the engagement.

Just when the snipers were feeling a sense of usefulness, another Viet Cong machine gun opened up, sending a flight of bullets through the brush just an inch above Toncar's head. Sanders and Toncar hit the deck and began digging with their bare hands into the sandy soil, trying desperately to hide under the incoming clusters of lead that flung themselves across the Marine lines in no particular pattern. The grunts braved the incoming fire to pop up sporadically and shoot quickly aimed snap shots back into the Communist bunkers. Dennis Toncar went back to work, with his M-14 rifle on semiautomatic firing rapid-fire groups of three to five rounds that coned with deadly precision into the Viet Cong positions. Knowing full well that the Marine small arms fire was insufficient to break the VC fire superiority, the skipper got on the radio to the 11th Marines Artillery Fire Direction Control back at An Hoa, requesting urgent fire support.

"Steel Curtain, this is Golf Actual. My troops under heavy fire vicinity AT915635 in northeast sector Antenna Valley. Give me one spotting round eight-inch gun with WP. Golf Actual will adjust fire. Over."

The captain and his troops huddled inside their perimeter and sporadically returned fire. The volume and accuracy of the incoming automatic weapons fire marked the enemy as one of the hardcore Viet Cong main force units that were turning the Que Son Valley into a Communist rest and refitting area. The enemy attack would have broken off long ago had the ambushers been a local Viet Cong guerilla unit trying to shake up the Marines. These hardcore VC were the NVA-led and trained professional killers who would definitely stand and fight. Fred Sanders glanced up toward the Que Son Mountains, awaiting the artillery-spotting round that was presently spiraling down through the heavy winter clouds toward Golf Company's platoons of weary men.

Sanders and Toncar looked at each other the moment the terrible scream of the huge 8-inch howitzer shell tore through the sky towards the fractured perimeter. The round shrieked its arrival and flung its heavy mass three hundred meters over the Marine perimeter, clearing the enemy ambush by a good two hundred meters. So closely were the two combatant forces locked in deadly combat that the Viet Cong seemingly hugged the Marines to ward off incoming artillery. The Golf skipper got back on the secure net to An Hoa and was immediately relayed to the 11th Marines Fire Direction Center.

"Steel Curtain," he said, "this is Golf Actual. My Six Position is static in perimeter a hundred meters west of enemy ambush. I have unknown number of KIA and WIA Marines requiring immediate medevac. Fire mission. Drop 150 meters from spotting round number one fired AT 915354. Fire WP spotting round number two using eight-inch gun. Golf Actual will adjust. Over."

The Golf captain had cut the range of the second white phosphorus spotting round by 150 meters. If the artillery adjusted the second shell impact just behind the enemy position, then the captain would call for two-gun fire mission close, switching to high explosive rounds. In a few short minutes a second heavy artillery shell slammed into the earth just over Viet Cong main force positions. The Golf skipper wasted no time in calling a "fire for effect" mission, with each of the 11th Marines' eight self-propelled guns firing a high explosive shell close into the chaos of the ambush site.

"Steele Curtain. This is Golf Actual. Fire mission. Drop another 50 meters. Repeat, drop five-zero meters to second spotting round at AT915354. Fire HE for effect 'danger close.' Repeat, enemy is a hundred meters east and locked up with Golf Marines in firefight. After fire mission run and secure, send immediate medevac my position. Approximately eight Marines KIA and WIA evacs Golf Actual, over."

"Golf Actual, this is Steele Curtain Fire Control," came the response. "Running fire mission. Fire for effect eight-inch guns with HE. Target VC ambush 200 meters drop from AT915354. Enemy emplaced 100 meters east your Six. Fire 'danger close.' Medevac is alerted. Estimated fifteen minutes ETA your position after fire mission secured. Running fire mission. Steele Curtain, out."

Fred Sanders lifted himself up on one elbow and sighted in on a standing Viet Cong in a camouflage pith helmet who wore a pistol in a leather holster strapped across his chest. His dark green uniform marked him as one of the Northern Vietnamese or Chinese advisors who helped plan the Viet Cong ambushes and defensive strategy in the Que Son Valley. Sanders knew he only had a brief moment to fire as the NVA officer waved, signaling his troops to swing closed the flank of their effective L-shaped ambush.

The trigger took up smooth and clean as the M1-D bucked hard in Sanders's sweaty grip. When the scopes settle back into the original position of aim, the Communist field commander was gone. Sanders's bullet had torn a gaping hole in the young officer's chest, and at no more than one hundred meters, the force of the bullet had pumped 173 grains of metal into his heart, expending 2,400 foot pounds of energy.

The venerable .30-06 bullet had a .308 diameter, which also would be utilized in the M-14's .308 NATO round. This bullet had the perfect ballistic and accuracy to cut through brush, logs, small trees, and light armor and still kill effectively with one shot. Later, in early spring, the Marines would be forced to equip their battle-proven riflemen with caliber .223 M-16 rifles, which delivered less than a third the punch and a third of the range of the M-1 and M-14 rifles. Needless to say, Fred Sanders was getting pretty salty, and another Marine would have had to choke Fred to fuckin' death to get that old M1-D away from him.

The first artillery shell blasted into the Viet Cong ambushers and tore deeply into the earth, throwing heaps of vegetation and dirt high into the sky. The second round plowed into the general vicinity of the first shell a few seconds later. God in Heaven, it must have been a hellacious surprise for any of the ambushers who looked up or got out of their holes to run after the first shell impacted. The Marine 8-inch gun threw a 2-4mm shell almost eleven miles with enough explosive power to wound or kill any soldiers within a hundred meters of its impact area, depending on the type of surface the round burst upon. In the rice valley, the earth was soft and muddy, laced with the runoff from the rice fields.

Fortunately for Fred Sanders and Dennis Toncar, the soft ground sucked up a significant amount of energy and shrapnel. The Marines were still terrified as they clustered in shallow, quickly dug holes as pieces of hot shrapnel big enough to cut a man in two whizzed overhead. The effects of a "danger close" fire mission were petrifying to the Marines near the impact area and absolutely murderous to the Viet Cong.

Sitting up to pepper the Marines with small arms fire, the Viet Cong soldiers had been caught dead to rights by the close artillery support from An Hoa. The 8-inch shell bursts had killed many of the VC riflemen by concussion. Others were literally ripped to pieces by the terrible explosion that threw earth and debris a hundred feet into the cold, gray sky.

As the second pair of rounds impacted, there was no more ambush site left to menace the Marines. Sanders hugged Toncar and let out a rebel yell in his glee to still be alive. Dennis Toncar, on the other hand, looked white as a sheet but still managed to stroke the worn wooden stock of his M-14 rifle, which had delivered him and his partner from another catastrophe at the hands of the elusive and combat-veteran Viet Cong. The remaining VC had hit their escape tunnels and only left half a dozen or so riflemen to face the Marines once they realized that heavy Marine artillery was on the way. The Viet Cong and their NVA advisors were cagey and jungle-wise soldiers, and if anything could be said about them in the way of praise, it was that they were damn hard to kill.

Sanders took in a full breath of cool air and looked at the Marine wounded that were being carried on stretchers and in ponchos into the awaiting choppers. The tattered bodies of the Marine KIAs would be lifted out in another chopper after being tagged and bagged. After preliminary ID at An Hoa, the dead heroes would be flown to Graves Registration in Da Nang for the long flight home to the land of milk and honey.

Sanders and Toncar walked through the fire teams and rifle squads of hard-faced kids who were growing old in battle. The young Marine survivors of 2/5 were quiet and sat smoking cigarettes, reflecting on the general value of life. Fred Sanders knew that he would always shoot straight and true to protect these young men. These brothers in the most misunderstood war in American history had made a silent bond that in all ways—from this day on— the surviving warriors would honor their dead and serve the living. Sanders smiled, glad to be alive, and thought about the spoiled teenagers back in the States who were bored, driving around with their girlfriends, with full bellies, and a soft warm bed to sleep in. Sanders was proud of himself and his fellow Marine grunts. They had faced the bullets like men and had come out on top, with stronger understanding of freedom and liberty than the protected would ever likely know.

"Daring beyond the
Point of Martial Prudence"

Chester G. Hearn

WHEN LIEUTENANT CHARLES W. READ REPORTED FOR DUTY ABOARD the *Florida* at Mobile Bay, John Newland Maffitt wrote in his journal, "Mr. Read is quiet and slow, and not much of a military officer of the deck, but I think him reliable and sure, though slow." Perhaps this first impression was influenced by Read's youth, for in a few short months, Maffitt would wire that he was, "daring beyond the point of Martial Prudence."

A June 1860 graduate of the U.S. Naval Academy, Read served only seven months before resigning to enter the service of his home state of Mississippi. During the lopsided battle of New Orleans, he had been one of the few Confederates cited for bravery. Taking command of the *McRae* from her fatally wounded captain, young Read continued to fight the ship until it became permanently disabled. He then retrieved and returned to action the CSS *Resolute*, which had been run ashore and abandoned early in the battle by a less courageous commander. After the Confederate surrender at New Orleans, Read distinguished himself as gunnery officer of the ironclad ram *Arkansas* in her battle with Farragut's overwhelming Union fleet at Vicksburg.

Read had watched the lackluster career of the *Lapwing* with interest. When the *Florida* captured the brig *Clarence* off the Cape San Roque, he saw a chance for his own command. Read presented Maffitt with a bold plan to take 20 men from the *Florida,* including an engineer and a transports, and "cut out a gunboat or a streamer of the enemy.... If it was found impossible to board a gunboat, or a merchant streamer, it would [still] be possible to fire the shipping in Baltimore."

The *Clarence* seemed ideal for the purpose. She carried 10,000 bags of Brazilian coffee consigned to a Baltimore merchant, and her genuine registry and clearance papers might get the vessel safely through the Union blockade at the Chesapeake's mouth and into the congested inner harbor. After destroying what shipping he could and escaping to sea with a steamer, Read planned to rejoin Maffitt and together destroy Northern commerce and harass the ports along the undefended New England Coast.

Maffitt was reminded of a proposal he had once made to Secretary Mallory to raid and burn the New York Navy Yard. Mallory had rejected the plan as too risky, but Mallory had no say here. Maffitt enthusiastically approved the plan, added a brass 6-pounder howitzer to Read's store of small arms, and stated: "You might make a capture or two on the way up. You'll be on your own, no orders to hamper you. Your success will depend upon yourself, and your sturdy heart."

On May 7, 1863, the new Confederate cruiser *Clarence* dipped her new colors, filled her sails, and headed north. Among the many things going through the mind of her 23-year-old commander were Maffitt's final words of caution, "If you find it impossible to enter Hampton Roads, you will continue up the coast to Nantucket. The *Florida* should be there until July 4, unless . . ."

In the hazardous business of commerce destroying, eight weeks can be forever.

The *Clarence*, which turned out to be a mediocre sailor, approached the Windward Islands, but after two uneventful weeks she had chased many strange sail but captured none. With the brig's larder depleted, Read overhauled a British bark. When Assistant Engineer Eugene H. Browne boarded to ask for supplies, her master flew into a rage that he had been fired upon by what he believed to be a Union merchant ship. But when Read hoisted the Stars and Bars, the captain softened: "I'll give you the whole darned ship if you want it," he said, ordering his steward to break out the stores. Read reciprocated with 300 bags of coffee. The first crisis ended and fresh provisions filled the supply room.

Early in June the *Clarence* approached the American coast, with a startling transformation in her armament. As Averett had done on the

Lapwing, Read had his men convert surplus spars into an imposing battery of quaker guns, painted black and mounted on wooden carriages. The crew cut gun ports, placed the guns in position, and rehearsed firing a quaker broadside on command.

On June 6, 250 miles west of Bermuda, the *Clarence* captured her first prize, the bark *Whistling Wind* of Philadelphia. With a broadside run out, a puff of smoke spewing from the howitzer, and the Confederate colors fluttering over an unlikely assailant, the *Whistling Wind*'s master hauled up his courses and waited for the boarding officer. Read found the bark laden with coal for Admiral Farragut's squadron on the Mississippi. Gratified that he could destroy supplies bound for the enemy, Read burned the ship.

Early the next morning, the *Clarence* intercepted the schooner *Alfred H. Partridge* of New York, laden with arms and clothing that the master claimed were being shipped to Confederate forces in Texas via the neutral port of Matamoras, Mexico. At first Read doubted the skipper's claim, but he knew that many Northern merchants secretly traded with the South, exchanging a variety of goods for cotton to supply the empty mills of New England. Read bonded the prize for $5,000 and released the ship under the pledge that the bond would be cancelled if the cargo was faithfully delivered "to loyal citizens of the Confederate States." The captain kept his promise.

On June 9 the *Clarence* captured the Boston bark *Mary Alvina* bound for New Orleans with a cargo of commissary stores for the United States Army. Read burned her after removing what supplies he needed, including some recent newspapers. From these, and from information gathered from prisoners, Read learned that all vessels entering Hampton Roads were being stopped, searched, and prevented from entering unless their cargoes were specifically designated for the federal government. Gunboats watched all vessels, and sentries patrolled the wharves. Although the *Clarence*'s papers were legitimate, Read realized that he would never get past the blockade and "that it was impossible to carry out the instructions of Commander Maffitt."

Unclear as to his next move, Read decided to cruise along the coast and somehow capture a supply ship bound for Fortress Monroe with proper clearance papers. And he wanted a ship faster than the sluggish *Clarence*, but capturing one would require different tactics.

Just off the Virginia Capes on June 12 the lookout reported a sail six miles distant and running before a fair breeze. Read knew the *Clarence* couldn't catch her, and the brass six-pounder couldn't reach her, but he wanted that ship. With gun ports closed, Read hoisted the American flag upside down—the traditional signal of a ship in distress.

From the deck of the bark *Tacony*, in ballast from Port Royal, S.C., to Philadelphia, Captain William Munday peered through a light morning mist at what seemed to be a fellow sailor in serious trouble. But there was something unnatural about the brig. If it were really in trouble, it was close enough to shore for the crew to reach safely in the ship's boats. While intuition warned him to leave her alone, the law of the sea compelled him to offer help. And then there were lucrative salvage claims to consider. Munday eased toward the *Clarence*.

As the two ships drew closer, Munday observed a boat loaded with 10 sailors shove off the *Clarence* and pull toward his ship. As the boat bumped against the *Tacony*, the men scrambled hand over hand to the deck and "presented revolvers at the captain and mate and those on deck and ordered them into their boat and took them to the *Clarence* as prisoners." Read, who had let his reddish mustache grow and looked like an old-time buccaneer, led the boarding party. Learning from the ship's log that the *Tacony* was a much faster sailor than his coffee merchant, he decided to trade vessels and issued orders to transfer his "armament" and flag.

Hardly had the new orders been issued to transfer ships when the schooner *M. A. Schlinder*, in ballast from Port Royal to Philadelphia, approached the scene. For a second time Read took his boat and within half an hour had captured the schooner and set it afire.

Meanwhile, Captain George E. Teague of the schooner *Kate Stewart* noticed smoke rising from a burning vessel. As he drew nearer he saw two other vessels, apparently assisting the ship in flames. Read saw him coming, but his six-pounder was still in a boat en route to the *Tacony*. As *Stewart* came within hailing distance of the *Clarence*, the brig's gun ports popped open to reveal a broadside ready to fire into his ship. Teague jumped to his cabin roof and bellowed though a trumpet. "For God's sake don't shoot! I surrender!" Ordered to bring his papers to the *Clarence*, Teague gazed unbelievingly at the wooden guns that forced him to surrender.

The *Stewart*, which was owned by the same company as the *Tacony*, presented a problem: She carried passengers—20 ladies on their way to Mexico. With too many prisoners on board already, Read decided to bond the *Stewart* for $7,000 and have Teague take all 50 "guests" to shore. He knew that the moment the *Stewart* reached port Teague would warn the Union Navy, but there might be a way to turn this to his advantage. Read boasted privately to Teague that a great fleet of Southern ships would soon strike the Atlantic coast and destroy Union blockading force. The navy would be searching for ships far more formidable than the little *Tacony*.

Before the morning ended, the converted *Tacony* confirmed her superior sailing qualities by chasing and capturing the brig *Arabella* in less than 30 minutes. The *Arabella* carried a neutral cargo, and Read bonded her for $30,000, expressing regret that he had a few hours earlier bonded the *Kate Stewart*.

At noon Read returned to the *Clarence*, now cast adrift with more than 8,000 bags of coffee still in her hold. What a treat for Confederate troops, used to drinking chicory root and other concoctions, to be able to land her on a Southern shore, but this was impossible. As the ship burned, the pungency of scorched timbers and tarred rigging mixed with the aroma of roasted coffee. Forced to abandon a scheme to enter Hampton Roads, Read headed north for his rendezvous along longitude 70 with the *Florida*—unaware that Maffitt had wasted 15 days at Rocas Island waiting for the *Lapwing*.

On Saturday afternoon, June 13, Secretary Gideon Welles noted in his diary that "three vessels were yesterday captured by a pirate craft off Cape Henry and burnt. Sent [Gustavus Vasa] Fox at once with orders to telegraph to New York and Philadelphia, etc., for every vessel in condition to proceed to sea in search of this wolf that is prowling so near to us. . . ." Fox moved quickly. By evening, he had issued pursuit orders to naval commandants from Boston to Hampton Roads.

Meanwhile, the *Tacony*'s former master touched ashore at a small harbor on the New Jersey coast and caught the first train to Philadelphia. There he recounted a tale of fire, terror, and piracy to the ship's owners and waiting reporters. The press printed Teague's version of Read's fictional account of the great Confederate fleet poised to ravage the eastern seaboard, further sensationalizing it by including both the dreaded *Alabama* and the now infamous *Florida* in the armada. These rumors drifted into the Navy Office, intensifying the prevailing confusion.

The welter of pursuit orders fills more than 80 pages of the Official Records, and includes vessels ranging from warships to converted pleasure yachts. Typical of the messages sent was an order to Admiral Hiram Paulding, commanding the New York Navy Yard: "The privateer *Clarence*, a sailing vessel fitted out by the *Oreto*, made three captures yesterday . . . send what vessels [you] can in pursuit." Out went the *Tuscarora, Dai Ching*, and *Adela*, with a promise from Paulding that, "We hope to get the *Virginia* and *Kittantinny* off tomorrow."

The United States Navy would not be accused of apathy. Within three days, 30 armed ships cruised the coast in search of "the pirates," their commanders in search of prestige and promotion. Unfortunately, organization and planning had been overlooked in the scramble. The ships fanned out at random. As days passed, it became evident that the entire navy was looking in the wrong place. A few steamers executing a proper search within predetermined grids probably would have caught the wooden-gunned *Tacony* within a day or two.

Late on June 14, Secretary Welles heard of Read's change of ships from the owners of the *Tacony*; his navy was chasing the wrong vessel. Because most of his ships were out at sea and out of communication, Welles dispatched new orders to hunt for the Confederate: "Charter or seize half a dozen moderate-sized, fast vessels; put on board an officer, a dozen men, plenty of small arms and one or two howitzers. Send them out in various directions. Take any vessel that can be sent to sea within the next forty-eight hours."

The whereabouts of Read and the *Tacony* remained a mystery until June 15 when he captured and burned the brig *Umpire* about 300 miles off the Delaware River. When a suspicious steamer appeared on the horizon, Read stuffed his prisoners into the hold and waited for the vessel to pass. Later that night, a Union warship hailed the bark asking for news about the "piratical *Tacony*." Read trumpeted back, "Yes, we saw her at dusk chasing an East Indiaman." He added a bogus heading and waited, holding his breath until the Union commander accepted the reply and hurried off in pursuit.

Another Union warship unexpectedly appeared through the morning mist and stopped the *Tacony*, her commander raising the same question. Read, now well-rehearsed, replied with the same answer but gave different bearings. Once again the officer took the bait and raced away in the opposite direction. Read knew that the enemy had not yet obtained a good description of his ship. In the next few days, he gave them one.

On June 20 he overhauled the huge packet *Isaac Webb*, with 750 passengers aboard and en route to new homes in America. One blank shot from his popgun brought her into the wind. As the crowds on deck gazed down in awe at the row of guns ready at the broadside, Read went on board and talked to the master, knowing that he could not burn the ship. Settling for a $40,000 bond, he was returning to the *Tacony* when the curious skipper of the fishing schooner *Micabar* sailed over to investigate. His curiosity ended when three black-painted barrels poked through the *Tacony's* gun ports. In full view of the *Webb's* panicked passengers, Read ordered the schooner torched. Many of the immigrants dropped to their knees and raised their voices to heaven, unaware that they had already been spared.

The following day, as Read continued looking for the *Florida*, he captured the fine new clipper ship *Byzantium*, out of Newcastle for New York with a large cargo of coal. Read considered retaining the ship to fuel the *Florida's* bunkers, but he was beginning to worry that Maffitt had encountered misfortune. With regrets he ordered the match.

Later in the day, the *Tacony* overhauled and burnt the bark *Goodspeed*, returning to New York in ballast from Londonderry. Upon reaching shore, her angry skipper concocted a story that a Union gunboat stood off a mile or two and watched cowardly as Read destroyed his vessel. The press, already faulting the navy, had a field day. Gideon Welles doubted the accusation, but the publicity forced him to undertake a formal, but inconclusive, investigation. It turned out naval vessels searching for the *Tacony* actually had passed the *Byzantium* and the *Goodspeed* earlier in the day, but they didn't stop to warn the commercial ships of Read's presence.

June 22 was an unfortunate day for New England fishing schooners, which dotted the sea in every direction, attracted by shoals of spawning cod and halibut. Before evening, there would be five fewer of them. Read captured the schooners *Marengo, Florence, Elizabeth Ann, Rufus Choate,* and *Ripple*, sparing only one. He noted in his journal, "The *Florence* being an old vessel I bonded her and placed seventy-five prisoners on her. The other schooners were burned."

Read continued north, keeping a sharp eye out for the smoke of an enemy steamer and wondering if the navy had simply decided to ignore him. On June 23 he captured and burned *Ada* and *Wanderer*, two more fishing schooners. From recent newspapers and talkative prisoners he learned that the navy now had an accurate description of the *Tacony* and had started to overhaul all ships of her kind. It was time for another change.

The following day he stopped the big clipper ship *Shatemuc*, bound from Liverpool to Boston with hundreds of Irish immigrants. Read boarded the vessel and threatened to burn the ship unless the captain signed a $150,000 bond. The captain, a crusty veteran whose face reddened quickly behind a stream of profanity, looked at the throng of anxious passengers frantically praying for help from above, decided the young sea raider might not be bluffing, and signed the bond.

Read wanted to burn the ship despite the huge passenger list, for the *Shatemuc*'s hold contained tons of iron plate and war supplies for the North. He wasted most of the day attempting to capture enough prizes to take off the prisoners, but was finally forced to set the ship free.

That evening, just before dark, the mackerel schooner *Archer* became Read's twentieth prize. Out of ammunition for the howitzer, he had to invent new ways of punishing the enemy. In his diary he noted, "During the night we transferred all our things on board the schooner *Archer*. At 2 a.m. set fire to the *Tacony* and stood west. The schooner *Archer* is a fishing vessel of 90 tons, sails well, and is easily handled. No Yankee gun boat would ever dream of suspecting us. I therefore think we will dodge our pursuers for a short time. It is my intention to go along the coast with a view to burning the shipping in some exposed port and of cutting out a steamer."

By morning only a charred, unidentifiable hulk remained of the *Tacony*. Read had destroyed his trail. While more than 38 Union ships prowled the Atlantic searching for the *Tacony*, and the powerful mayors of large port cities pressuring Welles for more action, Read and his crew commissioned the tiny schooner *Archer* as a new Confederate man-of-war. Three cheers and a ration of grog accompanied the raising of the flag.

By the morning of June 26, the *Archer*, looking like any other fishing schooner, lay off Portland, Maine. Read picked up two local lobstermen who had been adrift in a dory throughout the night and fed them a hot breakfast. When Albert T. Bibber and Elbrige Titcomb were told they were prisoners of the Confederate States Navy, they thought it a joke, believing they were guests of fellow fishermen out for a frolic. They supplied information regarding Portland's defenses, which included the United States revenue cutter *Caleb Cushing*, schooner rigged and mounting a 12- and 32-pounder. This stirred Read's interest, but when he learned that the fast passenger liner *Chesapeake* lay at a wharf ready to sail for New York in the morning, his attention shifted to the larger vessel.

At sundown the *Archer*, piloted by the helpful lobstermen, crept into the harbor and anchored. For their reward, Bibber and Titcomb were clapped in irons and herded below. Read gathered his officers and informed them of his plans to capture the *Chesapeake*, burn the shipping in the harbor, and during the confusion dash back to sea. But Engineer Browne doubted his ability to manage the engines of the big *Chesapeake* without help from another engineer, and he worried that steam would be down and impossible to raise before morning—leaving the ship under the guns of the fort. Read changed his plan and decided to grab the *Caleb Cushing*.

"There's a good offshore breeze blowing," Read told his crew. "After getting beyond the fort, we'll go back and fire the shipping." All knelt for a short prayer. Every man felt the weight of his responsibility, and listened reverently as their captain implored heaven to bless the enterprise and bring independence to the Confederacy. From tired bodies came solemn "Amens."

When the moon set at 1:30 a.m., Read selected three men to take the *Archer* to sea and wait. He and 19 others split into two boats, and with muffled oars rowed silently toward the slumbering *Caleb Cushing*. Good fortune still favored the raiders. The cutter's captain had just died and his successor, Lt. James H. Merryman, was not expected to reach Portland until the morning. For one night only, the command fell into the youthful hands of Lt. Dudlay Davenport, a native of the South. Half the crew and three of her officers were on shore liberty. A dozen remained on board, but only two stood deck watch. At that moment, a good night's sleep was important. The cutter was under orders to put to sea in the morning to help track down the *Tacony*.

The two men drowsing on watch sighted Read's boats approaching and hurried below to awaken Davenport. By the time Davenport comprehended that his ship was being boarded, Read was already on the cutter's deck, his pistol leveled at the two men as they returned from their cabin. Nineteen men lined up behind Read, ready to shoot if necessary. "I'll kill you both if you make a sound," Read said. "Don't speak a word." Both men were ironed to the mast; the rest of the crew was captured while they slept in their hammocks. Everything had worked as planned. Read had the cutter, and not a sound had reached the shore. But at the very moment they were congratulating each other, the stiff offshore breeze eased, and before the fouled mooring cables could be slipped the flood tide began. Read discarded any thoughts of firing at the shipping: the problem now was survival.

Read placed oarsmen in two small boats, unshackled Titcomb to act as pilot, and towed the *Caleb Cushing* through Hussy Sound seaward against the tide. At dawn the cutter was still within range of Fort Preble, but no one seemed to notice. By early morning, the *Caleb Cushing* was five miles outside the harbor and safely beyond the guns. The breeze freshened enough to raise sail and Read recalled the boats. He felt safe enough to order breakfast for all and invited his old Annapolis classmate, Lt. Davenport, to join him. Between mouthfuls of captured bacon and eggs, Read chided his friend for deserting the South and choosing the wrong side.

While the men in gray enjoyed breakfast on their new flagship, the citizens of Portland awoke to the stunning news that the revenue cutter had mysteriously departed without orders. Church bells tolled the alarm. People swarmed to the waterfront. "Women and children filled the streets and were rushing hither and thither in aimless fright." Once word spread that Southern-born Davenport had been left in charge of the cutter, everyone concluded that he had either stolen the ship or was somehow involved in a broader conspiracy.

Amid mounting confusion, Port Collector Jedediah Jewett took matters into his own hands. Without authority or instructions, he commandeered the Boston Line sidewheeler *Forest City* and enlisted those of the *Cushing's* crew who had been on shore leave, and who were anxious to get even with Davenport for stealing their ship. Jewett collected 36 men from the 17th Regulars at Fort Preble and hustled them on board with two 12-pounder field howitzers. By 10 a.m., the *Forest City* had a head of steam, and with Jewett barking orders, the newly minted warship sliced through the harbor in pursuit of the *Caleb Cushing*.

The fast propeller steamer *Chesapeake*, impressed into service by Portland's mayor, Jacob McLellan, joined the chase. The local agent for the New York Line protested as he watched his ship armed and manned, and eventually succeeded in detaining the vessel long enough to see her vital parts protected by bales of cotton. With McLellan issuing orders, the steamer joined the pursuit with a detachment of the 7th Maine Volunteers and about 20 zealous citizens armed with squirrel rifles, ancient muskets, and rusty cutlasses. A makeshift battery of two 6-pound field guns were braced on her deck. An unarmed steam tug joined the pursuit at a safe distance, followed by a host of curious spectators in almost anything that would float.

From the deck of the *Caleb Cushing*, then 20 miles at sea and moving slowly under sail, Read saw the smoke from "Admiral-General" Jewett's attack fleet and promptly cleared for action. He had learned how to fight at New Orleans and prepared to do it again. The *Forest City* entered the pursuit ahead of the *Chesapeake*. As she came into range, Read opened with a 32-pounder that splashed about 50 yards off the *Forest City's* bow. Three more shots had her bracketed, the last falling close to her waterline. The marksmanship of Read's gunners quieted the enthusiasm of the citizen volunteers, and the *Forest City* backtracked to confer with McLellan on the faster *Chesapeake*. After a brief council of war, the two commanders decided to get a full head of steam and ram the cutter before her long gun caused serious damage.

The plan of attack might have proved disastrous for the impromptu Portland navy if Read had done a better job of checking his inventory before breakfast. Although he had 500 pounds of powder in the cutter's magazine, he could find no more than five or six 32-pound shot. Somewhere on board was a reserve shot chest, but Read couldn't find it, and prisoner-guest Davenport refused to reveal its hidden location.

Into the gun went the final rounds. When those were gone, the gun was reloaded with scraps of metal, hardware, and crushed cookware until there was nothing left to fire. Read knew it was the end, but when Browne came on deck with a ball of Dutch cheese from the officer's mess, they decided to make one final gesture, and it was rammed home and fired. Unlike many of the earlier shots, this one stuck home, and fragments of cheese splattered the deck of the *Chesapeake*, bewildering her defenders.

As the steamers crept closer, Read ordered everyone into the long boats, remaining behind with a few men long enough to fire the *Cushing*. Three hundred yards away the boats converged to watch the flames leap into her sails. A spark touched the powder, and the Confederate's twenty-second and final prize exploded into flaming splinters. By the time the *Chesapeake* reached the boats to collect their prisoners, Read and his men were waving white handkerchiefs tied to the tips of their oars. During the confusion the *Archer* almost made it safely back to sea. Only vigilance on the part of one of the liberated lobstermen caused her capture after a short chase.

Read and his men, their clothes in tatters after being ripped to pieces by a frenzied crowd in Portland, were hustled off to the protective walls of Boston's Fort Warren, where they were imprisoned for a year before being exchanged as prisoners of war. Read returned to fight again, but not until the war's final days.

Read and his men captured 22 prizes in 21 days, demonstrating just how much damage a few well-led men in a sluggish bark carrying no more firepower than a remounted 6-pound field howitzer could inflict on the Union merchant fleet. Admiral David Dixon Porter caustically wrote in later years: "A single Federal gunboat, under an intelligent captain, would have nipped Read's whole scheme in the bud." Porter must have forgotten his own ineffective search for the *Sumter*, which began in the Gulf of Mexico and extended as far as the coast of Brazil.

Inaccurate reports, false sightings, and exaggerated press coverage created hysteria all along the East Coast. Under pressure, Welles ordered every available ship into the search, but his staff could not differentiate between valid information and nonsense. Operating always on stale information, the vessels usually were two or three days behind the Confederates—and because Read changed vessels three times, they were often looking for the wrong ship. Whether Read was lucky, daring, or just extremely intelligent is moot. The fact remains, at least 38 Union warships steamed frantically up and down the northeastern seaboard, unable to stop a few determined Confederate raiders in a succession of slow, almost unarmed ships.

Jumping into North Korea

Michael E. Haas

FROM MAY TO NOVEMBER 1951 THE PARTISANS CLAIMED TO HAVE killed, wounded, or captured more than 14,000 of the enemy in 710 separate encounters. Many in the Eight Army regarded these numbers as exaggerated to an unknown extent, but the bigger problem noted was that even if the numbers were accurate, "they were inflicted on an enemy who apparently considered manpower as cheap." Limiting still further the impact of the enemy was that almost all of these casualties occurred near the coast, far from the decisive combat on the peninsula.

Even as early as 1951, the North Korean army was taking most of its casualties from shallow-penetration, commando-type raids launched by the partisans from their island bases. Soon this raiding pattern became virtually the only tactic available to the partisans for the duration of the war. For as the Communists themselves gradually lost their fear of the UN offensive, they began releasing combat units from the main lines of resistance to reinforce their rear-area security forces. With increasing frequency, the partisans found themselves engaging not rear-area security units but heavily armed infantry formations. And given their mutual hatred, the fighting between these two groups was savage.

Whether fighting under the names White Tigers or Donkeys, the ferocity of the partisans' combat went to a fanaticism seldom found in any army. Many of the Donkey units actually included a designated "suicide squad" comprised of volunteers who proudly fulfilled this role at the cost of their lives. One advisor witnessed this extreme commitment firsthand while accompanying 120 partisans on a Donkey 4 raiding party to the mainland on 14 July 1952. As he and a group of partisans became pinned down by an enemy machine gun, he watched the Donkey 4 leader react to the crisis: "The D-4 leader called on his [five-man] suicide squad to advance upon it . . . . When they reached the wire . . . four of them opened fire. The fifth man crawled under the wire and moved up to the pillbox, pulled the pins on two grenades and holding one in each hand, the man walked right into the position. This knocked out the position."

Perhaps one explanation for the extreme behavior that went far beyond simple patriotism can be found in postwar interviews provided by the partisan themselves. As these American studies confirmed, partisan combat with their Communist adversaries on the mainland was truly a vicious, "no quarter given or asked" affair: "In battle they [the partisans] exerted every effort to bring off their wounded. Capture by the enemy is a fate to be avoided at all costs. Instances were cited of officers committing suicide rather than be taken. One rescue party found some captured partisans so brutally tortured it was impossible to remove them. The victims were promptly dispatched along with their tormentors. Sentiment does not override prudence in such a crisis."

Such was the bleak "victory or death" life of the island partisans throughout the war. But as desperate as their combat proved during raids on the coast, the geography over which they fought did offer one small advantage. The proximity and availability of air and in particular naval support actually held an escape route open should circumstances dictate a fighting withdrawal seaward from the mainland. Even that small advantage, however, was denied those partisans who penetrated by parachute deep into North Korea's wild interior. If such a seemingly small tactical difference on a peninsula seems unworthy of note to some, in North Korea it proved large enough to spell the difference between survival and annihilation for the two separate partisan groups.

The postwar report revealed details of one mission:

"Three of the team were lost immediately . . . Mustang IV team [operated] for about 6 days before its members were captured or killed . . . No further word was received [after one radio report] . . . Teams were lost immediately . . Not one member of the team is known to have extracted

. . . The Hurricane team, apparently compromised, was lost soon after it was dropped . . . None of the partisans involved ever returned."

[A special group, the Baker Section] was active to train and then insert "special airborne sabotage agents" against carefully selected high-priority targets. And though it was the training aspect of this mission that consumed most of the unit's time and scarce assets during 1951, Baker did launch two significant airborne insertions into North Korea during that year. That proved unfortunate, for even with the benefit of a half-century of hindsight, the Virginia I and Spitfire missions still appear to be a sorry spectacle of U.S. leadership at its worst.

The Eighth Army launched "Virginia I" on March 1, 1951, with four U.S. Army Rangers and twenty Koreans recruited from the South Korean army's officer candidate school. The ranger volunteers were sent to Baker Section only ten days before the mission launch date, then lost the following six days of team preparation time before finally meeting their Korean teammates. To make matters worse, Eighth Army mission planners removed the team leader only hours before mission launch, belatedly realizing that his capture could lead to compromise of secret information. Having thus denied the group any chance to develop the team cohesion indispensable for such a high-risk mission, Baker Section then parachuted the leadership team into an unmarked drop zone, at night and in deep snow.

After being subjected to subzero winds blowing through the aircraft's open exit door for the entire 250-mile flight into North Korea, the Virginia I team finally parachuted into the freezing night, eight miles south of the correct drop zone. Ranger Martin Watson came down in the middle of a small village, waking in the process all the dogs and most of its inhabitants, who took notice of the big Caucasian intruder. After exhausting slogging for hours through deep snow, the team arrived at its target, a supposedly remote and lightly defended railroad tunnel 30 miles inland from the North Korean coastline. Following a brief reconnaissance, the team discovered that its target was in fact so heavily defended as to make suicidal any attempt at blowing it up.

For the next two weeks, the cold and exhausted team successfully evaded Communist search parties and it moved eastward through the mountains toward its extraction point on the east coast. On 30 March, U.S. Navy helicopters extracted three of the Rangers under heavy enemy fire before North Korean gunners terminated the extraction by downing one of the helicopters. Ranger Watson, Helicopter pilot Lt. (jg) John H. Thornton, and five partisans escaped the extraction site in the subsequent confusion, but without the team radio or any other means of arranging a second extraction attempt. The doomed mission was over, though it took another full week before the tragedy came to its final, inevitable conclusion.

Watson and Thornton were captured, interrogated, and brutally tortured before being sent to North Korea's infamous POW camps. Both survived the war, though Watson was among the last Americans released in the final exchange of prisoners (Operation Big Switch) nearly six months after the armistice was signed. Some weeks after the capture of the Americans, two of the five remaining South Korean participants struggled back to friendly lines. That proved to be their undoing, however, as the South Korean army subsequently executed both soldiers upon learning they had been captured then released after promising to spy for the Communists.

Undeterred by the Virginia I fiasco, McGee's Miscellaneous Division soon turned its attention to planning another, much more ambitious airborne insertion. Unlike the quick "slash and dash" plans for the failed railroad sabotage mission, Operation Spitfire was intended to set up a long-term, partisan base deep in Communist-controlled territory. The projected area of operations for this group formed a huge rectangle from twenty to eighty miles behind the Communists' main line of resistance, nearly five thousand square miles of central North Korea. The unusual makeup of the Spitfire team reflected McGee's hopes of avoiding the mistakes committed in the Virginia I mission.

Selected by McGee to command the operation was Captain Ellery Anderson, a British officer and former Special/Air services operative with behind-the-scenes combat experience in Europe during World War II. Already in the Miscellaneous Division, Anderson had volunteered months earlier to lead missions in North Korea if the opportunity ever arose. McGee also allowed Anderson to bring into the mission a second

British officer, a lieutenant who, unknown to McGee, had no special operations experience or even parachute training.

Though short in experience, Lt. Samuel Adams-Acton proved long in motivation and of potentially greater value to McGee, fluent in the Chinese he spoke as a result of his upbringing in China. During this period McGee also succeeded in recruiting for Spitfire a third British soldier and two Americans (including one of the three surviving Rangers from the Virginia I operation). Completing the Spitfire team was a total of thirteen Koreans, all selected on the basis of the familiarity with the proposed area of operation and their willingness to undergo parachute training.

To avoid earlier problems of dropping the main team in the wrong location, a pathfinder team comprised of Anderson, two American sergeants, and two Korean partisans parachuted at night into their designated area on 8 June 1951, a week before the arrival of the main party. During the parachute landing Anderson injured his back to such an extent he was subsequently evacuated by helicopter four days later. Four days later another night drop delivered Adams-Acton, the third British soldier, and eleven Koreans.

All jumpers in this second group were injured to varying degrees after being dispatched into trees and rocky terrain some distance from the drop zone marked by the pathfinder team. As the days progressed the problems with air support continued to bedevil the Spitfire team. Inexperienced aircrews proved incapable of finding the drop zone, even when the team marked the spot with multiple flashlights and established radio contact with the aircraft overhead. This lack of army–air force coordination and properly trained special air mission crews led to a final calamity during a scheduled resupply drop on the night of 5-6 July.

Failing to locate the drop zone that night, the aircrew returned to its airfield at dawn, refueled, and retuned immediately to fly a low-altitude search for the team's "secret" location, in broad daylight. After having unwittingly alerted every Communist unit in the area as to the general location of the team, the aircrew dropped the resupply bundles, by accident right on top of the team's hidden base camp some distance from the drop zone. Irretrievably compromised and running for their lives, the Spitfire soldiers lasted only hours before being caught by Communist troops hot on their trail. In the end only half the team managed to walk back to friendly lines. Never heard from again were six Koreans, one American, and one British sergeant. Spitfire had been decimated in less than three weeks without coming close to accomplishing its mission of setting up a partisan base behind enemy lines.

The fallout from the Spitfire calamity extended beyond the mission itself. Returning to Baker Section from his hospitalization in Japan, now-major Anderson encountered a cold reception as doubt was cast on the true extent of his injuries that resulted in the helicopter extraction from the operational area. When word leaked out that Anderson was about to be appointed the new chief of Baker Section, every American in the unit reportedly asked for reassignment from the section. Whatever the truth, the appointment was shelved and Anderson later transferred quietly back to the British army.

The determined adventurer Adams-Acton survived his first taste of behind-the-scene warfare, and after recovering from his wounds, was later assigned to a group of west coast partisans operating from islands north of Leopard Base. Only six months later, in December 1951, the lieutenant and two other UN advisors were captured as the Chinese overran the forward island outpost. After eighteen months of imprisonment and torture and less than two weeks before the armistice was finally signed, Adams-Acton and a U.S. Army lieutenant assaulted a prison guard in a futile attempt to escape their camp on 16 July 1953. Though the American survived his recapture and was returned to UN control shortly thereafter in Operation Big Switch, it appears from his reports that Adams-Acton was shot to death in a fashion strongly suggesting deliberate execution.

The abortive end of the Virginia I and Spitfire operations generated a fateful discussion within the Miscellaneous Division staff regarding the feasibility of future parachute infiltration operations. From this, two major decisions were reached. First, airborne insertions of sabotage and intelligence-gathering teams would continue despite the experience to date. Second, no American or British soldiers would accompany the Korean teams sent on these missions. Varying reasons were given for removing UN personnel from future airborne missions.

These reasons included the high-profile presence of Caucasians in an Asian culture, foreign language problems, even the difference in food requirements to sustain American and Korean appetites in the field. Although not without merit, none of these factors played a significant role in the failures of the Virginia I and Spitfire missions. Apparently overlooked in these discussions was the fundamental fact that it was the incredibly poor mission planning by these same officers that doomed the two efforts before any of the above noted factors could have possibly affected the missions' outcome.

Failing to emerge from their discussions, perhaps to save face, was the obvious decision to either cease such operations or insist on the resources and time necessary for adequate mission preparation. What did emerge was the American decision to cut the U.S. Army and British losses while continuing to parachute Koreans into North Korea, and that is precisely what happened for the duration of the war.

In the following two years, Baker Section alone parachuted more than 350 additional Korean partisans deep behind enemy lines. This number does not include the untold hundreds that appear to have been parachuted into North Korea by CIA and KLO operations. The most exhaustive postwar report on these missions describes the results with depressingly repetitive phrases: "Three of the teams were lost immediately" . . . Mustang IV team [operated] for about 6 days before its members were captured or killed . . . No further word was received [after one radio report] . . . Teams were lost immediately . . . Not one member of the above teams is known to have extracted . . . The Hurricane team, apparently compromised, was lost soon after it was dropped . . . None of the partisans involved ever returned . . . ."

The report summarizes this unconscionable two-year-long continuance of suicide missions with the terse conclusions found in the epitaph:

"In most cases there is no information whatsoever as to what happened [after the Korean parachutists landed] although it is possible that some teams were able to operate for a time . . . These decisions to use partisans against enemy supply routes in airborne operations appears to have been futile and callous."

If any of the senior American officers privy to the classified results of these missions protested orders to continue the slaughter, there is no record of their statements in any of the government records or personal memoirs uncovered by this author.

As the war drew to a close in the spring of 1953, the partisans became a major "bargaining chip" in the long-running UN-Communist negotiations. The Communists obviously wanted them disarmed and withdrawn from the islands north of the thirty-eighth parallel before the armistice agreements were signed. For obvious reasons, the UN chose to keep the still-potent force on the islands as an inducement to keep the negotiations on track, and not surprisingly, the South Korean government and army remained extremely wary of accepting thousands of armed and bitter North Koreans as new citizens in their war-torn country. The South Koreans could hardly be faulted for what some might consider a lack of charity toward a wartime ally. The Americans had made little attempt during the war to consult the South Koreans on a partisan force that was in all but name an extension of the U.S. Army in South Korea.

Two months before the armistice agreements were finally signed, the partisans were withdrawn from all but five islands (agreed upon in the armistice negotiations), in Operation Pappy. Thousands of partisans, their families, and tons of equipment were moved in a sealift completed in multiple stages. Tensions ran high as the partisans were gradually disarmed and sent to South Korea as stateless refugees, citizens of no country. Thousands deserted rather than be drafted into the South Korean army, a military plan scheduled from completion by February 1954.

Eventually the Eighth Army emptied the remaining five islands, and most of the once-again refugees began their painful integration into South Korean society; most but not all. Many apparently returned to North Korea either to continue the fight or attempt to blend back into their prewar communities. In the months following the signing of the armistice a few frantic radio transmissions pleading for weapons and ammunition continued to come from those who chose to continue fighting in the North. But the calls were received by Americans already instructed not to respond to the politically awkward transmissions coming from these surviving "expendables" . . . and eventually the calls died out.

The Green Faced Frogmen,
An Oral History

Mike Beamon

My team was originally assigned to a barge floating in the middle of the Mekong, that was for security reasons; we were about a half mile from either shore. We worked with the Provincial Reconnaissance Units, the PRUs, on the Phoenix Program in the Ben Tre and My Tho areas.

The provincial recon units were made up by and large of guys who were doing time for murder, rape, theft, and assault in Vietnam. The CIA would bail them out of jail under the condition that they would work in these mercenary units. And we, the SEAL team, but primarily the CIA, would give them a certain bounty for weapons they would bring in, sometimes ears, depending on what the target was. If they were to assassinate a certain individual, they would have to bring back evidence that the person had been killed. Sometimes that consisted of ears or whatever. Going after weapons became kind of a comedy. One time a South Vietnamese armory was sort of assaulted, the PRUs snuck in and took out a bunch of weapons and sold them back to the CIA, and of course the CIA said, "that was very good to get these weapons, but you got them from the wrong side."

Sometimes we'd go out with a whole pack of mercenaries. They were very good going in, but once we got there and made our target, they would completely pillage the area, which created a lot of ruckus. They would rob everything. It was a complete carnival going back, so we would try to get way ahead of them so they could have their little carnival and if they got ambushed they'd have to deal with it.

At the time the PRU adviser I was working with was a SEAL who subsequently was killed. He was one of the original SEALs, and that's who they had usually working directly with the PRUs. They bring us in for backup support on specific missions, like one time we were going to knock out a Viet Cong weapons factory.

The other kinds of missions we went on were more with our team. Our team was fifteen SEALs, but we would usually break into groups of seven. Assigned to us were LD&Ns, basically SEAL-trained Vietnamese. I would usually scout with a Vietnamese person. Those kinds of targets consisted sometimes of ambushes.

I can remember ambushing a lot of tax collectors. After they made all the collections, you'd hit them in the morning and rob them of all the money, and of course kill them, and then report that all the money was destroyed in the firefight. They'd carry a thousand dollars at a time, so we'd have quite a party.

We were really deep in the delta. The terrain was heavy—heavy vegetation. Some of the places would be well irrigated, so we'd use the irrigation ditches to move through. We'd never be moving on land, just the irrigation ditches, in water up to your chest. We would just wade through the water. That became not a bad place to be because it was quiet for movement; you could relieve yourself very easily as you walked along. If you got shot you had water surrounding you and that tends to slow a bullet down. I don't think a bullet will travel much more than six feet from the time if hits the surface of the water. You could duck underwater and hide.

The Phoenix Program was a very carefully designed program to disrupt the infrastructure of the Viet Cong village systems. And apparently on some occasions the plan was to come in and assassinate a village chief and make it look like the Viet Cong did it. It was a really difficult program for me because I didn't totally understand it when I was in Vietnam.

I was just a scout, and my responsibility was to scout in and get us to a village. Get us to a particular spot, go in there and get the person out that we wanted for questioning. And then they would be handled. It was my understanding that these people were wanted for questioning. They would be high-level Viet Cong. What I have come to understand since then, and what I really feel was going on at the time, was that we were just going in there to make it look like the Viet Cong came through and killed this person. Now, understand that we were going into areas that had not been touched by Americans. They were Viet Cong strongholds.

There were booby traps all over the place. I was barefoot, we didn't want to make any boot prints. We were walking along barefoot, and Americans don't go into jungles barefoot. I had no identification on me except for a morphine syringe around my neck. If I was hit, I'd shoot morphine. My number was 50. It was on all my clothes. My face was completely painted black. Often I would wear a black pajama top. I learned how to walk like a Viet Cong, think like a Viet Cong.

I'm a tall person. I had to learn how to walk small and slump over. There's a certain way you walk through the jungle when you're comfortable with it and I got very comfortable in that style of walking. It's more of an experience. It's like a cat who walks and knows where he's going and what he's doing. Most Americans didn't know where they were going or what they were doing in Vietnam. They were kind of tromping around out there. I was moving slowly, hesitating, blending in with my environment, moving up to a structure, getting close to it, trying to blend in all the time. I had one occasion, a Viet Cong called to me and talked to me, that's how good I was at moving in this fashion. That was the only way I was going to survive out there, to look like a Viet Cong.

We would walk in and we wouldn't be carrying American-made weapons, either. There were no silhouettes on us that made us look like Americans. At a glimpse we would look like we were a group of men with some guns. Once again, the whole idea was to blend in like the Viet Cong, and at the time it was totally tuned to filling that role. Since I was the scout, I had to look more like a Viet Cong than anybody else.

I was the point man for that unit. We carried a heavy-equipment person with us, carried an M-60 machine gun fully loaded, ready to knock through trees. We were prepared to hit anything. We hit regimental point units sometimes, just five of us. We were prepared to make contact with anything.

We'd be dropped off in an area that was probably pretty dangerous, in about four or five miles, and we patrolled two or three miles. Sometimes it could take an hour to go one hundred yards, the jungle was that thick. We'd have to crawl underneath it all. We were in there pretty deep. Once again, there were no front lines, but we were in an area that was very, very dangerous. Consequently we had complete air support. When we were out on a certain mission, the pilots had to be in their planes on our frequencies. We would scramble them that quickly, so it was, by military standards, very, very high-level missions going on.

On the Phoenix program we would go in. . . . I had flown over the area the day before in a helicopter, so I knew exactly what it looked like in the daytime, and I'd translate that in my mind at nighttime. Usually I was the only one who knew where we were. Everybody had other specialties: the radioperson's specialty was a whole set of frequencies he had to deal with. The officer's specialty was to execute some of the orders. The medic had another specialty. Each person was an incredibly skilled technician.

I had to be totally tuned up. We were doing Dexedrine. When we'd go out on a mission, we'd take a whole handful of pills and some of those were Dexedrine. When I hit Dexedrine I'd just turn into a pair of eyeball and ears. That's probably why I don't remember too many of the details real well, because it was just like I was on a speed trip the whole time I was in the field. When I came in the crash would be so hard it would totally wipe out anything I'd been through, and I'm sure that works when you need people to go out and do the kind of things that we were doing, because it would be very hard to debrief us if we were ever wounded or captured. We had the morphine around our neck and we could shoot up immediately, which would make us incoherent for twenty-four hours at least, enough time to shift all the plans around that were predicated on that particular mission.

So when we would go in, I'd be barefoot. I would move up to a hootch. This is maybe during a real stormy night; they're not expecting Americans to be out there in the middle of a storm. They're not expecting them to come walking in at two o'clock in the morning in the middle of a Viet Cong stronghold. A stronghold is a village where they felt really secure. We would go into the hootch. I'd step in and I'd stand there and listen to everybody breathe. If I noticed a change in breathing patterns of the people sleeping, then I was immediately on alert. I carried with me, more often than not, a duckbill shotgun. A duckbill throws your four-buck [buckshot] at a horizontal; you get a nice wide spray if you have to open fire. God, it was really intense, because you had a whole family sleeping in this one room and you're standing in the middle of them all.

What I would do is, around my head I wore a triangular green bandage. I'd take it off and tie it into a knot in the center and walk over to the bed—I knew exactly what bed this guy was sleeping in. I had a Navy K-bar knife, which is one of the best knives you can get. The blade is about seven or nine inches long, razor sharp—you could shave with it. I would go over to the person and I would hold their nose so they'd take a breath with their mouth and I'd take this rag, which had a couple of knots in the middle of it, and cram it down their throat so it would get down to their larynx, so that if they moved at all they would be cutting their own throat.

So the person would obviously freeze. With that motion I would take the gag, grab it from behind their head, the knife under their throat, and literally pick them up just by the head. They were small people, usually sleeping in their black pajamas, and I'd just pick them up and carry them out.

Now, if anybody moved in the hootch, the other scout with me, who's Vietnamese, would start talking to them very quietly. He'd have them all lay down on the ground, face down. By then I'd have the person outside. I'd have his elbows secured behind his back. I would pass him to the prisoner handler. All this time no words are spoken. This is all well-rehearsed. This has all taken about a minute, maybe a minute and a half. We would go back inside. The scout would then instruct these people that if they made a move, there's going to be a person at the door that's going to completely blow them away. Our little group would pull back. We'd have only five or six people and we were dispersed to cover ourselves. We would pull back and start to move for our exit. I would usually sit by the hootch for about five minutes and listen and, while I was doing that, hook a hand grenade on the door so if anybody opened it up, they would drop the grenade and of course they would be killed.

I would sit by the doorway there and be very, very quiet and let them start mustering a bit. Then I'd make a little noise outside so that they knew I was there. Once I did that, I'd leave and haul ass back to the unit to scout on the way back. If anybody came out we would hear the grenade for about a mile and half if it went off. And these are like families, little kids and stuff, so it was something you just didn't think about. You just did it. It was that second you had to cover.

We did one mission, God, we spent half the night in a pigsty. We got into the area around one o'clock in the morning and climbed into a pigsty, a feeding area, and buried ourselves beneath all the manure and straw. We were looking through the wall. It was like a barn, there were little tiny cracks. We were waiting for our target to come into the marketplace, a tax collector who collected during market time, about eight o'clock in the morning. It was a sizable little village for Vietnam—must have been twenty hootches with a center courtyard—and he came into the area. I'll never forget that. He came waking into the area after we'd been sitting there all the time and he jumped up and knocked the entire wall down as we came out shooting. We just blasted everything, bodies were flying around, I just started running for the guy we wanted. It was my job to search him completely. I picked up an arm that had been blown across the courtyard and searched the sleeve. I had to search all parts of the body. The body would be strewn all over the place, kicking and squirming and puking, eyeballs rolling around . . . it was like picking through a broken car . . . it wasn't a human body any longer.

What blows me away is that my father is a meat-cutter. I couldn't stand the sight of blood as a kid and I still can't. And I can't stand the feeling of pain either for myself or somebody else. What's incredible is that I was able to do that so quickly without hesitation and so calmly. I just did it. I don't think I made a habit of shooting people unnecessarily, but at the same time my fear level was so high that if it meant me being afraid or them being dead, usually the person was dead.

On another mission we went out and we didn't do any face paint—we were getting tired of that; we'd been out for about five months and that was considered to be quite an accomplishment for a SEAL team to be intact that long—we made contact as soon as we came in. A fellow came walking down the road—I guess this is around midnight—and he had a lantern. If he'd have come over any closer he'd have seen our footprints coming from the river. We opened up on him, since we couldn't afford to have anybody else see us. It looked like he had a rifle sling on, and he did, the rifle sling was connected to a little basket. He was out plucking minnow, so we blew him away, and I went over to grab him and drag him into an irrigation ditch and sink the body—we didn't want to leave any bodies around—and I'll never forget, when I went to grab him I searched the front of him and I flipped him over to search the back and he just opened up like a hamburger. I just took all the pieces and stuff and scooped him into the water—I was in the water by then—and I was scooping this all over me, and he was sinking . . . I couldn't. . . . Usually I would stab him in the lungs to sink him, which would fill the lungs with water and that weight would keep him underwater.

We patrolled in further and we noticed as we were walking along that behind us about another hundred yards somebody was following us. We could hear the brush moving, so we zigzagged back though the canals, which ran in all directions. We had another three hours before our pickup came at sunrise, so we kind of laid out there by a real wide-open palm grove. Palms are so high they block out all the light along the ground. It's usually real flat, so it's like a playground and we were just lying there.

⌐⌐◆⌐⌐

The people who had followed us started shooting in the direction we were lying. It's incredibly frightening to be lying there and know that somebody knows your there and they're shooting at you. What they were attempting to do was get us to shoot back so they could identify our position. There were sixteen of them, and they had the perfect advantage over us because we had no cover at all. But we didn't shoot back and they were shooting all around me. Finally we heard them say, "The assholes have left." They thought that we had pulled out and gotten our boat and split.

We were digging holes in the ground with the buttons on our shirts, we were so goddamned scared. And we couldn't move. As soon as you move in that position, they can see the shadow of your movement, so our only hope was to make ourselves look like a pile of logs, so we became a pile of logs. It's incredible to explain what you can become, the illusions that you can present to people. You can become a bush, a log, if you just concentrate hard enough on being that. They told us in our training that you could become a master of illusion if you believe enough in the illusion. And it worked. I couldn't believe it. Also the power of your eyes—not to look directly at something but to look off to the side of it. You wouldn't concentrate your focus because if you look at something too long, it'll look back at you, and you don't want them to turn around and see you.

We flew into this place in the U Minh Forest on the southern tip. Our intelligence, our intelligence there said there were twenty-five POW camps with South Vietnamese and American prisoners in them. The area we flew into was heavily defoliated and they were flying the Viet Cong flag in the middle of the day. We were broken into three-man teams and we were just going to search through each of the hootches.

The first hootch I stepped into had a wood carving of Ho Chi Minh on the wall, so I thought, "Oh, Jesus, these people are really committed if they have this kind of paraphernalia around in the middle of the day." They also had a lot of bunkers, so what we would do is, before we got into a hootch we would fire a 40-millimeter grenade from a little tube that fits underneath an M-16 so it could also be a grenade launcher. Our radio guy had that, I had a Vietnamese with me; he would fire into a hootch and then go in and search it. We knew they were in their bunker, and after firing we'd go in and search the place and set it on fire and move to the next hootch.

The problem was, I was so tuned to blending in that I just stood there and blended into one of the hootches and told the guy to fire and he fired into the one I was standing next to. Usually when you fire a grenade into something that close, you're dead. But because it hit below the dirt embankment around the hootch, what hit me was the blast and a lot of dirt. It blew me about ten or fifteen feet. I got I shrapnel in my left arm. I just happened to be holding up my gun; if it had been down, I would have gotten it right in the lungs. The guy ran back and said, "Oh"—I mean we were really close; all the people I was working with were very, very close—and he said, "Oh, God, Mike. Do you want morphine?" I said,

"No. Hey look at me. You've done enough damage." And the officer came running over and said, "Can you get us out of here?" and I said, "You're goddamned right I can get us out of here" because I knew which way to patrol. I was really pissed off because I didn't want to go in there in the daytime. So finally, they said, "We'll medevac you out."

They medivaced me to Binh Thuy, and in Binh Thuy I felt kind of embarrassed because I had this small shrapnel wound in my arm and there were all these guys sewn up like Thanksgiving turkeys—this was around Christmas time '68. I mean these guys were wired together.

The Final Battle for Murphy's Ridge

Marcus Luttrell

THE GROUND SHOOK. THE VERY FEW TREES SWAYED. THE NOISE WAS worse than any blast all day. . . . This was one gigantic Taliban effort to finish us. We hit the deck . . . to avoid the lethal flying debris, rock fragments and shrapnel.

Lieutenant Mike Murphy bellowed out the command, the third time he had done so in the battle. Same mountain. Same command.

"Fall back! Axe and Marcus first!"

He really meant Fall off! And so we were all getting real used to it. Axe and I sprinted for the edge, while Murph and Danny, tucked into the rocks, drew fire and covered our escape. I had no idea whether Danny could even move again, with all his wounds.

Lying right along the top of the cliff was a tree trunk with a kind of hollow underneath it, as if it had been washed out by the rains. Axe, who could think quicker on his feet than most people I've ever met, made straight for that hole because the tree trunk would give him cover as he plunged down to whatever the hell was over the goddamned cliff.

The slimly built Axe hit the ground like a javelin, skidded fast into the hollow, shot straight under the log, and out into space. I hit the ground like a Texas longhorn and came to a grinding halt, stuck fast under the log. Couldn't go forward, couldn't go back. Fuck me. Was this a bummer or what?

The Taliban had seen me by now. I was the only one they could see, and I heard a volley of bullets screaming around me. One shot smacked into the tree just to my right. The rest were hitting the dirt and sending up puffs of dust. I heaved at the log. I heaved with all my might, but I could not move that sucker. I was pinned down.

I was trying to look backward, wondering if Mikey had seen me and might try a rescue, when suddenly I saw the stark white smoke trail of an incoming RPG against the mountain. The RPG smashed into the tree trunk right next to me and exploded with a shattering blast as I tried frantically to turn away from it. I can't tell what happened next, but it blew the goddamned trunk clean in half and shot me straight over the cliff.

I guess it was about fifteen feet down to where Axe was moving into firing position, and I landed close. Considering I'd just been blown over the ledge like a freakin' human cannonball, I was pretty lucky to still be standing. And there right next to me on the ground was my rifle, placed there by the Hand of God Himself.

I reached down to pick it up and listened again for His voice. But this time there was no noise, just one brief second of silence in my mind, amid all the chaos and malevolence of this monstrous struggle for supremacy, apparently being conducted on behalf of His Holy Prophet Muhammad.

I was not sure whether either of them would have approved. I don't know much about Muhammad, but, by all that's holy, I don't think my own God wished me to die. If He had been indifferent to my plight, He surely would not have taken such good care of my gun, right? Because how on earth that was still with me, I will never know.

That rifle had so far fought three separate battles in three different places, been ripped out of my grasp twice, been blown over a cliff by a powerful grenade, fallen almost nine hundred feet down a mountain, and was still somehow right next to my outstretched hand. Fluke? Believe what you will. My own faith will remain forever unshaken.

Anyhow, I picked it up and moved back into the rocks where Axe was now picking up fire from the enemy. But he was well positioned and fighting back, blazing away on the left, the flank for which he'd fought so desperate for so long. Actually it had been about forty minutes, but it seemed like ten years, and we were both still going.

So, for that matter, were Mikey and Danny, and somehow they had both made the leap down here to the lower level, near the stream, where the Taliban assault was not quite so bad.

Yet.

We looked, by the way, shocking, especially Danny, who was covered head to toe in blood. Axe was okay but badly battered, and Mikey was soaked in blood from that stomach wound; not as bad as Danny, but not very pretty.

When that grenade blew me over the cliff, it probably should have killed me, but the only new injury I had sustained was a broken nose, which I got when I hit the deck semiconscious. To be honest it hurt like hell, along with my back, and I was bleeding all over my gear. However, I had not been seriously shot, as two of my team had.

Axe was holding the tribesmen off, leaning calmly on a rock, firing up the hill, the very picture of an elite warrior in combat. No panic, rock steady, firing accurately, conserving his ammunition, missing nothing. I was close to him in a similar stance, and we were both hitting them pretty good. One guy suddenly jumped up from nowhere a little above us, and I shot him dead, about thirty yards range.

But we were trapped again. There were still around eight of these maniacs coming down at us and that's a heck of a lot of enemies. I'm not sure what their casualty rate was, because both Mikey and I estimated Sharmak had thrown 140 minimum into this fight. Whatever, they were still there, and I was not sure how long Danny could keep going.

Mikey worked his way alongside me and said with vintage Murphy humor, "Man, this really sucks."

I turned to face him and told him, "We're gonna fucking die out here—if we're not careful."

"I know," he replied.

And the battle raged on. The massed, wild gunfire of a very determined enemy against our more accurate, better-trained response, superior concentration, and war-fighting know-how. Once more, hundreds of bullets ricocheting around our rocky surroundings. And once more, the Taliban went to the grenades, blasting the terrain around us to pieces. Jammed between rocks, we kept firing, but Danny was in all kinds of trouble, and I was afraid he might lose consciousness.

That was when they shot him again, right at the base of the neck. I watched in horror as Danny went down, this beautiful guy, husband of

Patsy, a friend of mine for four years, a guy who had provided our covering fire until he couldn't stand anymore.

And now he lay on the ground, blood pouring from his five wounds. And I was supposed to be a fucking SEAL medic, and I could not do a damn thing for him without getting us all killed. I dropped my rifle and climbed over the rock, running across open ground to get to him. All right. All right. No hero bullshit. I was crying like a baby.

Danny was saturated in blood, still conscious, still trying to fire his rifle at the enemy. But he was in facedown position. I told him to take it easy while I turned him over.

"C'mon, Dan, we're gonna be all right."

He nodded, and I knew he could not speak and would probably never speak again. What I really remember is, he would not let go of his rifle. I raised him by the shoulders and hauled him into an almost sitting position. Then, grasping him under the arms, I started to drag him backwards, toward cover. And would you believe, that little iron man opened fire at the enemy once again, almost lying on his back, blasting away up the hill while I kept dragging.

We'd gone about eight yards when everything I dreaded came true. Here I was, just about defenseless, trying to walk backward, both hands full, when a Taliban fighter suddenly loomed up out of the rocks to our right. He was right on top of us, looking down, a smile on his face as he aimed that AK-47 straight at my head.

Neither of us saw him in time to return fire. I just said a quick prayer and stared back at him. Which was precisely when Axe banged two bullets right between his eyes, killed that tribesman stone dead instantly. I didn't have time to thank him, because the grenades were still coming in, and I just kept trying to drag Danny to safety. And like Axe, Danny kept firing.

I got him to the rock face just a few yards from Mikey. And it was clear the enemy had nearly managed to surround us for the fourth time today. We could tell by the direction of the gunfire and occasionally the RPGs. Danny was still alive and willing to fight, and Mikey was now fighting shoulder to shoulder with Axe, and they were inflicting heavy damage.

I still thought we had a chance of getting out, but once more the only option was down, toward that village and onto the flat ground. Fighting uphill, as we had been doing since this battle started, did, in the words of our mission officer, really suck.

I yelled out loudly, "Axe! Moving!" He had time to shout back, "Roger that!" before they shot him in the chest. I watched his rifle fall from his grasp. He slumped forward and slipped down the rock he'd been leaning on, all the way to the ground.

I absolutely froze. This could not be happening. Matt Axelson, a family fixture, Morgan's best friend, a part of our lives. I started calling his name, irrationally, over and over. Privately I thought Danny was dying, and all I could see was a stain of blood gathering in the red dirt where Axe was slumped. For a brief moment I thought I might be losing it.

But then Axe reached for his rifle and got up. He leveled the weapon, got a hold of another magazine, shoved it into the breech and opened fire again, blood pumping out of his chest. He held his same firing position, leaning against the rock. He showed the same attitude of a solid Navy SEAL know-how, the same formidable steadiness, staring through his scope, those brilliant blue eyes of his scanning the terrain.

When Axe got up, it was the bravest thing I ever saw. Except for Danny. Except for Mikey, still commanding us after taking a bullet through his stomach so early in the battle.

And now Murph was masterminding a way down the escarpment. He had chosen the route and called up to Axe to follow him down. And still the bullets were humming around us as the Taliban started their pursuit. Mikey and Axe were about seventy-five yards in front and I was dragging Danny along while he did everything he could to help, trying to walk, trying to give us covering fire.

"It's okay, Danny," I kept saying, "We just need to catch up with the others. It's gonna be all right."

Right then a bullet caught him full in the upper part of his face. I heard it hit home, I turned to help him, and the blood from his head wound spilled over both of us. I called out to him. But it was too late. He wasn't fighting against the terrible pain anymore. And he couldn't hear me. Danny Dietz died right there in my arms. I don't know how quickly hearts break, but that nearly broke mine.

And the gunfire never abated. I dragged Danny off the open ground maybe five feet, and then I said good-bye to him. I lowered him down, and I had to leave him or else die out here with him. But I knew one thing for certain. I still had my rifle and I was not alone, and neither was Danny, a devout Roman Catholic. I left him with God.

And now I had to get back to help my team. It was the hardest thing I've ever done in my life.

To this day I have nightmares about it, a chilling dream where Danny's still talking to me, and there's blood everywhere, and I have to walk away and I don't even know why. I always wake up in tears, and it will always haunt me, and it's never going to go away.

And now I could hear Murph yelling to me. I grabbed my rifle, ducked down, slipped and fell off a rock, then started to run toward him and Axe while they provided heavy covering fire nonstop aimed at the Taliban's rocky redoubt, maybe another forty yards back.

I reached the edge, ran almost blindly into a tree, bounced off, skidded down the slope, which was not very deep, and landed on my head right in the fucking stream. Like any good frogman, I was seriously pissed because my boots got wet. I really hate that.

Finally I caught up with them. Axe was out of ammunition and I gave him a new magazine. Mikey wanted to know where Danny was, and I had to tell him that Danny had died. He was appalled, completely shocked, and so was Axe. Although Mikey would not say it, I knew he wanted to go back for the body. But we both knew there was no time and reason. We had nowhere to take the remains of a fallen teammate, and we could not continue this firefight while carrying around a body.

Danny was dead. And strangely, I was the first to pull myself together. I said suddenly, "I'll tell you what. We have to get down this goddamned mountain or we'll all be dead."

And as if to make up our minds for us, the Taliban were again closing in, trying to make that 360-degree movement around us. And they were doing it. Gunfire was coming from underneath us now. We could see the tribesman still swarming, and I tried to count them as I had been trying to do for almost an hour.

I thought there were now only about fifty, maybe sixty, but the bullets were still flying. The grenades were still coming in, blasting close, sending up dust clouds of smoke and dirt with flying bits of rock. There had never been a lull in the amount of ordnance the enemy was piling down on us.

Right now, again tucked low behind rocks, the three of us could look down and see the village one and a half miles distant, and it remained our objective.

Again I told Mikey, "If we can just make it down there and get some cover, we'll take 'em all out on the flat ground."

I knew we were not in great shape. But we were still SEALs. Nothing can ever take that away. We were still confident. And we were never going to surrender. If it came down to it, we would fight to the death with our knives against their guns.

"Fuck surrender," said Mikey. And he had no need to explain further, either to Axe or me. Surrender would have been a disgrace to our community, like ringing the bell at the edge of the grinder and putting your helmet in the line. No one who had made it through this far, to this no-man's-land in the Afghan mountains, would have dreamed of giving up.

Remember the philosophy of the U.S. Navy SEALs: "I will never quit. . . . My Nation expects me to be physically harder and mentally stronger than my enemies. If knocked down, I will get back up, every time. I will draw on every remaining ounce of strength to protect my teammates. . . . I am never out of the fight."

Those words have sustained many brave men down the years. They were engraved upon the soul of every SEAL. And they were in the minds of all of us.

Mikey suddenly said, above the rage of the battle, "Remember, bro, we're never out of it."

I nodded tersely. "It's only about another thousand yards to flat ground. If we can just get down there, we got a chance."

Trouble was, we couldn't get down there, at least not right then. Because once more we were pinned down. And we faced the same dilemma: the only escape was to go down, but our only defensive strategy was to go up. Once more, we had to get off this ground, away from the ricochets. Back up the left flank.

We were trying to fight the battle our way. But even though we were still going, we were battered half to death. I led the way back up the rocks, blasting away, shooting down anyone I could see. But they caught on to that real quick, and now they really unloaded on us, Russian-made rocket grenades. Coming straight down their right flank, our left.

The ground shook. The very few trees swayed. The noise was worse than any blast all day. Even the walls of this little canyon shook. The stream splashed over its banks. This was one gigantic Taliban effort to finish us. We hit the deck, jamming ourselves into our rocky crevasse, heads down to avoid lethal flying debris, rock fragments and shrapnel. As before they did not kill anyone with this type of thunderous bombardment, and as before they waited till the dust had cleared and then opened fire again.

Above me I could see the tree line. It was not close, but it was nearer than the village. But the Taliban knew our objective, and as we tried to fight our way forward, they drove us back with sheer weight of fire.

We'd tried, against all the odds, and just could not make it. They'd knocked us back again. And we retreated down, making a long pathetic loop, back the way we'd come. But once more we landed up in a good spot, a sound defensive position, well protected by the rock face on either side. Again we tried to take the fight to them, picking our targets and driving them back, making some new ground toward the village.

They were up and screaming at us, yelling as the battle almost became close quarters. We yelled right back and kept firing. But there were still so many of them, and then they got into better position and shot Mike Murphy through the chest.

He came toward me, asking if I could give him another magazine. And then I saw Axe stumbling toward me, his head pushed out, blood running down his face, bubbling out of the most shocking head wound.

"They shot me, bro," he said. "The bastards shot me. Can you help me, Marcus?" What could I say? What could I do? I couldn't help except trying to fight off the enemy. And Axe was standing there right in my line of fire.

I tried to help get him down behind a rock. And I turned to Mikey, who was obviously badly hurt now. "Can you move, buddy?" I asked him.

And he groped in his pocket for his mobile phone, the one we had dared not to use because it would betray our position. And then Lieutenant Murphy walked into the open ground. He walked until he was more or less in the center, gunfire all around him, and he sat on a small rock and began punching in the numbers to HQ.

I could hear him talking. "My men are taking heavy fire . . . we're getting picked apart. My guys are dying out here . . . we need help."

And right then Mikey took a bullet straight to the back. I saw the blood spurt from his chest. He slumped forward, dropping his phone and rifle. But then he braced himself, grabbed them both, sat upright again, and once more put the phone to his ear.

I heard him speak again. "Roger that, sir. Thank you." Then he stood up and staggered out to our bad position, the one guarding our left, and Mikey started fighting again, firing at the enemy.

He was hitting them too, having made that one last desperate call to base, the one that might yet save us if they could send help in time, before we were overwhelmed.

Only I knew what Mikey had done. He'd understood we had only one realistic chance, and that was to call in help. He also knew there was only one place from which he could possibly make that cell phone work: out in the open, away from the cliff walls.

Knowing the risk, understanding the danger, in the full knowledge the phone call could cost him his life, Lieutenant Michael Patrick Murphy, son of Maureen, fiancé of the beautiful Heather, walked out into the firestorm.

His objective was clear: to make one last valiant attempt to save his two teammates. He made the call, made the connection. He reported our approximate position, the strength of our enemy, and how serious our situation was. When they shot him, I thought mortally, he kept talking.

Roger that, sir. Thank you.

Will those words ever dim in my memory, even if I lived to be a hundred? Will I ever forget them? Would you? And was there ever a greater SEAL team commander, an officer who fought to the last and, as perhaps his dying move, risked everything to save his remaining men?

I doubt there was ever anyone better than Mikey, cool under fire, always thinking, fearless about issuing the one-option command even if it was nearly impossible. And then the final, utterly heroic act. Not a gesture. An act of supreme valor. Lieutenant Mikey was a wonderful person and a very, very great SEAL officer. If they build a memorial to him as high as the Empire State Building, it won't ever be high enough for me.

Mikey was still alive, and he carried on, holding the left. I stayed on the right, both of us firing carefully and accurately. I was still trying to reach slightly higher ground. But the depleted army of the Taliban was determined that I should not get it, and every time I tried to advance even a few yards, get even a few feet higher, they drove me back. Mikey too was still trying to climb rock strata above where I was standing. It was a good spot from which to attack, but defensively poor. And I knew this must surely be Mikey's last stand.

Just then, Axe walked right by me in a kind of a daze, making only a marginal attempt at staying in the cover of the rocks. Then I saw the wound, the right side of his head almost blown away.

I shouted, "Axe! Axe!" C'mon, old buddy. Get down there, right down there.

I was pointing at the one spot in the rocks we might find protection. And he tried to raise his hand, an act of confirmation that he'd heard me. But he couldn't. And he kept walking slowly, hunched forward, no longer clutching his rifle. He was down to just his pistol, but I knew he could not hold that, aim, and fire. At least he was headed for cover, even though no one could survive a head wound like that. I knew Axe was dying.

Mikey was still firing, but suddenly I heard him scream my name, the most bone-chilling primeval scream: "Help me, Marcus! Please help me!" He was my best friend in all the world, but he was thirty yards up the mountain and I could not climb to him. I could hardly walk, and if I'd move two yards out of my protected position, they would have hit me with a hundred bullets.

Nonetheless, I edged out around the rocks to try to give him covering fire, to force these bastards back, give him a breather until I could find a way to get up there without getting mowed down.

And all the time, he was screaming, calling out my name, begging me to help him live. And there was nothing I could do except die with him. Even then, with only a couple of magazines left, I still believed I could nail these fuckers in the turbans and somehow save him and Axe. I just wanted Mikey to stop screaming, for his agony to end.

But every few seconds, he cried out for me again. And every time it happened, I felt like I'd been stabbed. There were tears welling uncontrollably out of my eyes, not for the first time on this day. I would have done anything for Mikey, I'd have laid down my own life for him. But my death here in this outcrop of rocks was not going to save him. If I could save him, it would be by staying alive.

And then, as suddenly as it began, the screaming stopped. There was silence for a few seconds, as if even these Taliban warriors understood that Mikey had died. I moved slightly forward and looked up there, in time to see four of them come down and fire several rounds into his fallen body.

The screaming had stopped. For everyone except me. I still hear Mikey, every night. I still hear that scream above all other things, even above the death of Danny Dietz. For several weeks I thought I might be losing my mind, because I could never push it aside. There were one or two frightening occasions when I heard it in broad daylight and found myself pressed against a wall, my hands covering my ears.

I always thought these kinds of psychiatric problems were suffered by other people, ordinary people, not by Navy SEALs. I now know the reality of them. I also doubt whether I will ever sleep through the night again.

Danny was dead. Mikey was now dead. And Axe was dying. Right now there were two of us, but only just. I resolved to walk down to where Axe was hiding and to die there with him. There was, I knew, unlikely to be a way out. There were still maybe fifty of the enemy, perhaps by now only hunting me.

It took me nearly ten minutes, firing back behind me sporadically to try to pin them down . . . just in case. I was firing on the wild chance there was a shot at survival, that somehow Mikey's phone call might yet have the guys up in here in time for a last-ditch rescue.

When I reached Axe, he was sitting in a hollow, and he'd fixed a temporary bandage on the side of his head. I stared at him, wondering where those cool blue eyes had gone. The eyes in which I could now see my own reflection were blood black, the sockets filled from the terrible wound in his skull.

I smiled at him because I knew we would not walk this way again, at least not together, not on this earth. Axe did not have long. If he'd been in the finest hospital in North America, Axe would still not have had long. The life was ebbing out of him, and I could see this powerful super-athlete growing weaker by the second.

"Hey, man," I said, "you're all fucked up!" And I tried, pitifully, to fix the bandage.

"Marcus, they got us good, man." He spoke with difficulty, as if trying to concentrate. And then he said, "You stay alive, Marcus. And tell Cindy I love her."

Those were his last words. I just sat there, and that was where I planned to stay the night, right there with Axe so he wouldn't be alone when the end came. I didn't give a flying fuck what happened to me any-more. Quietly, I made peace with God, and thanked Him for protecting me and saving my rifle. Which, somehow, I still had. I never took my eyes off Axe, who was semiconscious but still breathing.

Along with the other two, Axe will always be a hero to me. Through-out this brief but brutal conflict, he'd fought like a wounded tiger. Like Audie Murphy, like Sergeant York. They shot away his body, crippled his brain, but not his spirit. They never got that.

Matthew Gene Axelson, husband of Cindy, fired at the enemy until he could no longer hold his rifle. He was just past his twenty-ninth birth-day. And in his dying moments, I never took my eyes off him. I don't think he could hear me any longer. But his eyes were open, and we were still together, and I refused to allow him to die alone.

Right then, they must have seen us. Because one of those super-powerful Russian grenades came in, landed close, and blew me sideways, right out of the hollow, and across the rough ground, and over the edge of the goddamned ravine. I lost consciousness before I hit the bottom, and when I came to, I was in a different hollow, and my first thought was I'd been blinded by the explosion, because I couldn't see a thing.

However, after a few seconds, I gathered my wits and realized I was upside down in the freakin' hole. I still had my eyesight and a few other working parts, but my left leg seemed paralyzed and, to a lesser degree, so was my right. It took me God knows how long to wriggle out onto flat ground and claw my way into the cover of a rock.

My ears were zinging, I guess from the blast of the grenade. I looked up and saw I had fallen a pretty good way down, but I was too disoriented to put a number on it. The main difference between now and when I'd been sitting with Axe was that the gunfire had ceased.

If they'd reached Axe, who could not possibly have lived through the blast, they might not have bothered to go on shooting. They obviously had not found me, and I would have been real hard to locate, upside down in the hole. But whatever, no one seemed to be looking. For the first time in maybe an hour and a half, I was apparently not being actively hunted.

Aside from being unable to stand, I had two other very serious problems. The first was the total loss of my pants. They'd been blown right off me. The second was the condition of my left leg, which I could scarcely feel but which was a horrific sight, bleeding profusely and full of shrapnel.

I had no bandages, nothing medical. I had been able to do nothing for my teammates, and I could do nothing for myself, except try to stay hidden. It was not a promising situation. I was damn sure I'd broken my back and probably my shoulder; I'd broken my nose, and my face was a total mess. I couldn't stand up, never mind walk. At least one leg was wrecked, and maybe the other. I was paralyzed in both thighs, and the only way I could move was belly crawl.

Unsurprisingly, I was dazed. And through this personal fog of war, there was yet one more miracle for me to recognize. Not two feet from me where I was lying, half hidden by dirt and shale, well out of sight of my enemy, was my Mark 12 rifle, and I still had one and a half magazines left. I prayed before I grabbed it, because I thought it might just be a mirage and that when I tried to hold it . . . well, it might just disappear.

But it did not. And I felt the cold steel in the hot air as my fingers clasped it. I listened again for His voice. I prayed again, imploring Him for guidance. But there was no sound, and all I knew was that somehow I had to make it out to the right, where I'd be safe, at least for a while.

My God had not spoken again. But neither had He forsaken me. I knew that. For damned sure, I knew that.

I knew one other thing as well. For the first time, I was entirely alone. Here in these Taliban-controlled hostile mountains, there was no earthly teammate for me, and my enemy was all around. Had they heeded the words of the goatherds? That there were four of us and that right now they had only three bodies? Or did they assume I had been blown to pieces by the blast of the final Russian RPG?

I had no answer to these questions, only hope. With absolutely no one to turn to, no Mikey, no Axe, no Danny, I had to face the final battle by myself, maybe lonely, maybe desolate, maybe against formidable odds. But I was not giving up.

I had only one Teammate. And He moved, as ever, in mysterious ways. But I was a Christian, and He had somehow saved me from a thousand AK-47 bullets on this day. No one had shot me, which was well nigh beyond all comprehension.

And I still believed He did not wish me to die. And I would still try my best to uphold the honor of the United States Navy SEALs as I imagined they would have wished. No surrender. Fuck that.

When I judged I had fully gathered my senses and checked my watch, it was exactly 1342 local time. For a few minutes there was no gunfire, and I was beginning to assume they thought I was dead. Wrong, Marcus. The Taliban opened up again, and suddenly there were bullets flying everywhere, all around, just like before.

My enemy was coming up on me from the lower levels and from both sides, firing rapidly but inaccurately. Their bullets were ripping into the earth and shale across a wide range, most of them, thank Christ, well away from me.

It was clear they thought I might be still alive but equally clear they had not yet located me. They were conducting a kind of recon by fire, trying to flush me out, blazing away right across the spectrum, hoping someone would finally hit me and finish me. Or better yet, that I would come out with my hands high so the murdering little bastards could cut my head off or indulge in one of their other attractive little idiosyncrasies before telling that evil little television station Al-Jazeera how they had conquered the infidels.

I think I've mentioned my view about surrender. I rammed another magazine into the breech of my miraculous rifle and somehow crawled over this little hill, through the hail of bullets, right into the side of the mountain. No one saw me. No one hit me. I wedged myself into a rocky crevasse with my legs sticking out into a clump of bushes.

There were huge rocks to both sides, protecting me. Overall I judged I was jammed into a fifteen-foot-wide ledge on the mountain. It was not a cave, not even a shallow cave, because it had a kind of open top way above me. Rocks and sand kept falling down on me as the Taliban warriors scrambled around above my position. But this crevasse provided sensational cover and camouflage. Even I realized I would be pretty hard to spot. They'd have to get real lucky, even with their latest policy of trying to flush me out with sheer volume of fire.

My line of vision was directly ahead. I realized I couldn't move or change position, at least in broad daylight I couldn't, and it was imperative I hide the blood which was leaking from my battered body. I took stock of my injuries. My left leg was still bleeding pretty bad, and I packed the wounds with mud. I had a bug cut on my forehead, which I also packed with mud. Both legs were numb. I was not going anywhere. At least for a while.

I had no medical kit, no maps, no compass. I had my bullets, and I had my gun, and I had a decent view off my mountain. I had no pants, no buddies, but no one could see me. I was wedged in tight, my back to the wall in every possible sense.

I eased myself into a relatively comfortable position, checked my rifle, and laid it down the length of my body, aiming outward. If enough of them discovered me, I guess I'd quickly be going to join Danny, Axe, and Mikey. But not before I'd killed a whole lot more of them. I was, I knew in a perfect position for a stubborn, defensive military action, protected on all sides, vulnerable to a frontal assault only, and that would have to be by weight of numbers.

I could still hear gunfire, and it was growing closer. They were definitely coming this way. I just thought, don't move, don't breathe, do not make a sound. I think it was about then I understood how utterly alone I was for the very first time. And the Taliban was hunting me. They were not hunting for a SEAL platoon. They were hunting for me alone. Despite my injuries, I knew I had to reach deep. I was starting to lose track of time. But I stayed still. I actually did not move an inch for eight hours.

As the time passed, I could see the Taliban guys right across the canyon, running up and down, seemed like hundreds of them, plainly searching, scouring the mountain they knew so well, looking for me. I had some feeling back in my legs, but I was bleeding real bad, and was in a lot of pain. I think the loss of blood may have started to make me feel lightheaded.

Also I was scared to death. It was the first time in my entire six-year career as a Navy Seal I had been really scared. At one point, late in the afternoon, I thought they were all leaving. Across the canyon, the mountainside cleared, everyone running hard to the right, swarms of them, all headed for the same place. At least that's how it seemed to me across my narrow vision.

I now know where they were going. While I was lying in my crevasse, I had no idea what the hell was going on. But now I shall recount, to the best of my gathered knowledge, what happened elsewhere on that saddest of afternoons, that most shocking massacre high in the Hindu Kush, the worst disaster to ever to befall the SEALs in any conflict in our more than forty-year history.

The first thing to remember is that Mikey had succeeded in getting through to the quick reaction force (QRF) in Asadabad, a couple of mountain ranges over from where I was still holding out. That last call, the one on his cell phone that essentially cost him his life, was successful. From all accounts, his haunting words—my guys are dying out here . . . we need help—ripped around our base like a flash fire. SEALs are dying!

That's a five-alarm emergency that stops only just on the north side of frenzy.

Lieutenant Commander Kristensen, our acting CO, sounded the alarm. It's always a decision for the QRF, to launch or not to launch. Eric took a billionth of a second to make it. I know the vision of us four—his buddies, his friends and teammates, Mikey, Axe, Danny, and me fighting for our lives, hurt, possibly dead, surrounded by a huge fighting force of bloodthirsty Afghan tribesmen—flashed through his mind as he summoned the boys to action stations.

And the vision of terrible loss stood stark before him as he roared down the phone, ordering the men of the 160th Special Operation Aviation Regiment (SOAR), the fabled Night Stalkers, to get the big army MH-47 helo ready, right there on the runway. It was the same one that had taken off just before us on the previous day, the one we tracked in our ops area.

Guys I've already introduced charged into position, desperate to help, cramming as much ammunition as they could into their pouches, grabbing rifles and running for the Chinook, its rotors already screaming. My SDV Team 1 guys were instantly there. Petty Officers James Suh and Shane Patton reached the helo first. Then, scrambling aboard, came the massively built Senior Chief Dan Healy, the man who had masterminded Operation Redwing, who apparently looked as if he'd been shot as he left the barracks.

Then came the SEAL Team 10 guys, Lieutenant Mike McGreevy Jr. of New York, Chief Jacques Fontan of New Orleans, Petty Officers First Class Jeff Lucas from Oregon and Jeff Taylor from West Virginia. Finally, still shouting that his boys needed every gun they could get, came Lieutenant Commander Eric Kristensen, the man who knew perhaps better than anyone that the eight SEALs in that helo were about to risk a lethal daytime insertion in a high mountain pass, right into the jaws of an enemy that might outnumber them by dozens to one.

Kristensen knew he did not have to go. In fact, perhaps he should not have gone, stayed instead at his post, central to control and command. Right then, we had the skipper in the QRF, which was, at best, a bit unorthodox. But Kristensen was a SEAL to his fingertips. And what he knew above all else was that he had heard a desperate cry for help. From his brothers, from a man he knew well and trusted.

There was no way Eric was not going to answer that call. Nothing on God's earth could have persuaded him not to go. He must have known we were barely holding in, praying for help to arrive. There were after all, only four of us. And to everyone's certain knowledge, there were a minimum of a hundred Taliban.

Eric understood the stupendous nature of the risk, and he never blinked. Just grabbed his rifle and ammunition and raced aboard that aircraft yelling at everyone else to hurry. . . . "Move it, guys! Let's really move it!" That's what he always said under pressure. Sure, he was a commanding officer, and a hell of a good one. But more than that, he was a SEAL, a part of that brotherhood forged in blood. Even more important, he was a man. And right now he was answering an urgent, despairing cry from the very heart of his own brotherhood. There was only one way Eric Kristensen was headed, straight up the mountain, guns blazing, command or no command.

Inside the MH-47, the men of the 160th SOAR waited quietly, as they had done so many times before on these hair-raising air-rescue ops, often at night. They were led by a terrific man, Major Steve Reich of Connecticut, with Chief Warrant Officers Chris Scherkenbach of Jacksonville, Florida, and Corey J. Goodnature of Clarks Grove, Minnesota.

Master Sergeant James W. Ponder was there, with Sergeants First Class Marcus Muralles of Shelbyville, Indiana, and Mike Russell of Stafford, Virginia. Their group was completed by Staff Sergeant Shamus Goare of Danville, Ohio, and Sergeant Kip Jacoby of Pompano Beach, Florida. By any standards, it was a crack army fighting force.

The MH-47 took off and headed over the two mountain ranges. I guess it seemed to take forever. Those kinds of rescues always do. It came in to land at just about the same spot we had fast-roped in at the start of the mission, around five miles from where I was now positioned.

The plan was for the rescue team to rope it down just the same, and when the "Thirty Seconds!" call came, I guess the lead guys edged toward the stern ramp. What no one knew was the Taliban had some kind of bunker back there, and as the MH-47 tilted back for the insert and the ropes fell away for the climb down, the Taliban fired a rocket-propelled grenade straight through the open ramp.

It shot clean past the heads of the lead group and blew with a shattering blast against the fuel tanks, turning the helo into an inferno, stern and midships. Several of the guys were blown out and fell, some of them burning, to their deaths, from around thirty feet. They smashed into the mountainside and tumbled down. The impact was so violent, our search-and-rescue parties later found gun barrels snapped in half among the bodies.

The helicopter pilot fought for control, unaware of the carnage behind him but certainly aware of the raging fire around and above him. Of course there was nothing he could do. The big MH-47 just fell out of the sky and crashed with thunderous impact onto the mountainside, swayed, and then rolled with brutal force over and over, smashing itself into pieces on a long two-hundred-yard downhill trail to extinction.

There was nothing left except scattered debris when our guys finally got up there to investigate. And, of course, no survivors. My close SDV Team 1 buddies James, Chief Dan, and young Shane were all gone. It was as well I did not know this as I lay there in my crevasse. I'm not sure I could have coped with it. It was nothing less than a massacre. Weeks later I broke down when I saw the photographs, mostly because it was me they were trying to rescue.

As I explained, at the time I knew nothing of this. I only knew something had happened that had caused a lot of Taliban to get very obviously excited. And soon I could see U.S. aircraft flying right along the canyon in front of me, A-10s and AH-64 Apache helicopters. Some of them were so close I could see the pilots.

I pulled my PRC-148 radio out of my pouch and tried to make contact. But I could not speak. My throat was full of dirt, my tongue was sticking to the roof of my mouth, and I had no water. I was totally unable to transmit. But I knew I was in contact because I could hear the aircrew talking. So I fired up my emergency distress beacon on the radio and transmitted that.

They picked it up. I know they did because I could hear them plainly. "Hey, you getting that beacon?" "Yeah, we got it . . . but no further information." Then they just flew off, over to my right, where I now know the MH-47 had gone down.

The trouble was, the Taliban steal those radios if they can, and they often used them to lure the U.S. helicopters down. I was unaware of this at the time, but now it's obvious to me, the American pilots were extremely jumpy about trying to put down a response to a U.S. beacon because they did not know who the hell was aiming that beacon, and they might get shot down.

Which would have been, anyway, little comfort to me, lying there on the mountainside only half alive, bleeding to death and unable to walk. And now it was growing dark, and I was plainly running out of options. I guessed my only chance was to attract the attention of one of the pilots who were still flying down my canyon at pretty regular intervals.

My radio headset had been ripped away during my fall down the mountain, but I still had the wires. And I somehow rigged up two of my chem lights, which glow when you break them in half, and fixed them to the defunct radio wires. And then I whirled this homemade slingshot around my head in a kind of luminous buzz saw the first moment I saw a helicopter in the area.

I also had an infrared strobe light that I could fire up, and I had the laser from my rifle, which I took off and aimed at the regular U.S. flyby. Jesus Christ! I was a living, breathing distress signal. *There's got to be someone watching these mountains. Someone's got to see me.* I was using this procedure only when I actually saw a helicopter. And soon my optimism turned to outright gloom. No one was paying attention. From where I was lying, it looked like I'd been abandoned for dead.

By now, with the sun declining behind the mountains, I had almost all of the feeling back in my legs. And this gave me hope that I might be able to walk, although I knew the pain might be a bit fierce. I was getting dangerously thirsty. I could not get the clogged dust and dirt out of my throat. It was all I could do to not breathe, never mind speak. I had to find water, and I had to get the hell out of the death trap. But not until the veil of darkness fell over these mountains.

I knew I had to get myself out, first to water and then to safety, because it sure as hell didn't look like anyone was going to find me. I remember Axe's final words. They still rang clearly in my mind: "You stay alive, Marcus. And tell Cindy I love her." For Axe, and for Danny, and above all for Mikey, I knew I must stay alive.

I saw the last, long rays of the mountain sun cast their gigantic shadows through the canyon before me. And just as certainly, I saw the glint of the silver barrel of an AK-47 right across from me, dead ahead, on the far cliff face, maybe 150 yards. It caught the rays of the dying sun twice, which suggested the sonofabitch who was holding it was making a sweep across the wall of the mountain, right past the crevasse inside of which I was still lying motionless.

And now I could see the tribesman in question. He was just standing there, his shirtsleeves rolled up, wearing a blue and white checkered vest, holding his rifle in the familiar low-slung grip of the Afghans, a split second short of raising it to the firing position. The only conclusion was he was looking for me.

I did not know how many of his buddies were within shouting range. But I did know if he got a clear sight across that canyon and somehow spotted me, I was essentially history. He could hardly miss, and he kept staring across, but he did not raise his rifle. Yet.

I decided this was not a risk I was prepared to take. My own rifle was loaded and suppressed. There would be little noise to attract anyone else's attention. And very carefully, hardly daring to breathe, I raised the Mark 12 into the firing position and drew down on the little man on the far ridge. He was bang in the crosshairs of my telescopic sight.

I squeezed the trigger and hit him straight between the eyes. I just had time to see the blood bloom out into the center of his forehead, and then I watched him topple over the edge, down into the canyon. He must have fallen two hundred feet, screaming with his dying breath all the way. I was not in any way moved, except to thank God there was one less.

Almost immediately two of his colleagues ran into the precise spot where he had been standing, directly across from me. They were dressed more or less the same, except for the different colors of their vests. They stood there staring down into the canyon where the first man had fallen. They both carried AK's, held in the firing position but not fully raised.

I thought they might just take off, but they stood there, now looking hard across the void which separated my mountain from theirs. From where I was, they seemed to be looking right at me, scanning the cliff face for any sign of movement. I knew they had no idea if their pal had been shot, simply fallen, or perhaps committed suicide.

However, I think option one was their instinct. And right now they were trying to find out precisely who had shot him. I remained motionless, but those little black eyes were looking straight at me, and I realized if they both opened fire at once on my rocky redoubt, the chances of an AK-47 bullet, or bullets, hitting me were good to excellent. They had to go. Both of them.

Once more, I slowly raised my rifle and drew a bead on an armed Taliban tribesman. My first shot killed the one on the right instantly, and I watched him tumble over the edge. The second one, understanding now there was an enemy at large, raised his gun and scanned the cliff face where I was still flat on my back.

I hit him straight in the chest, then I fired a second time in case he was still breathing and able to cry out. He fell forward without a sound and went to join his two buddies on the canyon floor. Which left me all alone and thus far undiscovered.

Just a few hours previously, Mike Murphy and I had made a military judgment which cost three lives, the lives of some of the best SEALs I ever met. Lying here on my ledge, surrounded on all sides by hostile Taliban warriors, I could not afford another mistake. I'd somehow, by the grace of God, been spared from the consequences of the first one, made way up there on that granite outcrop which ought to be named for Mikey, our superb leader. The Battle of Murphy's Ridge.

Every decision I made from now on would involve my own life or death. I needed to fight my way out, and I did not give a damn how many of the Taliban enemy I had to kill in order to achieve that. The key point was, I could not make another mistake. I could take no chances.

The far side of the canyon remained silent as the sun disappeared behind the high western peaks of the Hindu Kush. I figured the Taliban had probably split their search party in this particular area and that I'd gotten rid of one half. Out there, somewhere, in the deathly silence of the twilight, there would almost certainly be three more, looking for the one surviving American from that original four-man platoon that had inflicted such damage on their troops.

The friendly clatter of the U.S. Apaches had gone now. No one was looking for me. And by far my biggest problem was water. Aside from the fact that I was still bleeding and couldn't stand up, the thirst was becoming desperate. My tongue was still clogged with dust and dirt, and I still could not speak. I'd lost my water bottle on the mountain during the first crashing fall with Mikey, and it had now been nine hours since I'd had a drink.

Also I was still soaking wet from when I fell in the river. I understood I was very light-headed from loss of blood, but I still tried to concentrate. And the one conclusion I reached was that I had to stand up. If a couple of those Taliban came around that corner to my left, the only way to approach me, and they had any form of light, I'd be like a jackrabbit caught in someone's headlights.

My redoubt had served me well, but I had to get out of it right now. When the bodies of those three guys were found at first light, this mountain would be swarming with Taliban. I dragged myself to my feet and stood there in my boxers in the freezing cold mountain air. I tested my right leg. Not too bad. Then I tested my left, and that hurt like a devil. I tried to brush some of the shale and dirt away from where I'd packed the wound, but the shards of the shrapnel were jutting out of my thigh, and whenever I touched one, I nearly jumped through the ceiling. At least I would have, if there'd been one.

One of my main problems was I had no handle on the terrain. Of course I knew that the mountain reared up behind me and that I was trapped on the cliff face with no way to go except up. Which from where I stood, almost unable to hobble, was a seriously daunting task. I tested my left leg again, and at least it wasn't worse.

But my back hurt like hell. I never realized how much pain three cracked vertebrae could inflict on a guy. Of course, I never realized I had three cracked vertebrae either. I could move my right shoulder despite a torn rotator cuff, which I also didn't realize I had. And my broken nose throbbed a bit, which was kid's stiff compared with the rest. I knew one side of my face was shredded by the fall down the mountain and the big cut on my forehead was pretty sore.

But my overriding thought was my thirst. I was only slightly comforted by the closeness of several mountain streams up here. I had to find one, fast, both to clean my wounds and to drink. That way I had a shot at yelling through the radio and locating an American helicopter or fighter aircraft in the morning.

I gathered up my gear, radio, strobes, and laser and repacked them into my pouch. I checked my rifle, which had about twenty rounds left in the magazine, with a full magazine remaining in the harness I still wore across my chest.

Then I stepped out of my redoubt, into absolute pitch black and the deadly silence of the Hindu Kush. There was no moon, and it was just starting to rain, which meant there wasn't going to be a moon in the foreseeable future.

I tested the leg again. It held my weight without giving way. I felt my direction around the huge rock which had been guarding my left flank all day. And then, with the smallest, most timid strides I had ever taken, I stepped out onto the mountain.

The Marauders' First Mission:
Walawbum

By 24 February 1944 the Chinese 22d and 38th Divisions had driven 60 miles into the Hukawng Valley and were advancing southward against the Japanese 18th Division, which had about 7,000 men near and north of Maingkwan. Strong jungle-hidden defensive positions, each manned by 40 to 100 Japanese, protected the Kamaing Road, the only motor route through the valley, the main supply artery for the enemy, and the key to control of the valley by either side.

The Chinese forces were making their main drive along the axis of this road. The 112th and 113th Regiments of the 38th Division, having taken Taihpa Ga and cleared the area between the Tawang and Tanai Hka rivers north of the road, were attacking south toward Maingkwan. Twenty miles to the west, beyond a 4,000-foot range of hills, the 65th Regiment of the 22d Division had captured Taro on 2 February and was working southeast in an advance that covered the right flank of the main effort.

General Stilwell planned to coordinate the employment of the 5307th with the main operations in the Hukawng Valley by sending the Marauders on wide encircling movements east of the Chinese forces to establish road blocks behind the Japanese front lines. For their first mission he ordered the Marauders to cut the Kamaing Road in the vicinity of Walawbum and to attack a forward command post believed to be near there. The Marauders were to move from Ningbyen to Tanja Ga and await General Stilwell's instructions to jump off. These instructions were to be given at the moment when Chinese operations along the road to the north of Maingkwan would most benefit by an attack in the rear of the Japanese lines.

To get into position for the jump-off, the 1st Battalion at 0600 on 24 February started over the trail from Ningbyen on a five-day march to Tanja Ga. The 2d Battalion followed at 0900; the 3d at 1100. Each battalion moved out in a column of combat teams, and the order of march afforded maximum protection. The I and R (Intelligence and Reconnaissance) Platoon was the point of the column and was followed by a rifle platoon. A rifle company, with half the heavy weapons platoon, was next in line. Combat team headquarters and the medical detachment, in the middle of the formation, preceded another rifle platoon and the rest of the heavy weapons.

In order to prevent surprise attacks, the I and R platoons scouted the trails in advance of the main elements of the combat teams and on the flanks. On the 25th the I and R Platoon of Orange Combat Team ran into an enemy patrol near Nzang Ga. In a sharp exchange of shots one Japanese was killed and one Marauder, Cpl. Warner Katz, was slightly wounded. On the same day, Pvt. Robert W. Landis, leading scout of Blue Combat Team's I and R Platoon, was killed by machine-gun fire as he approached Lanem Ga.

When the Marauders arrived in the vicinity of Tanja Ga on the afternoon of 28 February, they received orders from General Stilwell to proceed as quickly as possible to Walawbum. The steady advance of the Chinese on Maingkwan, forcing the enemy to retreat southward on the Kamaing Road, required the immediate employment of the 5307th. Coordinated with the Chinese operations, the Marauders' first mission was to hasten the enemy's withdrawal south of Walawbum by cutting his supply lines to forward troops.

Walawbum was 40 miles away; 3 days' march put the Marauders within striking distance. On 2 March, during a halt after the crossing of the Tanai River, General Merrill issued combat orders for this first mission. Moving out at 1600, the 3d Battalion was to pass through Sabaw Ga and Lagang Ga and secure control of the Kamaing Road at Walawbum by seizing the high ground along the Numpyek River east of the road. The 2d Battalion was to proceed via Wesu Ga, cut a trail through the jungle westerly to strike the Kamaing Road just east of the

Nambyu River at a point twenty-two miles west of Walawbum, and there construct and hold a road block.

The 1st Battalion was to block the trails at Sana Ga and Nchet Ga, with a minimum of one platoon at each point. One combat team of the battalion was to establish combat patrols along the Nambyu River between Shimak Ga and Uga Ga. The rest of the battalion was to constitute a reserve at Wesu Ga. The Marauders were to hold their positions blocking the Kamaing Road until the Chinese, following up an enemy withdrawal, could occupy the area and relieve them.

—◆—

By dawn on 3 March all battalions of the 5307th had started for Walawbum, fifteen miles away. Until their presence was known by the Japanese in this rear area, about twenty miles behind the front lines, the Marauders met only small parties of the enemy moving to and from supply dumps, rear hospitals, or command posts established in and around the small villages near Walawbum. At Lagang Ga a group of seven, carrying one casualty, encountered members of the 3d Battalion Headquarters as they were passing through the village about noon. The headquarters section opened fire when the enemy party was fifty yards away and killed five Japanese before their machine gunner was able to fire effectively.

Orange Combat Team led the 3d Battalion and bivouacked for the night within a half mile of Walawbum, protected on its right flank by the I and R Platoon, under Lt. Logan E. Weston. During the afternoon Major Lew had sent Weston's platoon, relieved of acting as point of the column, across the Numpyek River. The platoon of forty-eight men with three automatic rifles dug in for the night on the west bank of the stream, a few hundred yards west of Orange Combat Team.

The night of 3 March found the 1st Battalion 2 miles east of Wesu Ga and the 2d Battalion in the same general area. All elements put out heavy local security, consisting of trail blocks and listening posts, and before morning many of these had tangled with small Japanese patrols and foraging parties. No casualties were suffered.

It seemed evident that the enemy had been confused by the sudden appearance of the 5307th in the Walawbum area. Early on 4 March the Japanese began to feel out the Marauder positions. At 0630 an enemy force of 30 vigorously attacked the Lagang Ga air strip, which Khaki Combat Team had constructed and had since been protecting for L-4 and L-5 liaison planes. The enemy arrived just as the Marauders were preparing their breakfast. Conditions of fog, as well as concealment offered by heavy brush and gullies, facilitated the enemy's approach. Nevertheless, a squad of riflemen, two light machine gunners, and 60-mm mortar men quickly drove off the force after ten of its number had been killed. Six men from Khaki Combat Team were wounded during the engagement, and four of these were evacuated by liaison plane from the strip.

Within another hour a Japanese force of ninety, coming from the direction of Walawbum, threatened Orange Combat Team's I and R Platoon in the heaviest fighting of the day. Lieutenant Weston had moved his unit to higher ground along the river about 300 yards southwest of the position he had occupied during the night. On this higher ground he could stop any attempted enemy crossing of the river either up or down stream toward the flank of Orange Combat Team. At 0720 the platoon brushed with an enemy patrol on the west side of the river and shortly afterward met resistance from a Japanese group to the north. A little later another enemy group came at the platoon's position from the northwest, and a fourth and a fifth group advanced on it from the north and northeast.

Japanese officers were heard shouting orders to their men for these movements. Sgt. Henry H. Gosho, Nisei interpreter with Weston's platoon, was able to translate this information in time for shifting automatic weapons to meet each attack successfully. Nevertheless, mortar fire began to come very close, and by 1100 the platoon was pressed on three sides by superior enemy forces.

When the fourth enemy group was turned back, Lieutenant Weston signaled Major Lew by radio and asked for mortar fire from his 81-mm section. During and after the enemy's fifth attack, Lt. William E. Woorner fired 235 rounds of light, heavy, and smoke shells according to

Lieutenant Weston's radioed directions. Under cover of mortar fire, the I and R Platoon waded the stream, carrying three litters. The Japanese attempted to follow but a squad from the team, forming a skirmish line, protected the crossing and stopped the enemy with heavy small-arms fire. The I and R Platoon, having held up a strong enemy attack on Orange Combat Team's right flank until it reached its objective, withdrew to the southwest and dug in with the team. The platoon and the mortar section had destroyed two-thirds of the Japanese attacking force, estimated at 90 men.

Orange Combat Team established a perimeter along the Numpyek River on the high ground facing Walawbum and was in position to block the Kamaing Road with mortars and machine guns. In the afternoon Major Lew's men threw about 100 shells into the village and on the road. The Japanese replied with some mortar and artillery fire. The mortar shells landed around the perimeter, but the artillery ranged over it to Lagang Ga, where planes were dropping supplies to Khaki Combat Team. Neither Khaki nor Orange Combat Team suffered casualties from this enemy fire.

North of Walawbum two Japanese soldiers infiltrated the Marauder lines and almost succeeded in reaching General Merrill's command post, established temporarily at Wesu Ga. When they were discovered one was setting up a machine gun with which he could have wiped out the entire command group. The other was found worming his way through the heavy growth surrounding the headquarters. Both Japanese escaped, but a pool of blood on the ground showed that at least one was wounded.

Northwest of Walawbum the men of the 2d Battalion had been chopping their way through the jungle toward the Kamaing Road. Meeting no serious resistance, they reached the road at dusk, constructed a block and a perimeter defense, and dug in for the night.

The 18th Division's telephone communications from the front to headquarters at Kamaing ran along the road and so passed through the perimeter of the road block established by the 2d Battalion. Tec. 4 Roy H. Matsumoto, a Nisei assigned to the 2d Battalion for intelligence operations, tapped the enemy's telephone line. One of the conversations he heard concerned the troubles of a Japanese sergeant in charge of an ammunition dump. The sergeant had with him only three soldiers armed with rifles and begged "help and advice" from his commanding officer because he had learned of the 2d Battalion's arrival at the road. The sergeant, in reporting the location of the 2d Battalion, gave away his own position. When American planes appeared for a supply drop, the 2d Battalion signaled the crews to send back to the enemy dump fighters or bombers with "help and advice" of an unexpected kind.

On 4 March, while guarding the rear of the 2d and 3d Battalions, two platoons of the 1st Battalion had established blocks near Sana Ga and Nchet Ga on the trails leading into Walawbum. Their patrols inflicted heavy casualties on unwary small parties of the enemy, but nothing approaching a large engagement materialized in that section. From Wesu Ga, where most of the 1st Battalion was in reserve, Red and White Combat Teams sent out strong reconnaissance groups to the air strip at Lagang Ga and across the Nambyu River to Ninghku Ga. Red Combat Team's patrol met no resistance. White's patrol ran into a group of Japanese near Ninghku Ga. The Marauders killed two of the group and dispersed the rest, averting another possible attack on the 5307th's command post.

On March 5 the Japanese made several efforts to dislodge the forces blocking their supply road. The 2d Battalion underwent considerable shelling and turned back six infantry attacks, at a cost of one man killed and five wounded. South of Walawbum, after heavy mortar fire and some 77mm artillery shelling, strong Japanese patrols moved toward Orange Combat Team with the evident intention of finding its flanks. Anticipating just such moves, Major Lew had prepared ambush positions along the east bank of the Numpyek River, and Orange Combat Team took heavy toll of the enemy as they were crossing the stream. Seventy-five Japanese dead were counted; Orange lost one killed and seven wounded. Toward evening all activity against the 2d and 3d Battalions slackened, but enemy reinforcements were on their way from Kamaing. Strafed and bombed by our planes en route, they nevertheless kept coming; the noisy slamming of tail gates after dark indicated that truck after truck was arriving and discharging its cargo of reinforcements.

Messages intercepted on the telephone-tap by the 2d Battalion proved that the Japanese were still confused by the American activities. Finally, Matsumoto reported that forward elements of the Japanese 18th Division had been ordered to withdraw from the Maingkwan area, crossing the Nambyu River south of Kumnyen. To screen the withdrawal of the main units, which were apparently not intending to use the Kamaing Road, the enemy was planning to attack the 2d Battalion at 2300 that night. The Japanese had artillery available for this attack, and the 2d Battalion, with only a limited amount of mortar and machine-gun ammunition, was in no condition to stop them from pushing through the road block. The battalion had fought for 36 hours without food or water. Colonel McGee explained the situation to General Merrill by phone. The General advised the 2d Battalion to withdraw after dark toward Wesu Ga and join the 3d Battalion east of the Numpyek River. The Marauders blocked the road with trees, placed booby traps in the area, and withdrew along the trail they had cut 2 days before. Fortunately, they themselves were alert to the danger of booby traps and drove a mule ahead of them. The mule was blown to bits. Arriving at Wesu Ga by noon the following day, 6 March, Colonel McGee and his men picked up an air drop of rations and ammunition, filled their canteens, and hurried toward Lagang Ga where they could support the 3d Battalion if they were needed.

After the 2d Battalion vacated its road-block position west of Walawbum on the night of 5 March, Orange Combat Team was holding the only position still commanding the Kamaing Road. Khaki Combat Team was withdrawn from the Lagang Ga air strip early on the morning of 6 March and moved out to strengthen Major Lew's position by advancing beyond his left flank to a point where the Numpyek River makes a sharp U bend. General Merrill also moved 4 miles nearer the position of the 3d Battalion, changing his command post from Wesu Ga to Lagang Ga.

From dawn the Japanese, in what was presumably a further effort to cover the withdrawal of their main force, poured a steady stream of mortar fire on Orange Combat Team and about midmorning supplemented the mortar fire by medium artillery. Major Lew's men, now standing the brunt of the whole attack, were well protected in fox holes roofed with logs and managed to keep the upper hand throughout the day.

Elements of the combat team disrupted the enemy's plans to organize an attacking force to the south. Sgt. Andrew B. Pung directed mortar fire from the 81-mm section on a concentration area for troops arriving from Kamaing. Perched in a tree thirty feet from the ground, he secured several direct hits, one of the shells landing in the bed of a truck from which reinforcements were being unloaded. As a result of this accurate fire, no assaults materialized from the south.

Equal success was obtained against enemy efforts from the west. At 1715 two enemy companies, following each other in line of skirmishers and strongly supported by heavy machine-gun, mortar, and 77-mm fire, attempted to cross the river to attack Orange Combat Team's position. Except for mortars, the Marauders held their fire until the enemy reached the western river bank, some 25 yards away. Then they let loose with their automatic weapons and tore great gaps in the Japanese line. Two heavy machine guns, placed on the river bank with clear fields of fire, used 5,000 rounds each with deadly effect. The attack wilted, and 400 Japanese lay dead on the open ground near the river.

By now Orange Combat Team's ammunition was low. Khaki Combat Team, which was still moving to get into position south of Orange, rushed up five mule loads of mortar shells and machine-gun cartridges. But before the ammunition arrived the Japanese had retired. The only casualties Orange Combat Team suffered were three slightly wounded. During the hour of combat the Japanese put in a great deal of small-arms fire, but they were aiming uphill and most of the fire passed overhead.

At Kasan Ga, more than an hour before the last Japanese attack at 1715, General Merrill met a Chinese battalion commander who had just arrived, ahead of his regiment, to arrange relief of the Marauders at Walawbum. General Merrill's present intelligence estimates indicated that the enemy was bringing in reinforcements from the south to make a stand at Walawbum. He therefore decided to disengage the Marauders, pull back, circle around to the east, and cut the Kamaing Road near Chanmoi, again maneuvering his forces to the rear of the Japanese. The Chinese regiment would take over the Marauder positions at Walawbum.

However, before General Merrill's orders for this move could be executed, the situation at Walawbum had changed. The Japanese had suddenly retired toward Kamaing after their costly attack on Orange Combat Team. Also, the Chinese 22d and 38th Divisions had captured Maingkwan and were pushing rapidly to the south in pursuit of the main enemy force retreating toward Chanmoi on a road which bypassed the Marauder position. Further American efforts were unnecessary.

The 38th Division arrived in the Walawbum area on 7 March. The Chinese made contact with the Marauders so quickly and unexpectedly that the first encounter resulted in an exchange of shots. The Chinese, failing to recognize the American helmets, fired on Red Combat Team disposed along the river east of Wesu Ga. The Marauders replied with rifle and mortar fire, and shooting continued until a Chinese interpreter identified the opposing force. The Americans quickly waded across the stream to find a major and three enlisted men badly wounded. Marauder doctors rushed to the scene, and men from Red Combat Team carried the injured Chinese to the air strip for evacuation.

Shortly after this incident, the Chinese 38th Division entered Walawbum with almost no opposition. At 1845 that evening General Merrill held a staff meeting to inform the assembled officers that the first phase of the Marauder operation had ended. He conveyed to the group General Stilwell's congratulations for a job well done and requested the officers to relay the message to their men. A 3-day rest period, he announced, was now in order.

During the rest period the men of the 5307th cleaned and over-hauled their equipment and made repairs and replacements wherever necessary. The Americans and nearby Chinese troops set up a joint perimeter around Sana Ga and Shikau Ga. The two groups exchanged rations, battle souvenirs, and money and went swimming together. Morale was superb.

In five days, from the jump-off on 3 March to the fall of Walawbum on 7 March, the Americans had killed 800 of the enemy, had cooperated with the Chinese to force a major Japanese withdrawal, and had paved the way for further Allied progress. This was accomplished at a cost to the Marauders of eight men killed and thirty-seven wounded. Up to this point nineteen patients had been evacuated with malaria, eight with other fevers (mostly dengue), ten with psychoneurosis, and thirty-three with injuries. Miscellaneous sicknesses totaled 109. Of the 2,750 men who started toward Walawbum, about 2,500 remained to carry on.

The First Rangers:
Fighting the French and Indians

M. J. Canavan

A FEW DAYS AFTER THIS AMOS AND I WENT UP TO CONCORD AND enlisted in the Rangers. We had no showy uniform. Our clothes were of strong homespun of a dull color that would not attract attention in the woods. We brought our own guns, and they gave each of us a blanket, a greatcoat, a hatchet, and a wooden bottle in which to carry our drink. We were also given rackets and skates.

We waited till the end of January, when Rogers marched into town with five companies of men whom he had collected in New Hampshire. Most of them were rough, stern frontiersmen from the Amoskeag Falls, skilled in Indian fighting.

The recruits from Middlesex were distributed among these companies, and Edmund had us placed in his squad. On my right in the ranks was McKinstry, a grizzled old trapper, and to the left was John Martin, a hardy fellow a few years older than myself. Both of them had served before with Rogers.

Four of the companies set sail from Boston for Cape Breton, to take part in the siege of that place, and our company, under Rogers, started on the march for Fort Edward. The snow was deep, and we travelled on snowshoes. Rogers made us march in single file, with a man some distance ahead, and another behind. On either side were flankers to detect the enemy. As we shuffled along over the snow he taught us how to act in a hostile country.

"Don't crowd up together. Keep several paces apart. Then if the enemy fires at you, one shot will not hit two men. When you come to low, marshy ground, change the order of your march and go abreast, for if you went in single file, you would wear a path in the ground that the enemy could follow. If you are to reconnoiter a place, make a stand in a safe spot when you get near it, and send a couple of men ahead to look the ground over. If you have to retreat and come to a river, cross it anywhere but at the usual ford, for that is where the enemy would hide on the farther side ready to pick you off. If your march is by a lake or river, keep at some distance from it, that you may not be hemmed in on one side and caught in a trap. When you go out, always return by a different way, and avoid the usual travelled paths."

Thus, as we marched along, Rogers kept talking to us, instructing us in the methods of wood-fighting.

We went through Worcester, Brookfield, and Northampton to Pontoosuc Fort, where a party of Mohegan Indians from Stockbridge joined us, under their chief Jacob. Then to a Dutch settlement called Kinderhook, and to the Hudson River. The weather was very cold, and the river was frozen over. Rogers told us to put on our skates, and we skated up the river to Fort Edward.

This was a very strong fort, with much artillery. The fort was on the left shore, and a very strong blockhouse was on the right bank. The Rangers' camp was on an island in the Hudson. Their barracks were made of logs, with bark roofs, and their camp was not in bad condition.

The Rangers were mostly frontiersmen from New Hampshire, who had lived in the woods all their lives, and had fought against wild beasts and Indians. The life they were now leading was simply their old life on a larger scale. Most of them were dressed in deerskin. They were rough, stern men, who had been so much exposed to danger, and were so used to it, that they seemed to have no fear. They looked upon the French and Indians as a dire plague, to be wiped off the earth by any means.

They had heard the war-whoop at their own homes, and had seen their close relatives scalped by Indians. No wonder they classed the redskins with wolves and snakes, as a plague to be wiped off the earth. Living in the woods so much, they seemed to have acquired the keen senses that wild animals have. They were ever on the alert. Their eyes and ears noticed all the signs and sounds of nature. They had fought savages for years, and their own ways were savage. Many of them took scalps.

I do not believe that a bolder or more adventurous set of men than these Rangers ever existed.

As I looked them over and saw what a lot of keen, fearless, and self-reliant men I was among, I was very proud to think that I was one of this chosen corps.

McKinstry said: "They're a tough set, Ben. But when you get in your first fight, you'll be glad you're with a tough set. Not much school learning among them; but they know all about the woods and Injun fighting, and that's what we want here."

Every evening at roll-call we formed on parade, equipped with a firelock, sixty rounds of powder and ball, and a hatchet, and were inspected, that we might be ready at a minute's warning. The guards were arranged and the scouts for the next day appointed.

After we had been at the camp a couple of days Rogers came out of his hut and said to me:—

"Come, Comee, I'm going over to the fort and may want someone to bring back a few things."

We crossed the ice to the shore and went up to the fort. It was a great sight for me to see the regulars in their bright scarlet coats, the Scotch Highlanders with their kilts and tartans, and our own provincial troops in blue, though there were not many of them, as they had mostly gone home for the winter.

Rogers walked up to the headquarters of Colonel Haviland, the commander.

"I shall be busy here some time. Come back in an hour and wait for me."

I went over to the Scotch regiment, the Black Watch it was called, and listened to them talking their curious language.

One of the men turned to me and asked if I was looking for any one.

"Well, I'm of Scotch descent, and I thought I'd see if there were any McComees or Munros among you."

He looked over to another group and shouted: "Hector! Hector Munro! Here's one of your kinsmen." A strong, active fellow of some twenty-eight or thirty years came over.

"How's that? I didn't know that any of our kin were over here."

"My grandmother was a Munro, and her father was taken prisoner while fighting for King Charles the First, and was sent to America."

"Hear that now! My brother Donald and myself were out with Charlie in forty-five, and we had a hard time of it afterward, hunted about till they made up their minds to form some Highland regiments and give pardon to those who enlisted, and here we are fighting for King George."

He led me to his brother and made me acquainted with him. We went to their quarters, and I learned more about the clan in a short time than I ever heard before or since. It seemed as if most of the great generals in almost every army were Munros, and they traced their ancestry back to the time of Noah.

At last I said that I must go to headquarters to meet Captain Rogers.

"So you belong to the Rangers? They're a braw set of men, and there's many a gude Scotchman among them. We'll come over and see you."

I returned and waited for Rogers, and when he came out, he said: "Come over to the sutler's hut; I want to buy some things we haven't got on the island."

Rogers made some purchases and then listened to two English officers who were seated at a table, drinking. They had reached a maudlin state, and were bewailing the fate of England.

"This is a sad day for old England, my boy."

"Yes, the country will never be able to stand up under the great debt that we have incurred for these miserable Provinces."

Rogers went over to them and said:—

"Don't let that trouble you, my friends. Make yourselves easy on that score, for I will pay half the national debt, and my good friend here says he will take the other half on his shoulders, and the nation will be rid of her difficulties."

"By Gad! I'm blessed if you're not fine fellows. Sit down and have a drink with us."

Rogers introduced me to them as the Earl of Middlesex. They took off their hats to me and ordered some grog for us. I barely tasted mine, for I had no heart to drink with the besotted fools. We bade them good-by, I took up the things which Rogers had bought, and we walked away.

"Well, Comee, we've settled the nation's debt. That's one good thing off our hands. There's another thing I wish we could get rid of as easily. The old country has sent us over some curious commanders. There was Braddock, who threw away his army and his life; Webb, who was a coward; Loudon, our present commander, is always running hither and thither, giving orders, but effecting nothing. He is like the pictures of St. George on the tavern signs,—always on horseback, but never getting anywhere.

"But this Colonel Haviland, the commandant here, beats them all hollow. A worse specimen of stupidity or rascality I never saw. Captain Israel Putnam of the Connecticut troops was sent out on a scout a week ago. Before he went Haviland said publicly that on his return he should send me out against the French with four hundred men. One of Putnam's men deserted to the enemy and one of the Rangers was captured, so that the enemy knew all about it. Putnam says there are about six hundred Indians near Ticonderoga; and now this Haviland sends me out, not with four hundred men, but with one hundred and eighty, all told. You will see all the fighting you want inside the next week and I hope we may both get through it alive."

When I returned to the island, I told Edmund and Amos what Rogers had said, and we felt pretty glum. "It looks to me," said Edmund, "as if the rest of the campaign wouldn't interest us very much."

On the 10th of March we set forth on snowshoes and travelled through the thick forest. That night we encamped at a brook. The Rangers built shelters of boughs in a short time. Big fires were made, and after we had our suppers and a pull at the pipe, we rolled ourselves up in our blankets and went to sleep.

The next morning we reached Lake George, and saw the blackened ruins of Fort William Henry, where the massacre had taken place some eight months before.

Of course I knew the story, but Martin had been there, and told me how the fort was besieged by Montcalm; and after it was battered to pieces, the garrison surrendered. They had given up their arms and were marching back to the English army, when the drunken Indians set upon them and killed and scalped most of the force. Martin caught up a little boy whose parents had been killed, and escaped through the dense woods.

We marched down the lake in three files, threading our way among the islands and skirting the steep cliffs. The lake stretched out before us, covered with thick ice. On the further side were the woods and mountains.

We camped near the First Narrows that night. The next day we turned away from the lake and went to a cape called Sebattis Point.

"What's the matter, Martin? Why do we halt?"

"Didn't you see a dog run across the lake, some distance down?"

"Yes, I saw something go across."

"Well, it was a dog, and if there was a dog, there were probably Indians with him. What would a dog be doing out here alone?"

We camped in the woods, and after it was dark skated down the lake.

Our advanced guard sent back word that they thought they had seen a fire on an island. We hid our hand-sleighs and packs and went there, but could find no signs of a fire.

Rogers said that very likely it was the light from some old rotten stumps, but Martin was not of this opinion.

"There was a fire there. First we see the dog, and then the fire. The fire could be put out, and it would be difficult to find the burnt sticks in the dark. If it were the light from old wood, some one of all this party would have seen it. The French are no fools. They knew we were coming, and some Indians are watching us. We'll have a hot time before we get back."

We now left the lake, lest we should be seen, and marched through the woods back of the mountain which overlooked Fort Ticonderoga. At noon we halted.

Rogers said: "We are about two miles from the advanced guard of the French. We will wait here a couple of hours, and then go on. When night comes, we will make an ambush in the paths, and capture some of the guards as they come out in the morning."

We started on again, with a brook on our left and a steep mountain on our right.

We kept a sharp watch on the brook, for the enemy would probably travel on it, as the snow was four feet deep.

Our advanced guard came back and reported that the enemy were ahead. That there were ninety of them, mostly Indians. They were coming down the brook. The bank of the brook was higher than the ground where we were, and Rogers gave the order:—

"Come, boys! Stretch out in a line behind the bank. Lie down and keep hidden. Wait till I give the signal by firing my gun, and then jump up and give it to them."

Rogers hid in a clump of bushes, from which he could look over the bank. We lay without stirring, till Rogers fired and shouted, "Now, boys."

We jumped up and fired at them. It was the first time I had seen Indians, and very hideous they looked, as I stood up and saw them on the brook, dressed in moccasins, leggings, and breech clout, with a mantle or cloak of skins over their shoulders, a feather in the scalp-lock, and their faces and breasts painted with stripes of red and black.

When we fired, a great number of them fell, and the rest ran away. We supposed that they were defeated, and pursued them. But we got into a hornets' nest. For this was only the advanced guard, and as we ran after them, several hundred more French and Indians came up, fired at us, and killed nearly fifty of our men. I could hear the bullets whistle by me, and men dropped at my side.

We rallied and retreated; and having reloaded, poured a volley into them that drove them back again.

"What do you think about that fire on the island, Ben?" asked Martin.

They came on a third time, in front and on both sides of us. We kept up a continual fire and drove the flanking parties back, and they retreated once more.

When that great body of French and Indians appeared and their fierce war-whoops sounded through the woods, when the firing began and the men fell down close by me, I must confess I was nervous and frightened. But I looked on either side, and there stood the grim, stern frontiersmen picking off their men as cool as if they were at a turkey shoot. This brought my confidence back at once, and as the fight became hot, I found myself filled with an angry rage. I wanted to kill, to kill as many as I could, and pay off the old score.

We backed up against the steep mountain. The Indians now tried to go up it on our right, but a party was sent out and repulsed them. Another party attempted to ascend on our left. They, too, were driven back. Edmund, Amos, and I were with the main body, fighting, loading, and shooting as fast as we could. No time for talk. Sometimes the Indians were twenty yards from us, and at times we were all mixed up with them, fighting hand to hand.

When I had fired, I pulled out my hatchet, and as these devilish-looking savages in their red and black paint rushed at me, I cut and hacked with my hatchet in my right hand, and holding my firelock in my left, warded off the blows with it. A blow on my arm knocked the hatchet from my hand. Then I used my gun as a club. It was a long, heavy, old firelock, and anger and excitement added to my strength, so that it was a terrible weapon. I smashed away with it till nothing was left but the bent barrel.

When we drove them back, I picked up a French gun and a hatchet. There were plenty of them, for dead and dying men lay in heaps on the ground.

We struggled with them an hour and a half, during which time we lost over one hundred men.

Rogers was in the thick of the fight most of the time. Yet he saw what was going on round us, and directed our movements. Toward dark he cried out: "It's no use, boys; we must get out of this place. Follow me."

We ran up the mountain to a spot where Lieutenant Phillips and some men were fighting a flanking party of Indians, and there we had another lively scrimmage. We went along the side of the mountain. I had lost my rackets. One couldn't think of them and fight, as we had been fighting, too.

Rogers shouted: "Scatter, boys! Every man for himself. Meet at the First Narrows."

I loaded my gun and floundered along in the deep snow, making all possible haste.

Looking behind, I saw that an Indian on snowshoes was following me. I started up a side hill, where his rackets would not give him an advantage.

He fired, but missed me. I turned and shot him, as he raised his hand to throw his tomahawk. He fell and was quite dead by the time I reached him.

It's no pleasant sight to look on the face of a man you have just killed, even though you have right on your side, and he be only a redskin.

One glance at that face and the staring eyes was enough. I felt weak and guilty as I knelt by him, and picked up his rackets, gun, and ammunition. I took his fur mantle, too, for I had thrown away my blanket, and knew that I should be cold before the night was over.

I wandered through the woods till the moon rose, and gave me the direction to take. Then I came to the lake and went out on it, and at last got to the Narrows, where I found what was left of our party. Edmund and Amos were with them. Rogers had sent a messenger for assistance.

Over two-thirds of our party were killed or missing. And of those who remained, there were but few who did not have some cut or bullet wound.

We were exhausted. The men had thrown away their blankets, and the night was bitter cold.

We could not have fires, as they would have been beacon lights to the enemy, showing them where we were.

We huddled together like sheep for warmth, and I gave my mantle to a poor fellow who was badly wounded.

When the day began to break, we marched up the lake, and were met by Captain Stark with reënforcements, and sleds for our wounded, and then proceeded to Fort Edward.

The next day, as Edmund, Amos, and I were talking the fight over, Rogers came to us. He laughed, and said: "Well, boys! You haven't been here long. But you've had lots of fun, haven't you?"

"Yes, sir. Plenty! We are satisfied. We can stand a long spell of dull times now."

The Rangers lost so heavily in this fight that but little was required of them for some time. A few scouting-parties were sent out, but they were of little consequence.

Rebel Raider:
Mosby the Gray Ghost

H. Beam Piper

It was almost midnight, on January 2, 1863, and the impromptu party at the Ratcliffe home was breaking up. The guest of honor, General J. E. B. Stuart, felt that he was overstaying his welcome—not at the Ratcliffe home, where everybody was soundly Confederate, but in Fairfax County, then occupied by the Union Army.

About a week before, he had come raiding up from Culpepper with a strong force of cavalry, to spend a merry Christmas in northern Virginia and give the enemy a busy if somewhat less than happy New Year's. He had shot up outposts, run off horses from remount stations, plundered supply depots, burned stores of forage; now, before returning to the main Confederate Army, he had paused to visit his friend Laura Ratcliffe. And, of course, there had been a party. There was always a party when Jeb Stuart was in any one place long enough to organize one.

They were all crowding into the hallway—the officers of Stuart's staff, receiving their hats and cloaks from the servants and buckling on their weapons; the young ladies, their gay dresses showing only the first traces of wartime shabbiness; the matrons who chaperoned them; Stuart himself, the center of attention, with his hostess on his arm.

"It's a shame you can't stay longer, General," Laura Ratcliffe was saying. "It's hard on us, living in conquered territory, under enemy rule."

"Well, I won't desert you entirely, Miss Ratcliffe," Stuart told her. "I'm returning to Culpepper in the morning, as you know, but I mean to leave Captain Mosby behind with a few men, to look after the loyal Confederate people here until we can return in force and in victory."

Hearing his name, one of the men in gray turned, his hands raised to hook the fastening at the throat of his cloak. Just four days short of his thirtieth birthday, he looked even more youthful; he was considerably below average height, and so slender as to give the impression of frailness. His hair and the beard he was wearing at the time were very light brown. He wore an officer's uniform without insignia of rank, and instead of a saber he carried a pair of 1860-model Colt .44's on his belt, with the butts to the front so that either revolver could be drawn with either hand, backhand or crossbody.

There was more than a touch of the dandy about him. The cloak he was fastening was lined with scarlet silk and the gray cock-brimmed hat the slave was holding for him was plumed with a squirrel tail. At first glance he seemed no more than one of the many young gentlemen of the planter class serving in the Confederate cavalry. But then one looked into his eyes and got the illusion of being covered by a pair of blued pistol muzzles. He had an aura of combined ruthlessness, self-confidence, good humor and impudent audacity.

For an instant he stood looking inquiringly at the general. Then he realized what Stuart had said, and the blue eyes sparkled. This was the thing he had almost given up hoping for—an independent command and a chance to operate in the enemy's rear.

In 1855, John Singleton Mosby, newly graduated from the University of Virginia, had opened a law office at Bristol, Washington County, Virginia, and a year later he had married.

The son of a well-to-do farmer and slave-owner, his boyhood had been devoted to outdoor sports, especially hunting, and he was accounted an expert horseman and a dead shot, even in a society in which skill with guns and horses was taken for granted. Otherwise, the outbreak of the war had found him without military qualifications and completely uninterested in military matters. Moreover, he had been a rabid anti-secessionist.

It must be remembered, however, that, like most Southerners, he regarded secession as an entirely local issue, to be settled by the people of each state for themselves. He took no exception to the position that a state had the constitutional right to sever its connection with the Union if its people so desired. His objection to secession was based upon what he considered to be political logic. He realized that, once begun, secession was a process which could only end in reducing America to a cluster of impotent petty sovereignties, torn by hostilities, incapable of any concerted action, a fair prey to any outside aggressor.

However, he was also a believer in the paramount sovereignty of the states. He was first of all a Virginian. So, when Virginia voted in favor of secession, Mosby, while he deplored the choice, felt that he had no alternative but to accept it. He promptly enlisted in a locally organized cavalry company, the Washington Mounted Rifles, under a former U.S. officer and West Point graduate, William E. Jones.

His letters to his wife told of his early military experiences—his pleasure at receiving one of the fine new Sharps carbines which Captain Jones had wangled for his company, and, later, a Colt .44 revolver: his first taste of fire in the Shenandoah Valley, where the company, now incorporated into Colonel Stuart's First Virginia Cavalry, were covering Johnston's march to re-enforce Beauregard: his rather passive participation in the big battle at Manassas. He was keenly disappointed at being held in reserve throughout the fighting. Long afterward, it was to be his expressed opinion that the Confederacy had lost the war by failing to follow the initial victory and exploit the rout of McDowell's army.

The remainder of 1861 saw him doing picket duty in Fairfax County. When Stuart was promoted to brigadier general, and Captain Jones took his place as colonel of the First Virginia, Mosby became the latter's adjutant. There should have been a commission along with this post, but this seems to have been snarled in red tape at Richmond and never came through. It was about this time that Mosby first came to Stuart's personal attention. Mosby spent a night at headquarters after escorting a couple of young ladies who had been living outside the Confederate lines and were anxious to reach relatives living farther south.

Stuart had been quite favorably impressed with Mosby, and when, some time later, the latter lost his place as adjutant of the First by reason of Jones' promotion to brigadier general and Fitzhugh Lee's taking over the regiment, Mosby became one of Stuart's headquarters scouts.

Scouting for Jeb Stuart was not the easiest work in the world, nor the safest, but Mosby appears to have enjoyed it, and certainly made good at it. It was he who scouted the route for Stuart's celebrated "Ride Around MacClellan" in June, 1862, an exploit which brought his name to the favorable attention of General Lee. By this time, still without commission, he was accepted at Stuart's headquarters as a sort of courtesy officer, and generally addressed as "Captain" Mosby. Stuart made several efforts to get him commissioned, but War Department red tape seems to have blocked all of them. By this time, too, Mosby had become convinced of the utter worthlessness of the saber as a cavalryman's weapon, and for his own armament adopted a pair of Colts.

The revolver of the Civil War was, of course, a percussion-cap weapon. Even with the powder and bullet contained in a combustible paper cartridge, loading such an arm was a slow process: each bullet had to be forced in the front of the chamber on top of its propellant charge by means of a hinged rammer under the barrel, and a tiny copper cap had to be placed on each nipple. It was nothing to attempt on a prancing horse. The Union cavalryman was armed with a single-shot carbine—the seven-shot Spencer repeater was not to make its battlefield appearance until late in 1863—and one revolver, giving him a total of seven shots without reloading. With a pair of six-shooters, Mosby had a five-shot advantage over any opponent he was likely to encounter. As he saw it, tactical strength lay in the number of shots which could be delivered without reloading, rather than in the number of men firing them. Once he reached a position of independent command, he was to adhere consistently to this principle.

On July 14, 1862, General John Pope, who had taken over a newly created Union Army made up of the commands of McDowell, Banks and Fremont, issued a bombastic and tactless order to his new command, making invidious comparisons between the armies in the west and those in the east. He said, "I hear constantly of 'taking strong positions and holding them,' of 'lines of retreat,' and of 'bases of supplies.' Let us discard all such ideas. Let us study the probable lines of retreat of our opponents, and leave our own to take care of themselves."

That intrigued Mosby. If General Pope wasn't going to take care of his own rear, somebody ought to do it for him, and who better than John Mosby? He went promptly to Stuart, pointing out Pope's disinterest in his own lines of supply and communication, and asked that he be given about twenty men and detailed to get into Pope's rear and see what sort of disturbance he could create.

Stuart doubted the propriety of sending men into what was then Stonewall Jackson's territory, but he gave Mosby a letter to Jackson, recommending the bearer highly and outlining what he proposed doing, with the request that he be given some men to try it. With this letter, Mosby set out for Jackson's headquarters.

He never reached his destination. On the way, he was taken prisoner by a raiding force of New York cavalry, and arrived, instead, at Old Capitol jail in Washington. Stuart requested his exchange at once, and Mosby spent only about ten days in Old Capitol, and then was sent down the Potomac on an exchange boat, along with a number of other prisoners of war, for Hampton Roads.

The boat-load of prisoners, about to be exchanged and returned to their own army, were allowed to pass through a busy port of military embarkation and debarkation, with every opportunity to observe everything that was going on, and, to make a bad matter worse, the steamboat captain was himself a Confederate sympathizer. So when Mosby, from the exchange boat, observed a number of transports lying at anchor, he had no trouble at all in learning that they carried Burnside's men, newly brought north from the Carolinas. With the help of the steamboat captain, Mosby was able to learn that the transports were bound for Acquia Creek, on the Potomac; that meant that the re-enforcements were for Pope.

As soon as he was exchanged, Mosby made all haste for Lee's headquarters to report what he had discovered. Lee, remembering Mosby as the man who had scouted ahead of Stuart's Ride Around MacClellan, knew that he had a hot bit of information from a credible source. A dispatch rider was started off at once for Jackson, and Jackson struck Pope at

Cedar Mountain before he could be re-enforced. Mosby returned to Stuart's headquarters, losing no time in promoting a pair of .44's to replace the ones lost when captured, and found his stock with Stuart at an all-time high as a result of his recent feat of espionage while in the hands of the enemy.

So he was with Stuart when Stuart stopped at Laura Ratcliffe's home, and was on hand when Stuart wanted to make one of his characteristic gestures of gallantry. And so he finally got his independent command—all of six men—and orders to operate in the enemy's rear.

Whatever Stuart might have had in mind in leaving him behind "to look after the loyal Confederate people," John Mosby had no intention of posting himself in Laura Ratcliffe's front yard as a guard of honor. He had a theory of guerrilla warfare which he wanted to test. In part, it derived from his experiences in the Shenandoah Valley and in Fairfax County, but in larger part, it was based upon his own understanding of the fundamental nature of war.

The majority of guerrilla leaders have always been severely tactical in their thinking. That is to say, they have been concerned almost exclusively with immediate results. A troop column is ambushed, a picket post attacked, or a supply dump destroyed for the sake of the immediate loss of personnel or materiel so inflicted upon the enemy. Mosby, however, had a well-conceived strategic theory. He knew, in view of the magnitude of the war, that the tactical effects of his operations would simply be lost in the over-all picture. But, if he could create enough uproar in the Union rear, he believed that he could force the withdrawal from the front of a regiment or even a brigade to guard against his attacks and, in some future battle, the absence of that regiment or brigade might tip the scale of battle or, at least, make some future Confederate victory more complete or some defeat less crushing.

As soon as Stuart's column started southward, Mosby took his six men across Bull Run Mountain to Middleburg, where he ordered them to scatter out, billet themselves at outlying farms, and meet him at the Middleburg hotel on the night of January 10. Meanwhile he returned alone to Fairfax County, spending the next week making contacts with the people and gathering information.

On the night of Saturday, January 10, he took his men through the gap at Aldie and into Fairfax County. His first stop was at a farmhouse near Herndon Station, where he had friends, and there he met a woodsman, trapper and market hunter named John Underwood, who, with his two brothers, had been carrying on a private resistance movement against the Union occupation ever since the Confederate Army had moved out of the region. Overjoyed at the presence of regular Confederate troops, even as few as a half-dozen, Underwood offered to guide Mosby to a nearby Union picket post.

Capturing this post was no particularly spectacular feat of arms. Mosby's party dismounted about 200 yards away from it and crept up on it, to find seven members of the Fifth New York squatting around a fire, smoking, drinking coffee and trying to keep warm. Their first intimation of the presence of any enemy nearer than the Rappahannock River came when Mosby and his men sprang to their feet, leveled revolvers and demanded their surrender. One cavalryman made a grab for his carbine and Mosby shot him; the others put up their hands. The wounded man was given first aid, wrapped in a blanket and placed beside the fire to wait until the post would be relieved. The others were mounted on their own horses and taken to Middleburg, where they were paroled i.e., released after they gave their word not to take up arms again against the Confederacy. This not entirely satisfactory handling of prisoners was the only means left open to Mosby with his small force, behind enemy lines.

The next night, Mosby stayed out of Fairfax County to allow the excitement to die down a little, but the night after, he and his men, accompanied by Underwood, raided a post where the Little River Turnpike crossed Cub Run. Then, after picking up a two-man road patrol en route, they raided another post near Fryingpan Church. This time they brought back fourteen prisoners and horses.

In all, he and his sextet had captured nineteen prisoners and twenty horses. But Mosby still wasn't satisfied. What he wanted was a few more men and orders to operate behind the Union army on a permanent basis. So, after paroling the catch of the night before, he told John Underwood to get busy gathering information and establishing contacts, and he took his six men back to Culpepper, reporting his activities to Stuart and claiming that under his existing orders he had not felt justified in staying away from the army longer. At the same time, he asked for a larger detail and orders to continue operating in northern Virginia.

In doing so, he knew he was taking a chance that Stuart would keep him at Culpepper, but as both armies had gone into winter quarters after Fredericksburg with only a minimum of outpost activity, he reasoned that Stuart would be willing to send him back. As it happened, Stuart was so delighted with the success of Mosby's brief activity that he gave him fifteen men, all from the First Virginia Cavalry, and orders to operate until recalled. On January 18, Mosby was back at Middleburg, ready to go to work in earnest.

As before, he scattered his men over the countryside, quartering them on the people. This time, before scattering them, he told them to meet him at Zion Church, just beyond the gap at Aldie, on the night of the 28th. During the intervening ten days, he was not only busy gathering information but also in an intensive recruiting campaign among the people of upper Fauquier and lower Loudoun Counties.

In this last, his best selling-point was a recent act of the Confederate States Congress called the Scott Partisan Ranger Law. This piece of legislation was, in effect, an extension of the principles of prize law and privateering to land warfare. It authorized the formation of independent cavalry companies, to be considered part of the armed forces of the Confederacy, their members to serve without pay and mount themselves, in return for which they were to be entitled to keep any spoil of war captured from the enemy. The terms "enemy" and "spoil of war" were defined so liberally as to cover almost anything not the property of the government or citizens of the Confederacy. There were provisions, also, entitling partisan companies to draw on the Confederate government for arms and ammunition and permitting them to turn in and receive payment for any spoil which they did not wish to keep for themselves.

The law had met with considerable opposition from the Confederate military authorities, who claimed that it would attract men and horses away from the regular service and into ineffective freebooting. There is no doubt that a number of independent companies organized under the Scott Law accomplished nothing of military value. Some degenerated into mere bandit gangs, full of deserters from both sides, and terrible only to the unfortunate Confederate citizens living within their range of operations. On the other hand, as Mosby was to demonstrate, a properly employed partisan company could be of considerable use.

It was the provision about booty, however, which appealed to Mosby. As he intended operating in the Union rear, where the richest plunder could be found, he hoped that the prospect would attract numerous recruits. The countryside contained many men capable of bearing arms who had remained at home to look after their farms but who would be more than willing to ride with him now and then in hope of securing a new horse for farm work, or some needed harness, or food and blankets for their families. The regular Mosby Men called them the "Conglomerates," and Mosby himself once said that they resembled the Democrat party, being "held together only by the cohesive power of public plunder."

Mosby's first operation with his new force was in the pattern of the other two—the stealthy dismounted approach and sudden surprise of an isolated picket post. He brought back eleven prisoners and twelve horses and sets of small arms, and, as on the night of the 10th, left one wounded enemy behind. As on the previous occasions, the prisoners were taken as far as Middleburg before being released on parole.

For this reason, Mosby was sure that Colonel Sir Percy Wyndham, commander of the brigade which included the Fifth New York, Eighteenth Pennsylvania and the First Vermont, would assume that this village was the raiders' headquarters. Colonel Wyndham, a European-trained soldier, would scarcely conceive of any military force, however small, without a regular headquarters and a fixed camp. Therefore, Wyndham would come looking for him at Middleburg. So, with a companion named Fountain Beattie, Mosby put up for what remained of the night at the home of a Mr. Lorman Chancellor, on the road from Aldie a few miles east of Middleburg. The rest of the company were ordered to stay outside Middleburg.

Mosby's estimate of his opponent was uncannily accurate. The next morning, about daybreak, he and Beattie were wakened by one of the

Chancellor servants and warned that a large body of Union cavalry was approaching up the road from Aldie. Peering through the window shutters, they watched about 200 men of the Fifth New York ride by, with Colonel Wyndham himself in the lead. As soon as they were out of sight up the road, Mosby and Beattie, who had hastily dressed, dashed downstairs for their horses.

"I'm going to keep an eye on these people," Mosby told Beattie. "Gather up as many men as you can, and meet me in about half an hour on the hill above Middleburg. But hurry! I'd rather have five men now than a hundred by noon."

When Beattie with six men rejoined Mosby, he found the latter sitting on a stump, munching an apple and watching the enemy through his field glasses. Wyndham, who had been searching Middleburg for "Mosby's headquarters," was just forming his men for a push on to Upperville, where he had been assured by the canny Middleburgers that Mosby had his camp.

Mosby and his men cantered down the hillside to the road as Wyndham's force moved out of the village and then broke into a mad gallop to overtake them.

———

It was always hard to be sure whether jackets were dirty gray or faded blue. As the Union soldier had a not unfounded belief that the Virginia woods were swarming with bushwhackers (Confederate guerillas), the haste of a few men left behind to rejoin the column was quite understandable. The rearguard pulled up and waited for them. Then, at about twenty yards' range, one of the New Yorkers, a sergeant, realized what was happening and shouted a warning:

"They're Rebs!"

Instantly one of Mosby's men, Ned Hurst, shot him dead. Other revolvers, ready drawn, banged, and several Union cavalrymen were wounded. Mosby and his followers hastily snatched the bridles of three others, disarmed them and turned, galloping away with them.

By this time, the main column, which had not halted with the rearguard, was four or five hundred yards away. There was a brief uproar, a shouting of contradictory orders, and then the whole column turned and came back at a gallop. Mosby, four of his men, and the three prisoners, got away, but Beattie and two others were captured when their horses fell on a sheet of ice treacherously hidden under the snow. There was no possibility of rescuing them. After the capture of Beattie and his companions, the pursuit stopped. Halting at a distance, Mosby saw Wyndham form his force into a compact body and move off toward Aldie at a brisk trot. He sent off the prisoners under guard of two of his men and followed Wyndham's retreat almost to Aldie without opportunity to inflict any more damage.

During his stop at Middleburg, Wyndham had heaped coals on a growing opposition to Mosby, fostered by pro-Unionists in the neighborhood. Wyndham informed the townspeople that he would burn the town and imprison the citizens if Mosby continued the attacks on his outposts. A group of citizens, taking the threat to heart, petitioned Stuart to recall Mosby, but the general sent a stinging rebuke, telling the Middleburgers that Mosby and his men were risking their lives which were worth considerably more than a few houses and barns.

Mosby was also worried about the antipathy to the Scott Law and the partisan ranger system which was growing among some of the general officers of the Confederacy. To counteract such opposition, he needed to achieve some spectacular feat of arms which would capture the popular imagination, make a public hero of himself, and place him above criticism.

And all the while, his force was growing. The booty from his raids excited the cupidity of the more venturesome farmers, and they were exchanging the hoe for the revolver and joining him. A number of the convalescents and furloughed soldiers were arranging transfers to his command. Others, with no permanent military attachment, were drifting to Middleburg, Upperville, or Rectortown, inquiring where they might find Mosby, and making their way to join him.

There was a young Irishman, Dick Moran. There was a Fauquier County blacksmith, Billy Hibbs, who reported armed with a huge broadsword which had been the last product of his forge. There were Walter

Frankland, Joe Nelson, Frank Williams and George Whitescarver, among the first to join on a permanent basis. And, one day, there was the strangest recruit of all.

A meeting was held on the 25th of February at the Blackwell farm, near Upperville, and Mosby and most of his men were in the kitchen of the farmhouse, going over a map of the section they intended raiding, when a couple of men who had been on guard outside entered, pushing a Union cavalry sergeant ahead of them.

"This Yankee says he wants to see you, Captain," one of the men announced. "He came on foot; says his horse broke a leg and had to be shot."

"Well, I'm Mosby," the guerrilla leader said. "What do you want?"

The man in blue came to attention and saluted.

"I've come here to join your company, sir," he said calmly.

There was an excited outburst from the men in the kitchen, but Mosby took the announcement in stride.

"And what's your name and unit, sergeant?"

"James F. Ames: late Fifth New York Cavalry, sir."

After further conversation, Mosby decided that the big Yankee was sincere in his avowed decision to join the forces of the Confederacy. He had some doubts about his alleged motives: the man was animated with a most vindictive hatred of the Union government, all his former officers and most of his former comrades. No one ever learned what injury, real or fancied, had driven Sergeant Ames to desertion and treason, but in a few minutes Mosby was sure that the man was through with the Union Army.

Everybody else was equally sure that he was a spy, probably sent over by Wyndham to assassinate Mosby. Eventually Mosby proposed a test of Ames' sincerity. The deserter should guide the company to a Union picket post, and should accompany the raiders unarmed: Mosby would ride behind him, ready to shoot him at the first sign of treachery. The others agreed to judge the new recruit by his conduct on the raid. A fairly strong post, at a schoolhouse at Thompson's Corners, was selected as the objective, and they set out, sixteen men beside Ames and Mosby, through a storm of rain and sleet. Stopping at a nearby farm, Mosby learned that the post had been heavily re-enforced since he had last raided it. There were now about a hundred men at the schoolhouse.

Pleased at this evidence that his campaign to force the enemy to increase his guard was bearing fruit, Mosby decided to abandon his customary tactics of dismounting at a distance and approaching on foot. On a night like this, the enemy would not be expecting him, so the raiders advanced boldly along the road, Mosby telling Ames to make whatever answer he thought would be believed in case they were challenged. However, a couple of trigger-happy vedettes let off their carbines at them, yelled, "The Rebs are coming!" and galloped for the schoolhouse.

There was nothing to do but gallop after them, and Mosby and his band came pelting in on the heels of the vedettes. Hitherto, his raids had been more or less bloodless, but this time he had a fight on his hands, and if the men in the schoolhouse had stayed inside and defended themselves with carbine fire, they would have driven off the attack. Instead, however, they rushed outside, each man trying to mount his horse. A lieutenant and seven men were killed, about twice that number wounded, and five prisoners were taken. The rest, believing themselves attacked by about twice their own strength, scattered into the woods and got away.

Ames, who had ridden unarmed, flung himself upon a Union cavalryman at the first collision and disarmed him, then threw himself into the fight with the captured saber. His conduct during the brief battle at the schoolhouse was such as to remove from everybody's mind the suspicion that his conversion to the Confederate cause was anything but genuine. Thereafter, he was accepted as a Mosby man.

He was accepted by Mosby himself as a veritable godsend, since he was acquainted with the location of every Union force in Fairfax County, and knew of a corridor by which it would be possible to penetrate Wyndham's entire system of cavalry posts as far as Fairfax Courthouse itself. Here, then, was the making of the spectacular coup which Mosby needed to answer his critics and enemies, both at Middleburg and at army headquarters. He decided to attempt nothing less than a raid upon Fairfax Courthouse, with the capture of Wyndham as its purpose.

This last would entail something of a sacrifice, for he had come to esteem Sir Percy highly as an opponent whose mind was an open book and whose every move could be predicted in advance. With Wyndham eliminated, he would have to go to the trouble of learning the mental processes of his successor.

However, Wyndham would be the ideal captive to grace a Mosby triumph, and a successful raid on Fairfax Courthouse, garrisoned as it was by between five and ten thousand Union troops, would not only secure Mosby's position in his own army but would start just the sort of a panic which would result in demands that the Union rear be re-enforced at the expense of the front.

So, on Sunday, March 8, Mosby led thirty-nine men through the gap at Aldie, the largest force that had followed him to date. It was the sort of a foul night that he liked for raiding, with a drizzling rain falling upon melting snow. It was pitch dark before they found the road between Centreville and Fairfax, along which a telegraph line had been strung to connect the main cavalry camp with General Stoughton's headquarters. Mosby sent one of his men, Harry Hatcher, up a pole to cut the wire. They cut another telegraph line at Fairfax Station and left the road, moving through the woods toward Fairfax Courthouse. At this time, only Mosby and Yank Ames knew the purpose of the expedition.

It was therefore with surprise and some consternation that the others realized where they were as they rode into the courthouse square and halted. A buzz of excited whispers rose from the men.

"That's right," Mosby assured them calmly. "We're in Fairfax Courthouse, right in the middle of ten thousand Yankees, but don't let that worry you. All but about a dozen of them are asleep. Now, if you all keep your heads and do what you're told, we'll be as safe as though we were in Jeff Davis' front parlor."

He then began giving instructions, detailing parties to round up horses and capture any soldiers they found awake and moving about. He went, himself, with several men, to the home of a citizen named Murray, where he had been told that Wyndham had quartered himself, but here he received the disappointing news that the Englishman had gone to Washington that afternoon.

A few minutes later, however, Joe Nelson came up with a prisoner, an infantryman who had just been relieved from sentry duty at General

Stoughton's headquarters, who said that there had been a party there earlier in the evening and that Stoughton and several other officers were still there. Mosby, still disappointed at his failure to secure Wyndham, decided to accept Stoughton in his place. Taking several men, he went at once to the house where the prisoner said Stoughton had his head-quarters.

Arriving there, he hammered loudly on the door with a revolver butt. An upstairs window opened, and a head, in a nightcap, was thrust out.

"What the devil's all the noise about?" its owner demanded. "Don't you know this is General Stoughton's headquarters?"

"I'd hoped it was; I almost killed a horse getting here," Mosby retorted. "Come down and open up; dispatches from Washington."

In a few moments, a light appeared inside on the first floor, and the door opened. A man in a nightshirt, holding a candle, stood in the doorway.

"I'm Lieutenant Prentiss, on General Stoughton's staff. The general's asleep. If you'll give me the dispatches . . ."

Mosby caught the man by the throat with his left hand and shoved a Colt into his face with his right. Dan Thomas, beside him, lifted the candle out of the other man's hand.

"And I'm Captain Mosby, General Stuart's staff. We've just taken Fairfax Courthouse. Inside, now, and take me to the general at once."

The general was in bed, lying on his face in a tangle of bedclothes. Mosby pulled the sheets off of him, lifted the tail of his nightshirt and slapped him across the bare rump.

The effect was electric. Stoughton sat up in bed, gobbling in fury. In the dim candlelight, he mistook the gray of Mosby's tunic for blue, and began a string of bloodthirsty threats of court-martial and firing squad, interspersed with oaths.

"Easy, now, General," the perpetrator of the outrage soothed. "You've heard of John Mosby, haven't you?"

"Yes; have you captured him?" In the face of such tidings, Stoughton would gladly forget the assault on his person.

Mosby shook his head, smiling seraphically. "No, General. He's captured you. I'm Mosby."

"Oh my God!" Stoughton sank back on the pillow and closed his eyes, overcome.

Knowing the precarious nature of his present advantage, Mosby then undertook to deprive Stoughton of any hope of rescue or will to resist.

"Stuart's cavalry is occupying Fairfax Courthouse," he invented, "and Stonewall Jackson's at Chantilly with his whole force. We're all moving to occupy Alexandria by morning. You'll have to hurry and dress, General."

"Is Fitzhugh Lee here?" Stoughton asked. "He's a friend of mine; we were classmates at West Point."

"Why, no; he's with Jackson at Chantilly. Do you want me to take you to him? I can do so easily if you hurry."

It does not appear that Stoughton doubted as much as one syllable of this remarkable set of prevarications. The Union Army had learned by bitter experience that Stonewall Jackson was capable of materializing almost anywhere. So he climbed out of bed, putting on his clothes.

On the way back to the courthouse square, Prentiss got away from them in the darkness, but Mosby kept a tight hold on Stoughton's bridle. By this time, the suspicion that all was not well in the county seat had begun to filter about. Men were beginning to turn out under arms all over town, and there was a confusion of challenges and replies and some occasional firing as hastily wakened soldiers mistook one another for the enemy. Mosby got his prisoners and horses together and started out of town as quickly as he could.

The withdrawal was made over much the same route as the approach, without serious incident. Thanks to the precaution of cutting the telegraph wires, the camp at Centreville knew nothing of what had happened at Fairfax Courthouse until long after the raiders were safely away. They lost all but thirty of the prisoners—in the woods outside Fairfax Courthouse, they escaped in droves—but they brought Stoughton and the two captains out safely.

The results were everything Mosby had hoped. He became a Confederate hero over night, and there was no longer any danger of his being recalled. There were several half-hearted attempts to kick him upstairs—an offer of a commission in the now defunct Virginia Provisional Army, which he rejected scornfully, and a similar offer in the regular Confederate States Army, which he politely declined because it would deprive his men of their right to booty under the Scott Law. Finally he was given a majority in the Confederate States Army, with authorization to organize a partisan battalion under the Scott Law. This he accepted, becoming Major Mosby of the Forty-Third Virginia Partisan Ranger Battalion.

The effect upon the enemy was no less satisfactory. When full particulars of the Fairfax raid reached Washington, Wyndham vanished from the picture, being assigned to other duties where less depended upon him. There was a whole epidemic of courts-martial and inquiries, some of which were still smouldering when the war ended. And Stoughton, the principal victim, found scant sympathy. President Lincoln, when told that the rebels had raided Fairfax to the tune of one general, two captains, thirty men and fifty-eight horses, remarked that he could make all the generals he wanted, but that he was sorry to lose the horses, as he couldn't make horses. As yet, there was no visible re-enforcement of the cavalry in Fairfax County from the front, but the line of picket posts was noticeably shortened.

About two weeks later, with forty men, Mosby raided a post at Herndon Station, bringing off a major, a captain, two lieutenants and twenty-one men, with a horse apiece. A week later, with fifty-odd men, he cut up about three times his strength of Union cavalry at Chantilly. Having surprised a small party, he had driven them into a much larger force, and the hunted had turned to hunt the hunters. Fighting a delaying action with a few men while the bulk of his force fell back on an old roadblock of felled trees dating from the second Manassas campaign, he held off the enemy until he was sure his ambuscade was set, then, by feigning headlong flight, led them into a trap and chased the survivors for five or six miles. Wyndham and Stoughton had found Mosby an annoying nuisance; their successors were finding him a serious menace.

This attitude was not confined to the local level, but extended all the way to the top echelons. The word passed down, "Get Mosby!" and it was understood that the officer responsible for his elimination would find his military career made for him. One of the Union officers who saw visions of rapid advancement over the wreckage of Mosby's Rangers was a captain of the First Vermont, Josiah Flint by name. He was soon to have a chance at it.

On March 31, Mosby's Rangers met at Middleburg and moved across the mountain to Chantilly, expecting to take a strong outpost which had been located there. On arriving, they found the campsite deserted. The post had been pulled back closer to Fairfax after the fight of four days before. Mosby decided to move up to the Potomac and attack a Union force on the other side of Dranesville—Captain Josiah Flint's Vermonters.

They passed the night at John Miskel's farm, near Chantilly. The following morning, April 1, at about daybreak, Mosby was wakened by one of his men who had been sleeping in the barn. This man, having gone outside, had observed a small party of Union troops on the Maryland side of the river who were making semaphore signals to somebody on the Virginia side. Mosby ordered everybody to turn out as quickly as possible and went out to watch the signalmen with his field glasses. While he was watching, Dick Moran, a Mosby man who had billeted with friends down the road, arrived at a breakneck gallop from across the fields, shouting: "Mount your horses! The Yankees are coming!"

It appeared that he had been wakened, shortly before, by the noise of a column of cavalry on the road in front of the house where he had been sleeping, and had seen a strong force of Union cavalry on the march in the direction of Broad Run and the Miskel farm. Waiting until they had passed, he had gotten his horse and circled at a gallop through the woods, reaching the farm just ahead of them. It later developed that a woman of the neighborhood, whose head had been turned by the attentions of Union officers, had betrayed Mosby to Flint.

The Miskel farmhouse stood on the crest of a low hill, facing the river. Behind it stood the big barn, with a large barnyard enclosed by a high pole fence. As this was a horse farm, all the fences were eight feet

high and quite strongly built. A lane ran down the slope of the hill between two such fences, and at the southern end of the slope another fence
separated the meadows from a belt of woods, beyond which was the road
from Dranesville, along which Flint's column was advancing.

———

It was a nasty spot for Mosby. He had between fifty and sixty men,
newly roused from sleep, their horses unsaddled, and he was penned in
by strong fences which would have to be breached if he were to escape.
His only hope lay in a prompt counterattack. The men who had come
out of the house and barn were frantically saddling horses, without much
attention to whose saddle went on whose mount. Harry Hatcher, who
had gotten his horse saddled, gave it to Mosby and appropriated somebody else's mount.

As Flint, at the head of his cavalry, emerged from the woods, Mosby
had about twenty of his men mounted and was ready to receive him. The
Union cavalry paused, somebody pulled out the gate bars at the foot of
the lane, and the whole force started up toward the farm. Having opened
the barnyard end of the lane, Mosby waited until Flint had come about
halfway, then gave him a blast of revolver fire and followed this with a
headlong charge down the lane. Flint was killed at the first salvo, as were
several of the men behind him. By the time Mosby's charge rammed into
the head of the Union attack, the narrow lane was blocked with riderless
horses, preventing each force from coming to grips with the other. Here
Mosby's insistence upon at least two revolvers for each man paid off,
as did the target practice upon which he was always willing to expend
precious ammunition. The Union column, constricted by the fences on
either side of the lane and shaken by the death of their leader and by the
savage attack of men whom they had believed hopelessly trapped, turned
and tried to retreat, but when they reached the foot of the lane it was
discovered that some fool, probably meaning to deny Mosby an avenue of
escape, had replaced the gatebars. By this time, the rest of Mosby's force
had mounted their horses, breaches had been torn in the fence at either
side of the lane, and there were Confederates in both meadows, firing
into the trapped men. Until the gate at the lower end gave way under the

weight of horses crowded against it, there was a bloody slaughter. Within a few minutes Flint and nine of his men were killed, some fifteen more were given disabling wounds, eighty-two prisoners were taken, and over a hundred horses and large quantities of arms and ammunition were captured. The remains of Flint's force was chased as far as Dranesville. Mosby was still getting the prisoners sorted out, rounding up loose horses, gathering weapons and ammunition from casualties, and giving the wounded first aid, when a Union lieutenant rode up under a flag of truce, followed by several enlisted men and two civilians of the Sanitary Commission, the Civil War equivalent of the Red Cross, to pick up the wounded and bury the dead. This officer offered to care for Mosby's wounded with his own, an offer which was declined with thanks. Mosby said he would carry his casualties with him, and the Union officer could scarcely believe his eyes when he saw only three wounded men on horse litters and one dead man tied to his saddle.

The sutlers at Dranesville had heard the firing and were about to move away when Mosby's column appeared. Seeing the preponderance of blue uniforms, they mistook the victors for prisoners and, anticipating a lively and profitable business, unpacked their loads and set up their counters. The business was lively, but anything but profitable. The Mosby men looted them unmercifully, taking their money, their horses, and everything else they had.

—◆—

All through the spring of 1863, Mosby kept jabbing at Union lines of communication in northern Virginia. In June, his majority came through, and with it authority to organize a battalion under the Scott Law. From that time on, he was on his own, and there was no longer any danger of his being recalled to the regular Army. He was responsible only to Jeb Stuart until the general's death at Yellow Tavern a year later; thereafter, he took orders from no source below General Lee and the Secretary of War.

Even before this regularization of status, Mosby's force was beginning to look like a regular outfit. From the fifteen men he had brought up from Culpepper in mid-January, its effective and dependable strength had grown to about sixty riders, augmented from raid to raid by the

"Conglomerate" fringe, who were now accepted as guerrillas-pro-tem without too much enthusiasm. A new type of recruit had begun to appear, the man who came to enlist on a permanent basis. Some were Maryland secessionists, like James Williamson, who, after the war, wrote an authoritative and well-documented history of the organization, Mosby's Rangers. Some were boys like John Edmonds and John Munson, who had come of something approaching military age since the outbreak of the war. Some were men who had wangled transfers from other Confederate units. Not infrequently these men had given up commissions in the regular army to enlist as privates with Mosby. For example, there was the former clergyman, Sam Chapman, who had been a captain of artillery, or the Prussian uhlan lieutenant, Baron Robert von Massow, who gave up a captaincy on Stuart's staff, or the Englishman, Captain Hoskins, who was shortly to lose his life because of his preference for the saber over the revolver, or Captain Bill Kennon, late of Wheat's Louisiana Tigers, who had also served with Walker in Nicaragua. As a general thing, the new Mosby recruit was a man of high intelligence, reckless bravery and ultra-rugged individualism.

For his home territory, Mosby now chose a rough quadrangle between the Blue Ridge and Bull Run Mountain, bounded at its four corners by Snicker's Gap and Manassas Gap along the former and Thoroughfare Gap and Aldie Gap along the latter. Here, when not in action, the Mosby men billeted themselves, keeping widely dispersed, and an elaborate system, involving most of the inhabitants, free or slave, was set up to transmit messages, orders and warnings. In time this district came to be known as "Mosby's Confederacy," and, in the absence of any effective Confederate States civil authority, Mosby became the lawgiver and chief magistrate as well as military commander. John Munson, who also wrote a book of reminiscences after the war, said that Mosby's Confederacy was an absolute monarchy, and that none was ever better governed in history.

Adhering to his belief in the paramount importance of firepower, Mosby saw to it that none of his men carried fewer than two revolvers, and the great majority carried four, one pair on the belt and another on the saddle. Some extremists even carried a third pair down their boot-tops, giving them thirty-six shots without reloading. Nor did he underestimate the power of mobility. Each man had his string of horses, kept where they could be picked up at need. Unlike the regular cavalryman with his one mount, a Mosby man had only to drop an exhausted animal at one of these private remount stations and change his saddle to a fresh one. As a result of these two practices, Union combat reports throughout the war consistently credited Mosby with from three to five times his actual strength.

In time, the entire economy of Mosby's Confederacy came to be geared to Mosby's operations, just as the inhabitants of seventeenth century Tortugas or Port Royal depended for their livelihood on the loot of the buccaneers. The Mosby man who lived with some farmer's family paid for his lodging with gifts of foodstuffs and blankets looted from the enemy. There was always a brisk trade in captured U.S. Army horses and mules. And there was a steady flow of United States currency into the section, so that in time Confederate money was driven out of circulation in a sort of reversal of Gresham's law. Every prisoner taken reasonably close to Army pay day could be counted on for a few dollars, and in each company there would be some lucky or skillful gambler who would have a fairly sizeable roll of greenbacks. And, of course, there was the sutler, the real prize catch; any Mosby man would pass up a general in order to capture a sutler.

And Northern-manufactured goods filtered south by the wagonload. Many of the Mosby men wore Confederate uniforms that had been tailored for them in Baltimore and even in Washington and run through the Union lines.

By mid-June, Lee's invasion of Pennsylvania had begun and the countryside along Bull Run Mountain and the Blue Ridge exploded into a series of cavalry actions as the Confederate Army moved north along the Union right. Mosby kept his little force out of the main fighting, hacking away at the Union troops from behind and confusing their combat intelligence with reports of Rebel cavalry appearing where none ought to be. In the midst of this work, he took time out to dash across into Fairfax County with sixty men, shooting up a wagon train, burning wagons, and carrying off prisoners and mules, the latter being turned over to haul Lee's invasion transport. After the two armies had passed over the Potomac, he gathered his force and launched an invasion of Pennsylvania on his own, getting as far as Mercersburg and bringing home a drove of over 200 beef cattle.

He got back to Mosby's Confederacy in time to learn of Lee's defeat at Gettysburg. Realizing that Lee's retreat would be followed by a pursuing Union army, he began making preparations to withstand the coming deluge. For one thing, he decided to do something he had not done before—concentrate his force in a single camp on the top of Bull Run Mountain. In the days while Lee's army was trudging southward, Mosby gathered every horse and mule and cow he could find and drove them into the mountains, putting boys and slaves to work herding them. He commandeered wagons, and hauled grain and hay to his temporary camp. His men erected huts, and built corrals for horses and a stockade for prisoners. They even moved a blacksmith shop to the hidden camp. Then Mosby sat down and waited.

A few days later, Meade's army began coming through. The Forty-Third Partisan Ranger Battalion went to work immediately. For two weeks, they galloped in and out among the Union columns, returning to their hidden camp only long enough to change horses and leave the prisoners they had taken. They cut into wagon trains, scattering cavalry escorts, burning wagons, destroying supplies, blowing up ammunition, disabling cannon, running off mules. They ambushed marching infantry, flitting away before their victims had recovered from the initial surprise. Sometimes, fleeing from the scene of one attack, they would burst through a column on another road, leaving confusion behind to delay the pursuit.

Finally, the invaders passed on, the camp on the mountain top was abandoned, the Mosby men went back to their old billets, and the Forty-Third Battalion could take it easy again. That is to say, they only made a raid every couple of days and seldom fought a pitched battle more than once a week.

The summer passed; the Virginia hills turned from green to red and from red to brown. Mosby was severely wounded in the side and thigh during a fight at Gooding's Tavern on August 23, when two of his men were killed, but the raiders brought off eighty-five horses and twelve prisoners and left six enemy dead behind. The old days of bloodless sneak raids on isolated picket posts were past, now that they had enough men for two companies and Mosby rarely took the field with fewer than a hundred riders behind him.

Back in the saddle again after recovering from his wounds, Mosby devoted more attention to attacking the Orange and Alexandria and the Manassas Gap railroads and to harassing attacks for the rest of the winter.

In January, 1864, Major Cole, of the Union Maryland cavalry, began going out of his way to collide with the Forty-Third Virginia, the more so since he had secured the services of a deserter from Mosby, a man named Binns who had been expelled from the Rangers for some piece of rascality and was thirsting for revenge. Cole hoped to capitalize on Binns' defection as Mosby had upon the desertion of Sergeant Ames, and he made several raids into Mosby's Confederacy, taking a number of prisoners before the Mosby men learned the facts of the situation and everybody found a new lodging place.

On the morning of February 20, Mosby was having breakfast at a farmhouse near Piedmont Depot, on the Manassas Gap Railroad, along with John Munson and John Edmonds, the 'teen-age terrors, and a gun-smith named Jake Lavender, who was the battalion ordnance sergeant and engaged to young Edmonds' sister. Edmonds had with him a couple of Sharps carbines he had repaired for other members of the battalion and was carrying to return to the owners. Suddenly John Edmonds' younger brother, Jimmy, burst into the room with the news that several hundred Union cavalrymen were approaching. Lavender grabbed the two carbines, for which he had a quantity of ammunition, and they all ran outside.

Sending the younger Edmonds boy to bring re-enforcements, Mosby, accompanied by John Edmonds, Munson, and Jake Lavender, started to follow the enemy. He and Munson each took one of Lavender's carbines and opened fire on them, Munson killing a horse and Mosby a man. That started things off properly. Cole's Marylanders turned and gave chase, and Mosby led them toward the rendezvous with Jimmy Edmonds and the re-enforcements. Everybody arrived together, Mosby's party, the pur-suers, and the re-enforcements, and a running fight ensued, with Cole's men running ahead. This mounted chase, in the best horse-opera manner, came thundering down a road past a schoolhouse just as the pupils were being let out for recess. One of these, a 14-year-old boy named Cabell Maddox, jumped onto the pony on which he had ridden to school and joined in the pursuit, armed only with a McGuffy's Third Reader. Overtaking a fleeing Yank, he aimed the book at him and demanded his surrender; before the flustered soldier realized that his captor was unarmed, the boy had snatched the Colt from his belt and was covering him in earnest. This marked the suspension, for the duration of hostilities, of young Maddox's formal education. From that hour on he was a Mosby man, and he served with distinction to the end of the war.

―――

The chase broke off, finally, when the pursuers halted to get their prisoners and captured horses together. Then they discovered that one of their number, a man named Cobb, had been killed. Putting the dead man across his saddle, they carried the body back to Piedmont, and the next day assembled there for the funeral. The services had not yet started, and Mosby was finishing writing a report to Stuart on the previous day's action, when a scout came pelting in to report Union cavalry in the vicinity of Middleburg.

Leaving the funeral in the hands of the preacher and the civilian mourners, Mosby and the 150 men who had assembled mounted and started off. Sam Chapman, the ex-artillery captain, who had worked up from the ranks to a lieutenancy with Mosby, was left in charge of the main force, while Mosby and a small party galloped ahead to reconnoiter. The enemy, they discovered, were not Cole's men but a California battalion. They learned that this force had turned in the direction of Leesburg, and that they were accompanied by the deserter, Binns.

Mosby made up his mind to ambush the Californians on their way back to their camp at Vienna. He had plans, involving a length of rope, for his former trooper, Binns. The next morning, having crossed Bull Run Mountain the night before, he took up a position near Dranesville, with scouts out to the west. When the enemy were finally reported approaching, he was ready for them. Twenty of his 150, with carbines and rifles, were dismounted and placed in the center, under Lieutenant Mountjoy. The rest of the force was divided into two equal sections, under Chapman and Frank Williams, and kept mounted on the flanks. Mosby himself took his place with Williams on the right. While they waited, they could hear the faint boom of cannon from Washington, firing salutes in honor of Washington's Birthday.

A couple of men, posted in advance, acted as decoys, and the Union cavalry, returning empty-handed from their raid, started after them in hopes of bringing home at least something to show for their efforts. Before they knew it, they were within range of Mountjoy's concealed riflemen. While they were still in disorder from the surprise volley, the two mounted sections swept in on them in a blaze of revolver fire, and they broke and fled. There was a nasty jam in a section of fenced road, with mounted Mosby men in the woods on either side and Mountjoy's rifles behind them. Before they could get clear of this, they lost fifteen killed, fifteen more wounded, and over seventy prisoners, and the victorious Mosby men brought home over a hundred captured horses and large quantities of arms and ammunition. To their deep regret, however, Binns was not to be found either among the casualties or the prisoners. As soon as he had seen how the fight was going, the deserter had spurred off northward, never to appear in Virginia again. Mosby's own loss had been one man killed and four wounded.

For the rest of the spring, operations were routine—attacks on wagon trains and train wrecking and bridge burning on the railroads. With the cut-and-try shifting of command of the Union Army of the Potomac over and Grant in command, there was activity all over northern Virginia. About this time, Mosby got hold of a second twelve-pound howitzer, and, later, a twelve-pound Napoleon and added the Shenandoah Valley to his field of operations.

From then on, Mosby was fighting a war on two fronts, dividing his attention between the valley and the country to the east of Bull Run Mountain, his men using their spare horses freely to keep the Union rear on both sides in an uproar. The enemy, knowing the section from whence

Mosby was operating, resorted to frequent counter-raiding. Often, returning from a raid, the Mosby men would find their home territory invaded and would have to intercept or fight off the invaders. At this time, Mosby was giving top priority to attacks on Union transport whether on the roads or the railroads. Wagon trains were in constant movement, both moving up the Shenandoah Valley and bound for the Army of the Potomac, in front of Petersburg. To the east was the Orange and Alexandria Railroad, to the south, across the end of Mosby's Confederacy, was the Manassas Gap, and at the upper end of the valley was the B. & O. The section of the Manassas Gap Railroad along the southern boundary of Mosby's Confederacy came in for special attention, and the Union Army finally gave it up for a bad job and abandoned it. This writer's grandfather, Captain H. B. Piper, of the Eleventh Pennsylvania Volunteer Infantry, did a stint of duty guarding it, and until he died he spoke with respect of the abilities of John S. Mosby and his raiders. Locomotives were knocked out with one or another of Mosby's twelve-pounders. Track was torn up and bridges were burned. Land-mines were planted. Trains were derailed and looted, usually with sharp fighting.

By mid-July, Mosby had been promoted to lieutenant colonel and had a total strength of around 300 men, divided into five companies. His younger brother, William Mosby, had joined him and was acting as his adjutant. He now had four guns, all twelve-pounders—two howitzers, the Napoleon and a new rifle, presented to him by Jubal Early. He had a compact, well-disciplined and powerful army-in-miniature. After the Union defeat at Kernstown, Early moved back to the lower end of the Shenandoah Valley, and McCausland went off on his raid in to Pennsylvania, burning Chambersburg in retaliation for Hunter's burnings at Lexington and Buchanan in Virginia. Following his customary practice, Mosby made a crossing at another point and raided into Maryland as far as Adamstown, skirmishing and picking up a few prisoners and horses.

Early's invasion of Maryland, followed as it was by McCausland's sack of Chambersburg, was simply too much for the Union command. The Shenandoah situation had to be cleaned up immediately, and, after some top-echelon dickering, Grant picked Phil Sheridan to do the cleaning. On August 7, Sheridan assumed command of the heterogeneous

Union forces in the Shenandoah and began welding them into an army. On the 10th, he started south after Early, and Mosby, who generally had a good idea of what was going on at Union headquarters, took a small party into the valley, intending to kidnap the new commander as he had Stoughton. Due mainly to the vigilance of a camp sentry, the plan failed, but Mosby picked up the news that a large wagon train was being sent up the valley, and he decided to have a try at this.

On the evening of the 12th, he was back in the valley with 330 men and his two howitzers. Spending the night at a plantation on the right bank of the Shenandoah River, he was on the move before daybreak, crossing the river and pushing toward Berryville, with scouts probing ahead in the heavy fog. One of the howitzers broke a wheel and was pushed into the brush and left behind. As both pieces were of the same caliber, the caisson was taken along. A lieutenant and fifteen men, scouting ahead, discovered a small empty wagon train, going down the valley in the direction of Harper's Ferry, and they were about to attack it when they heard, in the distance, the rumbling of many heavily loaded wagons. This was the real thing. They forgot about the empty wagons and hastened back to Mosby and the main force to report.

Swinging to the left to avoid premature contact with the train, Mosby hurried his column in the direction of Berryville. On the way, he found a disabled wagon, part of the north-bound empty train, with the teamster and several infantrymen sleeping in it. These were promptly secured, and questioning elicited the information that the south-bound train consisted of 150 wagons, escorted by 250 cavalry and a brigade of infantry. Getting into position on a low hill overlooking the road a little to the east of Berryville, the howitzer was unlimbered and the force was divided on either side of it, Captain Adolphus Richards taking the left wing and Sam Chapman the right. Mosby himself remained with the gun. Action was to be commenced with the gun, and the third shot was to be the signal for both Richards and Chapman to charge.

————

At just the right moment, the fog lifted. The gun was quickly laid on the wagon train and fired, the first shot beheading a mule. The second shell hit the best sort of target imaginable—a mobile farrier's forge. There was a deadly shower of horseshoes, hand-tools and assorted ironmongery, inflicting casualties and causing a local panic. The third shell landed among some cavalry who were galloping up, scattering them, and, on the signal, Richards and Chapman charged simultaneously.

Some infantry at the head of the train met Richards with a volley, costing him one man killed and several wounded and driving his charge off at an angle into the middle of the train. The howitzer, in turn, broke up the infantry. Chapman, who had hit the rear of the train, was having easier going: his men methodically dragged the teamsters from their wagons, unhitched mules, overturned, looted and burned wagons. The bulk of the escort, including the infantry, were at the front of the train, with Richards' men between them and Chapman. Richards, while he had his hands full with these, was not neglecting the wagons, either, though he was making less of a ceremony of it. A teamster was shot and dragged from his wagon-seat, a lighted bundle of inflammables tossed into the wagon, and pistols were fired around the mules' heads to start them running. The faster they ran, the more the flames behind them were fanned, and as the wagon went careening down the road, other wagons were ignited by it.

By 8 a. m., the whole thing was over. The escort had been scattered, the wagons were destroyed, and the victors moved off, in possession of 500-odd mules, thirty-six horses, about 200 head of beef cattle, 208 prisoners, four Negro slaves who had been forcibly emancipated to drive Army wagons, and large quantities of supplies. In one of the wagons, a number of violins, probably equipment for some prototype of the U.S.O., were found; the more musically inclined guerrillas appropriated these and enlivened the homeward march with music.

—◦—

Of course, there was jubilation all over Mosby's Confederacy on their return. The mules were herded into the mountains, held for about a week, and then started off for Early's army. The beef herd was divided among the people, and there were barbecues and feasts. A shadow was cast over the spirits of the raiders, however, when the prisoners informed them, with considerable glee, that the train had been carrying upwards of a million dollars, the pay for Sheridan's army. Even allowing for exaggeration, the fact that they had overlooked this treasure was a bitter pill for the Mosbyites. According to local tradition, however, the fortune was not lost completely; there were stories of a Berryville family who had been quite poor before the war but who blossomed into unexplained affluence afterward.

Less than a week later, on August 19, Mosby was in the valley again with 250 men, dividing his force into several parties after crossing the river at Castleman's Ford. Richards, with "B" Company, set off toward Charlestown. Mosby himself took "A" toward Harper's Ferry on an uneventful trip during which the only enemies he encountered were a couple of stragglers caught pillaging a springhouse. It was Chapman, with "C" and "D," who saw the action on this occasion.

Going to the vicinity of Berryville, he came to a burning farmhouse, and learned that it had been fired only a few minutes before by some of Custer's cavalry. Leaving a couple of men to help the family control the fire and salvage their possessions, he pressed on rapidly. Here was the thing every Mosby man had been hoping for—a chance to catch house burners at work. They passed a second blazing house and barn, dropping off a couple more men to help fight fire, and caught up with the incendiaries, a company of Custer's men, just as they were setting fire to a third house. Some of these, knowing the quality of mercy they might expect from Mosby men, made off immediately at a gallop. About ninety of them, however, tried to form ranks and put up a fight. The fight speedily became a massacre. Charging with shouts of "No quarters!", Chapman's men drove them into a maze of stone fences and killed about a third of them before the rest were able to extricate themselves.

This didn't stop the house burnings, by any means. The devastation of the Shenandoah Valley had been decided upon as a matter of strategy, and Sheridan was going through with it. The men who were ordered to do the actual work did not have their morale improved any by the knowledge that Mosby's Rangers were refusing quarter to incendiary details, however, and, coming as it did on the heels of the wagon train affair of the 13th, Sheridan was convinced that something drastic would have to be done about Mosby. Accordingly, he set up a special company, under a Captain William Blazer, each man armed with a pair of revolvers and a Spencer repeater, to devote their entire efforts to eliminating Mosby and his organized raiders.

On September 3, this company caught up with Joe Nelson and about 100 men in the valley and gave them a sound drubbing, the first that the Mosby men had experienced for some time. It was a humiliating defeat for them, and, on the other side, it was hailed as the beginning of the end of the Mosby nuisance. A few days later, while raiding to the east of Bull Run Mountain, Mosby was wounded again, and was taken to Lynchburg. He was joined by his wife, who remained with him at Lynchburg and at Mosby's Confederacy until the end of the war.

During his absence, the outfit seems to have been run by a sort of presidium of the senior officers. On September 22, Sam Chapman took men into the valley to try to capture a cavalry post supposed to be located near Front Royal, but, arriving there, he learned that his information had been incorrect and that no such post existed. Camping in the woods, he sent some men out as scouts, and the next morning they reported a small wagon train escorted by about 150 cavalry, moving toward Front Royal. Dividing his force and putting half of it under Walter Frankland, he planned to attack the train from the rear while Frankland hit it from in front. After getting into position, he kept his men concealed, waiting for the wagons to pass, and as it did, he realized that his scouts had seen only a small part of it. The escort looked to him like about three regiments. Ordering his men to slip away as quietly as possible, he hurried to reach Frankland.

"Turn around, Walter!" he yelled. "Get your men out of here! You're attacking a whole brigade!"

"What of it?" Frankland replied. "Why, Sam, we have the bastards on the run already!"

Chapman, the erstwhile clergyman, turned loose a blast of theological language in purely secular connotation. Frankland, amazed at this blasphemous clamor from his usually pious comrade, realized that it must have been inspired by something more than a little serious, and began ordering his men to fall back. Before they had all gotten away, two of the three Union regiments accompanying the wagons came galloping up and swamped them. Most of the men got away but six of them, Anderson, Carter, Overby, Love, Rhodes and Jones, were captured.

Late that night some of the stragglers, making their way back to Mosby's Confederacy on foot, reported the fate of these six men. They had been taken into Front Royal, and there, at the personal order of General George A. Custer, and under circumstances of extreme brutality, they had all been hanged. Rhodes' mother, who lived in Front Royal, had been forced to witness the hanging of her son.

To put it conservatively, there was considerable excitement in Mosby's Confederacy when the news of this atrocity was received. The senior officers managed to restore a measure of calmness, however, and it was decided to wait until Mosby returned before taking any action on the matter.

In addition to the hangings at Front Royal, Custer was acquiring a bad reputation because of his general brutality to the people of the Shenandoah Valley. After the battle of the Little Bighorn, Sitting Bull would have probably won any popularity contest in northern Virginia without serious competition.

On September 29, Mosby was back with his command; his wound had not been as serious as it might have been for the bullet had expended most of its force against the butt of one of the revolvers in his belt. Operations against the railroads had been allowed to slacken during Mosby's absence; now they were stepped up again. Track was repeatedly torn up along the Manassas Gap line, and there were attacks on camps and strong points, and continual harassing of wood-cutting parties obtaining fuel for the locomotives. The artillery was taken out, and trains were shelled. All this, of course, occasioned a fresh wave of Union raids into the home territory of the raiders, during one of which Yank Ames, who had risen to a lieutenancy in the Forty-Third, was killed.

The most desperate efforts were being made, at this time, to keep the Manassas Gap Railroad open, and General C. C. Augur, who had charge of the railroad line at the time, was arresting citizens indiscriminately and forcing them to ride on the trains as hostages. Mosby obtained authorization from Lee's headquarters to use reprisal measures on officers and train crews of trains on which citizens were being forced to ride, and also authority to execute prisoners from Custer's command in equal number to the men hanged at Front Royal and elsewhere.

It was not until November that he was able to secure prisoners from Custer's brigade, it being his intention to limit his retaliation to men from units actually involved in the hangings. On November 6, he paraded about twenty-five such prisoners and forced them to draw lots, selecting, in this manner, seven of them—one for each of the men hanged at Front Royal and another for a man named Willis who had been hanged at Gaines' Cross Roads several weeks later. It was decided that they should be taken into the Shenandoah Valley and hanged beside the Valley Pike, where their bodies could serve as an object lesson. On the way, one of them escaped. Four were hanged, and then, running out of rope, they prepared to shoot the other two. One of these got away during a delay caused by defective percussion caps on his executioner's revolver.

A sign was placed over the bodies, setting forth the reason for their execution, and Mosby also sent one of his men under a flag of truce to Sheridan's headquarters, with a statement of what had been done and why, re-enforced with the intimation that he had more prisoners, including a number of officers, in case his messenger failed to return safely. Sheridan replied by disclaiming knowledge of the Front Royal hangings, agreeing that Mosby was justified in taking reprisals, and assuring the Confederate leader that hereafter his men would be given proper treatment as prisoners of war. There was no repetition of the hangings.

By this time the Shenandoah Valley campaign as such was over. The last Confederate effort to clear Sheridan out of the Valley had failed at Cedar Creek on October 19, and the victor was going methodically about his task of destroying the strategic and economic usefulness of the valley. How well he succeeded in this was best expressed in Sheridan's own claim that a crow flying over the region would have to carry his own rations. The best Mosby could do was to launch small raiding parties to harass the work of destruction.

By the beginning of December, the northern or Loudoun County end of Mosby's Confederacy was feeling the enemy scourge as keenly as the valley, and the winter nights were lighted with the flames of burning houses and barns. For about a week, while this was going on, Mosby abandoned any attempt at organized action. His men, singly and in small parties, darted in and out among the invaders, sniping and bushwhacking, attacking when they could and fleeing when they had to, and taking no prisoners. When it was over, the northern end of Mosby's Confederacy was in ashes and most of the people had "refugeed out," but Mosby's Rangers, as a fighting force, was still intact. On December 17, for instance, while Mosby was in Richmond conferring with General Lee, they went into the valley again in force, waylaying a column of cavalry on the march, killing and wounding about thirty and bringing off 168 prisoners and horses.

When Mosby came back from Lee's headquarters, a full colonel now, his brother William was made a lieutenant-colonel, and Richards became a major. The southern, or Fauquier County, end of Mosby's Confederacy was still more or less intact, though crowded with refugees. There was even time, in spite of everything, for the wedding of the Forty-Third's armorer, Jake Lavender, with John and Jimmy Edmonds' sister.

While the wedding party was in progress, a report was brought in to the effect that Union cavalry were in the neighborhood of Salem, a few miles away. Mosby took one of his men, Tom Love, a relative of one of the Front Royal victims, and went to investigate, finding that the enemy had moved in the direction of Rectortown, where they were making camp for the night. Sending a resident of the neighborhood to alert Chapman and Richards for an attack at daybreak, Mosby and Love set out to collect others of his command.

By this time, it was dark, with a freezing rain covering everything with ice. Mosby and Love decided to stop at the farm of Ludwell Lake for something to eat before going on; Love wanted to stay outside on guard, but Mosby told him to get off his horse and come inside. As they would have been in any house in the neighborhood, Mosby and his companion were welcomed as honored guests and sat down with the family to a hearty meal of spareribs.

❦

While they were eating, the house was surrounded by Union cavalry. Mosby rushed to the back door, to find the backyard full of soldiers.

He started for the front door, but as he did, it burst open and a number of Yankees, officers and men, entered the house. At the same time, the soldiers behind, having seen the back door open and shut, began firing at the rear windows, and one bullet hit Mosby in the abdomen. In the confusion, with the women of the Lake family screaming, the soldiers cursing, and bullets coming through the windows, the kitchen table was overturned and the lights extinguished. Mosby in the dark, managed to crawl into a first-floor bedroom, where he got off his tell-tale belt and coat, stuffing them under the bed. Then he lay down on the floor.

After a while, the shooting outside stopped, the officers returned, and the candles were relighted. The Union officers found Mosby on the floor, bleeding badly, and asked the family who he was. They said, of course, that they did not know, and neither did Tom Love—he was only a Confederate officer on his way to rejoin his command, who had stopped for a night's lodging. There was a surgeon with the Union detachment. After they got most of Mosby's clothes off and put him on the bed, he examined the wounded Confederate and pronounced his wound mortal. When asked his name and unit, Mosby, still conscious, hastily improvised a false identity, at the same time congratulating himself on having left all his documents behind when starting on this scouting trip. Having been assured, by medical authority, that he was as good as dead, the Union officers were no longer interested in him and soon went away.

Fortunately, on his visit to Lee's headquarters, Mosby had met an old schoolmate, a Dr. Montiero, who was now a surgeon with the Confederate Army, and, persuading him to get a transfer, had brought him back with him. Montiero's new C.O. was his first patient in his new outfit. Early the next morning, he extracted the bullet. The next night Mosby was taken to Lynchburg.

Despite the Union doctor's pronouncement of his impending death, Mosby was back in action again near the end of February, 1865. His return was celebrated with another series of raids on both sides of the mountains. It was, of course, obvious to everybody that the sands of the Confederacy were running out, but the true extent of the debacle was somewhat obscured to Mosby's followers by their own immediate successes. Peace rumors began drifting about, the favorite item of wish-thinking being that the Union government was going to recognize the Confederacy and negotiate a peace in return for Confederate help in throwing the French out of Mexico. Of course, Mosby himself never believed any such nonsense, but he continued his attacks as though victory were just around the corner. On April 5, two days after the Union army entered Richmond, a party of fifty Mosby men caught their old enemies, the Loudoun Rangers, in camp near Halltown and beat them badly. On April 9, the day of Lee's surrender, "D" Company and the newly organized "H" Company fired the last shots for the Forty-Third Virginia in a skirmish in Fairfax County. Two days later, Mosby received a message from General Hancock, calling for his surrender.

He sent a group of his officers—William Mosby, Sam Chapman, Walter Frankland and Dr. Montiero—with a flag of truce, and, after several other meetings with Hancock, the command was disbanded and most of the men went in to take the parole.

When his armistice with Hancock expired, Mosby found himself with only about forty irreconcilables left out of his whole command. As General Joe Johnston had not yet surrendered, he did not feel justified in getting out of the fight, himself. With his bloodied but unbowed handful, he set out on the most ambitious project of his entire military career— nothing less than a plan to penetrate into Richmond and abduct General Grant. If this scheme succeeded, it was his intention to dodge around the Union Army, carry his distinguished prisoner to Johnston, and present him with a real bargaining point for negotiating terms.

They reached the outskirts of Richmond and made a concealed camp across the river, waiting for darkness. In the meanwhile, two of the party, both natives of the city, Munson and Cole Jordan, went in to scout. Several hours passed, and neither returned. Mosby feared that they had been picked up by Union patrols. He was about to send an older man, Lieutenant Ben Palmer, when a canal-boat passed, and, hailing it, they learned of Johnston's surrender.

That was the end of the scheme to kidnap Grant. As long as a Confederate force was still under arms, it would have been a legitimate act of war. Now, it would be mere brigandage, and Mosby had no intention of turning brigand.

So Mosby returned to Fauquier County to take the parole. For him, the fighting was over, but he was soon to discover that the war was not. At that time, Edwin M. Stanton was making frantic efforts to inculpate as many prominent Confederates as possible in the Booth conspiracy, and Mosby's name was suggested as a worthy addition to Stanton's long and fantastic list of alleged conspirators. A witness was produced to testify that Mosby had been in Washington on the night of the assassination, April 14. At that time, Stanton was able to produce a witness to almost anything he wanted to establish. Fortunately, Mosby had an alibi; at the time in question, he had been at Hancock's headquarters, discussing armistice terms; even Stanton couldn't get around that.

However, he was subjected to considerable petty persecution, and once he was flung into jail without charge and held incommunicado. His wife went to Washington to plead his case before President Johnson, who treated her with a great deal less than courtesy, and then before General Grant, who promptly gave her a written order for her husband's release.

Then, in 1868, he did something which would have been social and political suicide for any Southerner with a less imposing war record. He supported Ulysses S. Grant for President. It was about as unexpected as any act in an extremely unconventional career, and, as usual, he had a well-reasoned purpose. Grant, he argued, was a professional soldier, not a politician. His enmity toward the South had been confined to the battlefield and had ended with the war. He had proven his magnanimity to the defeated enemy, and as President, he could be trusted to show fairness and clemency to the South.

While Virginia had not voted in the election of 1868, there is no question that Mosby's declaration of support helped Grant, and Grant was grateful, inviting Mosby to the White House after his inauguration and later appointing him to the United States consulate at Hong Kong. After the expiration of his consular service, Mosby resumed his law practice, eventually taking up residence in Washington. He found time to write several books—war reminiscences and memoirs, and a volume in vindication of his former commander, Jeb Stuart, on the Confederate cavalry in the Gettysburg campaign. He died in Washington, at the age of eighty-three, in 1916.

The really important part of John Mosby's career, of course, was the two years and three months, from January, 1863, to April, 1865, in which he held independent command. With his tiny force—it never exceeded 500 men—he had compelled the Union army to employ at least one and often as high as three brigades to guard against his depredations, and these men, held in the rear, were as much out of the war proper as though they had been penned up in Andersonville or Libby Prison.

In addition to this, every northward movement of the Confederate Army after January, 1863, was accompanied by a diversionary operation of Mosby's command, sometimes tactically insignificant but always contributing, during the critical time of the operation, to the uncertainty of Union intelligence. Likewise, every movement to the south of the Army of the Potomac was harassed from behind.

—◆—

It may also be noted that Sheridan, quite capable of dealing with the menace of Stuart, proved helpless against the Mosby nuisance, although, until they were wiped out, Blazer's Scouts were the most efficient anti-Mosby outfit ever employed. In spite of everything that was done against them, however, Mosby's Rangers stayed in business longer than Lee's army, and when they finally surrendered, it was not because they, themselves, had been defeated, but because the war had been literally jerked out from under them.

Mosby made the cavalry a formidable amalgamation of fire power and mobility and his influence on military history was felt directly, and survived him by many years. In his last days, while living in Washington, the old Confederate guerrilla had a youthful friend, a young cavalry lieutenant fresh from West Point, to whom he enjoyed telling the stories of his raids and battles and to whom he preached his gospel of fire and mobility. This young disciple of Mosby's old age was to make that gospel his own, and to practice it, later, with great success. The name of this young officer was George S. Patton, Jr.

The Marine Raiders of the Pacific

Major Jon T. Hoffman

IN FEBRUARY 1942, LIEUTENANT GENERAL THOMAS HOLCOMB, THE Commandant of the Marine Corps, ordered the creation of a new unit designated the 1st Marine Raider Battalion. This elite force, and its three sister battalions, went on to gain considerable fame for fighting prowess in World War II. There is more to the story of these units, however, than a simple tale of combat heroics.

Two completely independent forces were responsible for the appearance of the raiders in early 1942. Several historians have fully traced one of these sets of circumstances, which began with the friendship developed between Franklin D. Roosevelt and Evans F. Carlson. As a result of his experiences in China, Carlson was convinced that guerrilla warfare was the wave of the future. One of his adherents in 1941 was Captain James Roosevelt, the president's son. At the same time, another presidential confidant, William J. Donovan, was pushing a similar theme. Donovan had been an Army hero in World War I and was now a senior advisor on intelligence matters. He wanted to create a guerrilla force that would infiltrate occupied territory and assist resistance groups. He made a formal proposal along these lines to President Roosevelt in December 1941. In January 1942, the younger Roosevelt wrote to the Major General Commandant of the Marine Corps and recommended creation of "a unit for purposes similar to the British Commandos and the Chinese Guerrillas."

These ideas were appealing at the time because the war was going badly for the Allies. The Germans had forced the British off the continent of Europe, and the Japanese were sweeping the United States and

Britain from much of the Pacific. The military forces of the Allies were too weak to slug it out in conventional battles with the Axis powers, so guerrilla warfare and quick raids appeared to be viable alternatives. The British commandos had already conducted numerous forays against the European coastline, and Prime Minister Winston S. Churchill enthusiastically endorsed the concept to President Roosevelt. The Marine Commandant, Major General Thomas Holcomb, allegedly succumbed to this high-level pressure and organized the raider battalions, though he himself thought that any properly trained Marine unit could perform amphibious raids.

Two other men also were responsible for the genesis of the raiders. One was General Holland M. Smith, who eventually crystallized his new ideas about amphibious operations. He envisioned making future assaults with three distinct echelons. The first wave would be composed of fast-moving forces that could seize key terrain prior to the main assault. This first element would consist of a parachute regiment, an air infantry regiment (gliderborne troops), a light tank battalion, and "at least one APD [high-speed destroyer transport] battalion." With a relatively secure beachhead, the more ponderous combat units of the assault force would come ashore. The third echelon would consist of the reserve force and service units.

In June 1941 he personally had picked Lieutenant Colonel Merritt A. "Red Mike" Edson to command that battalion and had designated it to serve permanently with the Navy's APD squadron. Smith began to refer to Edson's outfit as the "light battalion" or the "APD battalion."

Edson's unit was unique in other ways. In a lengthy August 1941 report, the lieutenant colonel evaluated the organization and missions of his unit. He believed that the APD battalion would focus primarily on reconnaissance, raids, and other special operations—in his mind it was a waterborne version of the parachutists. In a similar fashion, the battalion would rely on speed and mobility, not firepower, as its tactical mainstay.

Since the APDs could neither embark nor offload vehicles, that meant the battalion had to be entirely foot mobile once ashore, again like the parachutists. To achieve rapid movement, Edson recommended a new table of organization that made his force much lighter than other infantry battalions. He wanted to trade in his 81mm mortars and heavy machine guns for lighter models. There also would be fewer of these weapons, but they would have larger crews to carry the ammunition. Given the limitations of the APDs, each company would be smaller than its standard counterpart. There would be four rifle companies, a weapons company, and a headquarters company with a large demolitions platoon. The main assault craft would be 10-man rubber boats.

Merritt A. Edson's military career began in the fall of 1915 when he enlisted in the 1st Vermont Infantry (a National Guard outfit). In the summer of 1916 he served in the Mexican border campaign. When the United States entered World War I in April 1917, he earned a commission as a Marine officer, but he did not arrive in France until just before the Armistice.

He ultimately more than made up for missing out on "the war to end all wars." In 1921 he began his long career in competitive shooting as part of the 10-man team that won the National Rifle Team Trophy for the Marine Corps. He earned his pilot's wings in 1922 and flew for five years before poor depth perception forced him back into the infantry. In 1927, he received command of the Marine detachment on board the *Denver* (CL 16). He and his men soon became involved in the effort to rid Nicaragua of Augusto Sandino. Edson spent 14 months ashore, most of it deep in the interior of the country. In the process, he won a reputation as an aggressive, savvy small-unit leader. He bested Sandino's forces in more than a dozen skirmishes, earned his first Navy Cross for valor, and came away with the nickname "Red Mike" (in honor of the colorful beard he sported in the field).

Edson spent the first half of the 1930s as a tactics instructor at the Basic School for new lieutenants, and then as ordnance officer at the Philadelphia Depot of Supplies. During the summers he continued to shoot; ultimately he captained the rifle team to consecutive national championships in 1935 and 1936. In the summer of 1937 he transferred to Shanghai to become the operations officer for the 4th Marines. He arrived just in time for a ringside seat when the Sino-Japanese War engulfed that city. That gave him ample opportunity to observe Japanese combat techniques at close range. In June 1941, Red Mike assumed command of the 1st Battalion, 5th Marines at Quantico.

Evans F. Carlson got an early start in his career as a maverick. He ran away from his home in Vermont at the age of 14 and two years later bluffed his way past the recruiters to enlist in the Army. When war broke out in 1917, he already had five years of service under his belt. Like Merritt A. Edson, he soon won a commission, but arrived at the front too late to see combat. After the war he tried to make it as a salesman, but gave that up in 1922 and enlisted in the Marine Corps. In a few months he earned a commission again. Other than a failed attempt at flight school, his first several years as a Marine lieutenant were unremarkable.

In 1927 Carlson deployed to Shanghai with the 4th Marines. There he became regimental intelligence officer and developed a deep interest in China that would shape the remainder of his days. Three years later, commanding an outpost of the *Guardia National* in Nicaragua, he had his first brush with guerrilla warfare. That became the second guiding star of his career. In his only battle, he successfully engaged and dispersed an enemy unit in a daring night attack. There followed a tour with the Legation Guard in Peking, and a stint as executive officer of the presidential guard detachment at Warm Springs, Georgia. In the latter job Carlson came to know Franklin D. Roosevelt.

Captain Carlson arrived in Shanghai for his third China tour in July 1937. Again like Edson, he watched the Japanese seize control of the city. Detailed to duty as an observer, Carlson sought and received permission to accompany the Chinese Communist Party's 8th Route Army, which was fighting against the Japanese. For the next year he divided his time between the front lines and the temporary Chinese capital of Hangkow. During that time he developed his ideas on guerrilla warfare and ethical indoctrination. When a senior naval officer censured him for granting newspaper interviews, Carlson returned to the States and resigned so that he could speak out about the situation in China. He believed passionately that the United States should do more to help the Chinese in their war with Japan.

During the next two years Carlson spoke and wrote on the subject, to include two books (*The Chinese Army* and *Twin Stars of China*), and made another trip to China. With war looming for the United States, he sought to rejoin the Corps in April 1941. The Commandant granted his request, made him a major in the reserves, and promptly brought him onto active duty. Ten months later he created the 2d Raider Battalion.

SHAPING THE RAIDERS

The two raider battalions bore the same name, but they could hardly have been more dissimilar. What they did have in common was excellent training and a desire to excel in battle.

The raider battalions soon received first priority in the Marine Corps on men and equipment. Edson and Carlson combed the ranks of their respective divisions and also siphoned off many of the best men pouring forth from the recruit depots. They had no difficulty attracting volunteers with the promise that they would be the first to fight the Japanese. Carlson's exactions were much greater than those required to fill out Edson's battalion, but both generated resentment from fellow officers struggling to flesh out the rapidly expanding divisions on a meager skeleton of experienced men. The raiders also had *carte blanche* to obtain any equipment they deemed necessary, whether or not it was standard issue anywhere else in the Corps.

Carlson and Roosevelt soon broke the shackles that Holcomb had attempted to impose on them. They rejected most of the men whom Edson sent them, and they adjusted the organization of their battalion to suit their purposes. They also inculcated the unit with an unconventional military philosophy that was an admixture of Chinese culture, Communist egalitarianism, and New England town hall democracy. Every man would have the right to say what he thought, and their battle cry would be "Gung Ho!"—Chinese for "work together." Officers would have no greater privileges than the men, and would lead by consensus rather than rank. There also would be "ethical indoctrination," which Carlson described as "giv[ing] conviction through persuasion." That process supposedly ensured that each man knew what he was fighting for and why.

The 2d Raiders set up their pup tents at Jacques Farm in the hills of Camp Elliot, where they remained largely segregated from civilization. Carlson rarely granted liberty, and sometimes held musters in the middle of the night to catch anyone who slipped away for an evening on the town. He even tried to convince men to forgo leave for family emergencies, though he did not altogether prohibit it.

Training focused heavily on weapons practice, hand-to-hand fighting, demolitions, and physical conditioning, to include an emphasis on long hikes. As the men grew tougher and acquired field skills, the focus shifted to more night work. Carlson also implemented an important change to the raider organization promulgated from Washington. Instead of a unitary eight-man squad, he created a 10-man unit composed of a squad leader and three fire teams of three men each. Each fire team boasted a Thompson submachine gun, a Browning automatic rifle (BAR), and one of the new Garand M-1 semiautomatic rifles. To keep manpower within the constraints of the carrying capacity of an APD, each rifle company had just two rifle platoons and a weapons platoon. Carlson's system of organization and training was designed to create a force suited "for infiltration and the attainment of objectives by unorthodox and unexpected methods." He and Roosevelt were developing the guerrilla unit they had envisioned.

Edson's battalion retained the table of organization he had designed. It was based on an eight-man squad, with a leader, two BAR men, four riflemen armed with the M-1903 Springfield bolt-operated rifle, and a sniper carrying a Springfield mounting a telescopic sight. (Later in the war he would champion the four-man fire team that became the standard for all Marine infantry.) With smaller squads, his companies contained three rifle platoons and a weapons platoon. His weapons company provided additional light machine guns and 60mm mortars. (The 81mm mortar platoon, added to the headquarters company by the Commandant, would not deploy overseas with the battalion.)

Training was similar to that in the 2d Raiders, except for more rubber boat work due to the convenient location of Quantico on the Potomac River. The 1st Raiders also strove to reach a pace of seven miles per hour on hikes, more than twice the normal speed of infantry. They did so by alternating periods of double-timing with fast walking. Although Red Mike emphasized light infantry tactics, his men were not guerrillas. Instead, they formed a highly trained battalion prepared for special operations as well as more conventional employment.

Edson's style of leadership contrasted starkly with that of his counterpart. He encouraged initiative in his subordinates, but rank carried both responsibility and authority for decision-making. He was a quiet man who impressed his troops with his ability on the march and on the firing ranges, not with speeches. His raiders received regular liberty, and he even organized battalion dances attended by busloads of secretaries from nearby Washington.

GETTING TO THE FIGHT

It did not take long for the raiders to move toward the sound of the guns. In early April 1942 the majority of the 1st Raiders boarded trains and headed for the West Coast, where they embarked in the *Zeilin*. They arrived in Samoa near the end of the month and joined the Marine brigades garrisoning that outpost. Company D, the 81mm mortar platoon, and a representative slice of the headquarters and weapons companies remained behind in Quantico. This rear echelon was under the command of Major Samuel B. Griffith II, the battalion executive officer. (He had recently joined the raiders after spending several months in England observing the British commandos.) This small force maintained some raider capability on the East Coast, and also constituted a nucleus for a projected third raider battalion.

The 2d Raiders spent the month of April on board ship learning rubber boat techniques. The Navy had transferred three of its APDs to the West Coast, and Carlson's men used them to conduct practice landings on San Clemente Island. In May the 2d Raiders embarked and sailed for Hawaii, arriving at Pearl Harbor on 17 May.

Carlson's outfit hardly had arrived in Hawaii when Admiral Chester W. Nimitz, commander-in-chief of the Pacific Fleet and the Pacific Ocean Areas, ordered two companies of raiders to Midway to reinforce the garrison in preparation for an expected Japanese attack. They arrived on 25 May. Company C took up defensive positions on Sand Island, while Company D moved to Eastern Island. Trained to fight a guerrilla campaign of stealth and infiltration, these raiders had to conduct a static defense of a small area. In the end, Navy and Marine aircraft turned back the invading force in one of the great naval victories of the war. Combat for the Marines on the ground consisted of a single large enemy air attack on the morning of 4 June. Although the Japanese inflicted considerable damage on various installations, the raiders suffered no casualties. Not long after the battle, the two companies joined the rest of the battalion back in Hawaii.

Makin

During the summer of 1942 Admiral Nimitz decided to employ Carlson's battalion for its designated purpose. Planners selected Makin Atoll in the Gilbert Islands as the target. They made available two large mine-laying submarines, the *Nautilus* and the *Argonaut*. Each one could carry a company of raiders. The force would make a predawn landing on Butaritari Island, destroy the garrison (estimated at 45 men), withdraw that evening, and land the next day on Little Makin Island. The scheduled D-day was 17 August, 10 days after the 1st Marine Division and the 1st Raiders assaulted the lower Solomons. The objectives of the operation were diverse: to destroy installations, take prisoners, gain intelligence on the area, and divert Japanese attention and reinforcements from Guadalcanal and Tulagi.

Companies A and B drew the mission and boarded the submarines on 8 August. Once in the objective area, things began to go badly. The subs surfaced in heavy rain and high seas. Due to the poor conditions, Carlson altered his plan at the last minute. Instead of each company landing on widely separated beaches, they would go ashore together. Lieutenant Oscar F. Peatross, a platoon commander, did not get the word; he and the squad in his boat ended up landing alone in what became the enemy rear. The main body reached shore in some confusion due to engine malfunctions and weather, then the accidental discharge of a weapon ruined any hope of surprise.

First Lieutenant Merwyn C. Plumley's Company A quickly crossed the narrow island and turned southwest toward the known enemy positions. Company B, commanded by Captain Ralph H. Coyt, followed in trace as the reserve. Soon thereafter the raiders were engaged in a firefight with the Japanese. Sergeant Clyde Thomason died in this initial action while courageously exposing himself in order to direct the fire of his platoon. He later was awarded the Medal of Honor, the first enlisted Marine so decorated in World War II.

The raiders made little headway against Japanese machine guns and snipers. Then the enemy launched two banzai attacks, each announced with a bugle call. Marine fire easily dispatched both groups of charging enemy soldiers. Unbeknownst to the Americans, they had nearly wiped out the Japanese garrison at that point in the battle.

At 1130 two enemy aircraft appeared over the island and scouted the scene of action. Carlson had trained his men to remain motionless and not fire at planes. With no troops in sight and no contact from their own ground force, the planes finally dropped their bombs, though none landed within Marine lines. Two hours later 12 planes arrived on the scene, several of them seaplanes. Two of the larger flying boats landed in the lagoon. Raider machine guns and Boys antitank rifles fired at them. One burst into flame and the other crashed on takeoff after receiving numerous hits. The remaining aircraft bombed and strafed the island for an hour, again with most of the ordnance hitting enemy-occupied territory. Another air attack came late in the afternoon.

The natives on the island willingly assisted the Americans throughout the day. They carried ammunition and provided intelligence. The latter reports suggested that enemy reinforcements had come ashore from the seaplanes and from two small ships in the lagoon. (The submarines later took the boats under indirect fire with their deck guns and miraculously sunk both.) Based on this information, Carlson was certain there was still a sizable Japanese force on the island. At 1700 he called several individuals together and contemplated his options. Roosevelt and the battalion operations officer argued for a withdrawal as planned in preparation for the next day's landing on Little Makin. Concerned that he might become too heavily engaged if he tried to advance, Carlson decided to follow their recommendation.

This part of the operation went smoothly for a time. The force broke contact in good order and a group of 20 men covered the rest of the raiders as they readied their rubber boats and shoved off. Carlson, however, forgot about the covering force and thought his craft contained the last men on the island when it entered the water at 1930. Disaster then struck in the form of heavy surf. The outboard engines did not work and the men soon grew exhausted trying to paddle against the breakers. Boats capsized and equipment disappeared. After repeated attempts several boatloads made it to the rendezvous with the submarines, but Carlson and 120 men ended up stranded on the shore. Only the covering force and a handful of others had weapons. In the middle of the night a small Japanese patrol approached the perimeter. They wounded a sentry, but not before he killed three of them.

With the enemy apparently still full of fight and his raiders disorganized and weakened, Carlson called another council of war. Without much input from the others, he decided to surrender. His stated reasons were concern for the wounded, and for the possible fate of the president's son (who was not present at the meeting). At 0330 Carlson sent his operations officer and another Marine out to contact the enemy. They found one Japanese soldier and eventually succeeded in giving him a note offering surrender. Carlson also authorized every man to fend for himself—those who wished could make another attempt to reach the submarines. By the next morning several more boatloads made it through the surf, including one with Major Roosevelt. In the meantime, a few exploring raiders killed several Japanese, one of them probably the man with the surrender note.

With dawn the situation appeared dramatically better. The two-man surrender party reported that there appeared to be no organized enemy force left on the island. There were about 70 raiders still ashore, and the able-bodied armed themselves with weapons lying about the battlefield. Carlson organized patrols to search for food and the enemy. They killed two more Japanese soldiers and confirmed the lack of opposition. The raider commander himself led a patrol to survey the scene and carry out the demolition of military stores and installations. He counted 83 dead Japanese and 14 of his own killed in action. Based on native reports, Carlson thought his force had accounted for more than 160 Japanese. Enemy aircraft made four separate attacks during the day, but they inflicted no losses on the raider force ashore.

The Marines contacted the submarines during the day and arranged an evening rendezvous off the entrance to the lagoon, where there was no surf to hinder an evacuation. The men hauled four rubber boats across the island and arranged for the use of a native outrigger. By 2300 the remainder of the landing force was back on board the *Nautilus* and *Argonaut*. Since the entire withdrawal had been so disorganized, the two companies were intermingled on the submarines and it was not until they returned to Pearl Harbor that they could make an accurate accounting of their losses. The official tally was 18 dead and 12 missing.

Only after the war would the Marine Corps discover that nine of the missing raiders had been left alive on the island. These men had become separated from the main body at one point or another during the operation. With the assistance of the natives the group evaded capture for a time, but finally surrendered on 30 August. A few weeks later the Japanese beheaded them on the island of Kwajalein.

The raid itself had mixed results. Reports painted it as a great victory and it boosted morale on the home front. Many believed it achieved its original goal of diverting forces from Guadalcanal, but the Japanese had immediately guessed the size and purpose of the operation and had not let it alter their plans for the Solomons. However, it did cause the enemy to worry about the potential for other such raids on rear area installations. On the negative side, that threat may have played a part in the subsequent Japanese decision to fortify heavily places like Tarawa Atoll, the scene of a costly amphibious assault later in the war. At the tactical level, the 2d Raiders had proven themselves in direct combat with the enemy. Their greatest difficulties had involved rough seas and poor equipment; bravery could not fix those limitations. Despite the trumpeted success of the operation, the Navy never again attempted to use submarines to conduct raids behind enemy lines.

Carlson received the Navy Cross for his efforts on Makin, and the public accorded him hero status. A few of those who served with him were not equally pleased with his performance. No one questioned his demonstrated bravery under fire, but some junior officers were critical of his leadership, especially the attempt to surrender to a non-existent enemy. Carlson himself later noted that he had reached "a spiritual low" on the night of the 17th. And again on the evening of the 18th, the battalion commander contemplated remaining on the island to organize the natives for resistance, while others supervised the withdrawal of his unit. Those who criticized him thought he had lost his aggressiveness and ability to think clearly when the chips were down. But he and his raiders would have another crack at the enemy in the not too distant future.

TULAGI

The Makin operation had not been Nimitz's first choice for an amphibious raid. In late May he had proposed an attack by the 1st Raiders against the Japanese seaplane base on Tulagi, in the lower Solomon Islands. The target was in the Southwest Pacific Area, however, and General Douglas MacArthur opposed the plan. But Tulagi remained a significant threat to the maritime lifeline to Australia. After the Midway victory opened the door for a more offensive Allied posture, the Japanese advance positions in the Solomons became a priority objective. In late June the Joint Chiefs of Staff shifted that region from MacArthur's command to Nimitz's Pacific Ocean Areas command, and ordered the seizure of Tulagi. The Americans soon discovered that the Japanese were building an airfield on nearby Guadalcanal, and that became the primary target for Operation Watchtower. The 1st Marine Division, with the 1st Raider Battalion attached, received the assignment.

In answer to Edson's repeated requests, the rear echelon of his battalion (less the 81mm mortar platoon) finally joined up with him on 3 July in Samoa. The entire unit then moved on to New Caledonia. The 1st Raiders received definitive word on Watchtower on 20 July. They would seize Tulagi, with the 2d Battalion, 5th Marines, in support. The 1st Parachute Battalion would take the conjoined islets of Gavutu-Tanambogo. The 1st Marine Division, less one regiment in reserve, would capture the incomplete airfield on Guadalcanal.

Edson offered to make amphibious reconnaissance patrols of the objectives, but the naval commander rejected that idea. Most of the information on Tulagi would come from three Australians, all former colonial officials familiar with the area. Tulagi was 4,000 yards long and no more than 1,000 yards wide, and a high ridge ran along its length, except for a low, open saddle near the southeast end. The only suitable landing beaches from a hydrographic standpoint were those on either side of this low ground, since coral formations fringed the rest of the island. Intelligence officers estimated that the island held several hundred men of the Japanese *Special Naval Landing Force*; these were elite troops of proven fighting ability. Aerial reconnaissance indicated they were dug in to defend the obvious landing sites. Planners thus chose to make the assault halfway up the western coast at a place designated as Beach Blue. They wisely decided to make the first American amphibious assault of the war against natural obstacles, not enemy gunfire.

The raiders sailed from New Caledonia on 23 July and joined up with the main task force for rehearsals on Koro Island in the Fijis. These went poorly, since the Navy boat crews and most of the 1st Marine Division were too green. On the morning of 7 August the task force hove to and commenced unloading in what would become known as Ironbottom Sound. Although Edson's men had trained hard on their rubber boats, they would make this landing from Higgins boats. After a preliminary bombardment by a cruiser and destroyer, the first wave, composed of Companies B and D, headed for shore. Coral forced them to debark and wade the last 100 yards, but there was no enemy opposition. Companies A and C quickly followed them. The four rifle companies spread out across the waist of the island and then advanced in line to the southeast. They met only occasional sniper fire until they reached Phase Line A at the end of the ridge, where they halted as planned while naval guns fired an additional preparation on the enemy defenses.

The attack jumped off again just before noon, and promptly ran into heavy Japanese resistance. For the remainder of the day the raiders fought to gain control of the saddle from the entrenched enemy, who would not surrender under any circumstances. The Marines quickly discovered that their only recourse was to employ explosives to destroy the men occupying the caves and bunkers. As evening approached, the battalion settled into defensive lines that circled the small ridge (Hill 281) on the tip of the island. The 2d Battalion, 5th Marines, had already scoured the remainder of the island and now took up positions in the rear of the raiders.

The Japanese launched their classic banzai counterattack at 2200 that night. The initial effort punched a small hole in the raider lines between

Companies A and C. A second assault, which might have exploited this gap, instead struck full against Company A's front. This time the raiders held their ground. For the remainder of the night the Japanese relied on infiltration tactics, with individuals and small groups trying to make their way into the American rear by stealth. By this means they attacked both the 2d Battalion's command post (CP) and the aid station set up near Blue Beach. They also came within 50 yards of the raider CP. Edson tried to call for reinforcements, but communications were out.

In the morning things looked much better, just as they had on Makin. At 0900 two companies of the 5th Marines passed through raider lines and swept over the southern portions of Hill 281. The remaining enemy were now isolated in a ravine in the midst of the small ridge. After a lengthy barrage by the 60mm mortars of Company E and their heavier 81mm cousins of the rifle battalion, infantrymen from both outfits moved through the final enemy pocket. Grenades and dynamite were the weapons of choice against the Japanese still holed up in their caves and dugouts. At 1500 Edson declared the island secured. That did not mean the fighting was entirely over. For the next few days Marines scoured the island by day, and fended off occasional infiltrators at night, until they had killed off the last enemy soldier. In the entire battle, the raiders suffered losses of 38 dead and 55 wounded. There were an additional 33 casualties among other Marine units on the island. All but three of the 350 Japanese defenders had died.

On the night of 8 August a Japanese surface force arrived from Rabaul and surprised the Allied naval forces guarding the transports. In a brief engagement the enemy sank four cruisers and a destroyer, damaged other ships, and killed 1,200 sailors, all at minimal cost to themselves. The American naval commander had little choice the next morning but to order the early withdrawal of his force. Most of the transports would depart that afternoon with their cargo holds still half full. The raiders were in a particularly bad way. They had come ashore with little food because the plan called for their immediate withdrawal after seizing the island. Moreover, since they had not cleared the enemy from the only usable beaches until D plus 1, there had been little time to unload anything. The result would be short rations for some time to come.

The 1st Raiders performed well in their initial exposure to combat. Like their compatriots in the 2d Raiders, they were both brave and daring. Major Kenneth D. Bailey demonstrated the type of leadership that was common to both units. When an enemy machine gun held up the advance of his company on D-day, he personally circled around the bunker, crawled on top, and pushed a grenade into the firing port. In the process he received a gunshot wound in the thigh. Edson established his reputation for fearlessness by spending most of his time in the front lines, where he contemptuously stood up in the face of enemy fire. More important, he aggressively employed his force in battle, while many other senior commanders had grown timid after years of peacetime service. Major General Alexander A. Vandegrift, commander of the 1st Marine Division, soon wrote Commandant Holcomb that "Edson is one of the finest troop leaders I ever saw."

TASIMBOKO

As August progressed the Japanese moved a steady stream of reinforcements to Guadalcanal in nightly runs by destroyers and barges, a process soon dubbed the "Tokyo Express." The Marines repulsed the first enemy attack at the Tenaru River on 21 August, but Vandegrift knew that he would need all the strength he could muster to defend the extended perimeter surrounding the airfield. At the end of the month he brought the raiders and parachutists across the sound and placed them in reserve near Lunga Point. The latter battalion had suffered heavily in its assault on Gavutu-Tanambogo, to include the loss of its commander, so Vandegrift attached the parachutists to Red Mike's force.

Edson quickly established a rapport with Lieutenant Colonel Thomas, the division operations officer, and convinced him to use the raiders offensively. The first product of this effort was a two-company patrol on 4 September to Savo Island, where intelligence believed the enemy had an observation post. While Griffith commanded that operation, Red Mike planned a reconnaissance-in-force against Cape Esperance for the next day. When the Savo patrol returned in the late afternoon on *Little* (APD 4) and *Gregory* (APD 3), the men began debarking before they received the order to remain on board in preparation for the next mission. Once he became aware of the mix-up, Edson let the offload process proceed to completion. That night Japanese destroyers of the Tokyo Express sank the two APDs. It was the second close escape for the raiders. During the shift to Guadalcanal, enemy planes had sunk the *Colhoun* (APD 2) just after it had unloaded a company.

Marine attention soon shifted from Cape Esperance as it became evident that the primary terminus of the Tokyo Express was the village of Tasimboko. On 6 September Edson and Thomas won permission from Vandegrift to raid the area on the eighth. After the loss of three of their APDs, shipping was at a premium, so the raiders boarded the *McKean* (APD 5), *Manley* (APD 1), and two converted tuna boats for the operation. The raider rifle companies would comprise the first echelon; the ships then would shuttle back to the Lunga for the weapons company and the parachutists. Native scouts reported there were several thousand Japanese in the area, but division planners discounted that figure. However, Edson did rely on their reports that the enemy defenses faced west toward Marine lines. He decided to land beyond the village at Taivu Point and then advance overland to take the target from the rear.

When the raiders went ashore just prior to dawn on 8 September, they quickly realized the scouting reports had been accurate. As they moved along the coast toward Tasimboko, they discovered more than a thousand life preservers placed in neat rows, a large number of foxholes, and even several unattended 37mm antitank guns. In previous days Major General Kiyotaki Kawaguchi had landed an entire brigade at Tasimboko, but it was then advancing inland. Only a rearguard of about 300 men secured the village and the Japanese supply dumps located there, though this force was nearly as big as the raider first echelon. The Marines soon ran into stubborn resistance, to include 75mm artillery pieces firing point-blank down the coastal road and the orderly rows of a coconut plantation. While Edson fixed the attention of the defenders with two companies, he sent Griffith and Company A wide to the left flank.

Concerned that he might be facing the enemy main force, Red Mike radioed a plea for a supplemental landing to the west of Tasimboko. The last part of the message indicated there was trouble: "If not, request instructions regarding my embarkation." Forty-five minutes later Edson again asked for fresh troops and for more air support. Division responded the same way each time—the raiders were to break off the action and withdraw. Red Mike ignored that order and continued the attack. Not long afterwards, enemy resistance melted away, and both wings of the raider force entered the village around noon. The area was stockpiled with large quantities of food, ammunition, and weapons ranging up to 75mm artillery pieces. Vandegrift radioed a "well done" and repeated his order to withdraw yet again.

The raider commander chose to stay put for the time being, and his men set about destroying as much of the cache as they could. Troops wrecked a powerful radio station, bayoneted cans of food, tore open bags of rice and urinated on the contents or spilled them on the ground, tied guns to landing boats and towed them into deep water, and then finally put the torch to everything that was left. They also gathered all available documents. As the sun went down, the men reembarked and headed for the perimeter, many of them a little bit heavier with liberated chow, cigarettes, and alcohol.

The raid was a minor tactical victory in terms of actual fighting. The Marines counted 27 enemy bodies and estimated they had killed 50. Their own losses were two dead and six wounded. But the battle had important repercussions. The raiders had put a serious dent in Japanese logistics, fire support, and communications. The intelligence gathered had more far-reaching consequences, since it revealed many of the details of the coming Japanese offensive. Finally, the setback hurt the enemy's morale and further boosted that of the raiders. They had defeated the Japanese yet again, and were literally feasting on the fruits of the victory.

EDSON'S RIDGE

The next day Red Mike discussed the situation with division planners. Intelligence officers translating the captured documents confirmed that 3,000 Japanese were cutting their way through the jungle southwest of Tasimboko. Edson was convinced that they planned to attack the currently unguarded southern portion of the perimeter. From an aerial photograph he picked out a grass-covered ridge that pointed like a knife at the airfield. His hunch was based on his own experience in jungle fighting and with the Japanese. He knew they liked to attack at night, and that was also the only time they could get fire support from the sea. And a night attack in the jungle only had a chance if it moved along a well-defined avenue of approach. The ridge was the obvious choice. Thomas agreed. Vandegrift did not, but they convinced the general to let the raiders and parachutists shift their bivouac to the ridge in order to get out of the pattern of bombs falling around the airfield.

The men moved to the new location on 10 September. Contrary to their hopes, it was not a rest zone. Japanese planes bombed the ridge on the 11th and 12th. Native scouts brought reports of the approaching enemy column, and raider patrols soon made contact with the advance elements of the force. The Marines worked to improve their position under severe handicaps. There was very little barbed wire and no sandbags or engineering tools. Troops on the ridge itself could not dig far before striking coral; those on either flank were hampered by thick jungle that would conceal the movement of the enemy. Casualties had thinned ranks, while illness and a lack of good food had sapped the strength of those still on the lines.

Edson and Thomas did the best they could with the resources available. Red Mike used the spine of the ridge as the dividing point between his two rump battalions. One company of parachutists held the left of his line, with the rest of their comrades echeloned to the rear to protect that flank. Two companies of raiders occupied the right, with that flank anchored on the Lunga River. A lagoon separated the two raider units. Edson attached the machine guns to the forward companies and kept the remaining raiders in reserve. (Company D was no larger than a platoon now, since Red Mike had used much of its manpower to fill holes in the other three rifle companies.) He set up his forward command post on Hill 120, just a few hundred yards behind the front lines.

Thomas placed the 2d Battalion, 5th Marines, in reserve between the ridge and the airfield. Artillery forward observers joined Edson and registered the howitzers. The Marines were as ready as they could be, but the selection of the ridge as the heart of the defense was a gamble. To the west of the Lunga there were only a few strongpoints occupied by the men from the pioneer and amphibious tractor battalions. To the east of Red Mike's line there was nothing but a mile of empty jungle.

Kawaguchi was having his own problems. In addition to the setback at Tasimboko, his troops were having a tough time cutting their way through the heavy jungle and toiling over the many ridges in their path. Some of his difficulties were self-inflicted. His decision to attack from the south had required him to leave his artillery and most of his supplies behind, since they could not be hauled over the rough jungle trail. Thus he would go into battle with little fire support and poor logistics. He then detailed one of his four battalions to make a diversionary attack along the Tenaru. This left him with just 2,500 men for the main assault. Finally, he had underestimated the time needed to reach his objective.

On the evening of 12 September, as the appointed hour for the attack approached, Kawaguchi realized that only one battalion had reached its assigned jumpoff point, and no units had been able to reconnoiter the area of the ridge. He wanted to delay the attack, but communications failed and he could not pass the order. Behind schedule and without guides, the battalions hastily blundered forward, only to break up into small groups as the men fought their way through the tangled growth in total darkness. At 2200 a Japanese plane dropped a series of green flares over the Marine perimeter. Then a cruiser and three destroyers opened up on the ridge. For the next 20 minutes they poured shells in that direction, though most rounds sailed over the high ground to land in the jungle beyond, some to explode among the Japanese infantry.

When the bombardment ceased, Kawaguchi's units launched their own flares and the first piecemeal attacks began. The initial assault concentrated in the low ground around the lagoon. This may have been an attempt to find the American flank, or the result of lack of familiarity with the terrain. In any case, the thick jungle offset the Marine advantage in firepower, and the Japanese found plenty of room to infiltrate between platoon strongpoints. They soon isolated the three platoons of Company C, each of which subsequently made its way to the rear. The Marines on the ridge remained comparatively untouched. As daylight approached the Japanese broke off the action, but retained possession of Company C's former positions. Kawaguchi's officers began the slow process of regrouping their units, now scattered over the jungle and totally disoriented.

In the morning Edson ordered a counterattack by his reserve companies. They made little headway against the more-numerous Japanese, and Red Mike recalled them. Since he could not restore an unbroken front, he decided to withdraw the entire line to the reserve position. This had the added benefit of forcing the enemy to cross more open ground on the ridge before reaching Marine fighting holes. In the late afternoon the B Companies of both raiders and parachutists pulled back and anchored themselves on the ridge midway between Hills 80 and 120. Thomas provided an engineer company, which Edson inserted on the right of the ridge. Company A of the raiders covered the remaining distance between the engineers and the Lunga. The other two parachute companies withdrew slightly and bulked up the shoulder of the left flank. The remains of Companies C and D assumed a new reserve position on the west slope of the ridge, just behind Hill 120. Red Mike's command post stayed in its previous location.

The Japanese made good use of the daylight hours and prepared for a fresh effort. This time Kawaguchi would not make the mistake of getting bogged down in the jungle; he would follow the tactics Edson had originally expected and concentrate his attack on the open ground of the ridge. The new assault kicked off just after darkness fell. The initial blow struck Company B's right flank near the lagoon. A mad rush of screaming soldiers drove the right half of the raider company out of position and those men fell back to link up with Company C on the ridge. Inexplicably, Kawaguchi did not exploit the gap he had created. Possibly the maneuver had been a diversion to draw Marine reserves off the ridge and out of the way of the main effort.

Edson had to decide quickly whether to plug the hole with his dwindling reserve or risk having the center of his line encircled by the next assault. The enemy soon provided the answer. By 2100 Japanese soldiers were massing around the southern nose of the ridge, making their presence known with the usual barrage of noisy chants. They presumably were going to launch a frontal assault on the center of the Marine line. Red Mike ordered Company C of the raiders and Company A of the parachutists to form a reserve line around the front and sides of Hill 120. Japanese mortar and machine-gun fire swept the ridge; the Marines responded with artillery fire on suspected assembly areas.

The assault waves finally surged forward at 2200. The attack, on a front all across the ridge, immediately unhinged the Marine center. As Japanese swarmed toward the left flank of his Company B, Captain Harry L. Torgerson, the parachute battalion executive officer, ordered it to withdraw. The parachutists in Company C soon followed suit. Torgerson gathered these two units in the rear of Company A's position on Hill 120, where he attempted to reorganize them. The remaining Company B raiders were now isolated in the center. The situation looked desperate.

At this point, the Japanese seemed to take a breather. Heavy fire raked the ridge, but the enemy made no fresh assaults. Edson arranged for more artillery support, and got his own force to provide covering fire for the withdrawal of the exposed raiders of Company B. For a time it looked like the series of rearward movements would degenerate into a rout. As a few men around Hill 120 began to filter to the rear, Red Mike took immediate steps to avert disaster. From his CP, now just a dozen yards behind the front, he made it known that this was to be the final stand. The word went round: "Nobody moves, just die in your holes." Major Bailey ranged up and down the line raising his voice above the din and breathing fresh nerve into those on the verge of giving up. The commander of the Parachute Battalion broke down; Edson relieved him on the spot and placed Torgerson in charge.

The new position was not very strong, just a small horseshoe bent around the hill, with men from several units intermingled on the bare slopes. Red Mike directed the artillery to maintain a continuous barrage close along his front. When the Japanese renewed their attack, each fresh wave of Imperial soldiers boiled out of the jungle into a torrent of steel and lead. In addition to the firepower of artillery and automatic weapons, men on the lines tossed grenade after grenade at whatever shapes or sounds they could discern. Supplies of ammunition dwindled rapidly, and division headquarters pushed forward cases of belted machine gun ammunition and grenades.

One of the Japanese assaults, probably avoiding the concentrated fire sweeping the crest, pushed along the jungle edge at the bottom of the slope and threatened to envelop the left flank. Edson ordered Torgerson to launch a counterattack with his two reorganized parachute companies. These Marines advanced, checked the enemy progress, and extended the line to prevent any recurrence. Red Mike later cited this effort as "a decisive factor in our ultimate victory."

At 0400 Edson asked Thomas to commit the reserve battalion to bolster his depleted line. A company at a time, the men of the 2d Battalion, 5th Marines, filed along the top of the ridge and into place beside those who had survived the long night. By that point the Japanese were largely spent. Kawaguchi sent in two more attacks, but they were hit by artillery fire as the troops assembled and never presented much of a threat. A small band actually made it past the ridge and reached the vicinity of the airfield; the Marines providing security there dealt with them.

The onset of daylight brought an end to any organized effort, though remnants of Japanese assault units were scattered through the fringing jungle to the flanks and rear of the Marine position. Squads began the long process of rooting out these snipers. Edson also ordered up an air attack to strike the enemy units clinging to the southern end of the ridge. A flight of P-400s answered the call and strafed the exposed enemy groups. Kawaguchi admitted failure that afternoon and ordered his tattered brigade to retreat.

The raiders and parachutists had already turned over the ridge to other Marines that morning. The 1st Raiders had lost 135 men, the 1st Parachute Battalion another 128. Of those, 59 men were dead or missing-in-action. Seven hundred Japanese bodies littered the battlefield, and few of Kawaguchi's 500 wounded would survive the terrible trek back to the coast.

The battle was much more than a tremendous tactical victory for the Marines. Edson and his men had turned back one of the most serious threats the Japanese were to mount against Henderson Field. If the raiders and parachutists had failed, the landing strip would have fallen into enemy hands, and the lack of air cover probably would have led to the defeat of the 1st Marine Division and the loss of Guadalcanal. Such a reversal would have had a grave impact on the course of the war and the future of the Corps.

Vandegrift wasted no time in recommending Edson and Bailey for Medals of Honor. Red Mike's citation noted his "marked degree of cool leadership and personal courage." At the height of the battle, with friendly artillery shells landing just 75 yards to the front, and enemy bullets and mortars sweeping the knoll, Edson had never taken cover. Standing in the shallow hole that passed for a CP, he had calmly issued orders and served as an inspiration to all who saw him. War correspondents visiting the scene the day after the battle dubbed it "Edson's Ridge."

MATANIKAU

The depleted parachutists (55 percent casualties in the campaign) left Guadalcanal on 17 September on board the convoy that brought in the 7th Marines. The 1st Raiders (33 percent casualties) remained, and received precious little rest. Just six days after the battle, Vandegrift ordered them to make a reconnaissance south of Edson's Ridge and destroy any Japanese stragglers. The raiders passed through their old position, now strongly defended by the 7th Marines, and followed the track of their beaten foe, a trail marked by abandoned weapons and bodies. Edson made liberal use of artillery and his crew-served weapons against the slightest sign of resistance. At a cost of three wounded, the raiders captured a single dismantled howitzer and killed 19 enemy soldiers. The greatest point of danger in the operation turned out to be the return trip. As the battalion neared friendly lines, the jittery new arrivals of the 7th Marines opened fire on the raiders. Luckily no one was hit.

That same day Vandegrift shipped out several excess colonels and reorganized the senior ranks of the division. Edson took command of the 5th Marines and Griffith succeeded him as head of the 1st Raiders. Red Mike's departure did not take the raider battalion out of the spotlight. Lieutenant Colonel Lewis B. "Chesty" Puller's 1st Battalion, 7th Marines, departed the perimeter on 23 September with the mission of clearing enemy units from the vicinity of the Matanikau River. Once that was accomplished, division wanted to place the raiders in a patrol base near Kokumbona to prevent the enemy's return. That would keep Japanese artillery out of range of the airfield.

On the 24th Puller's men surprised a Japanese unit and routed it, but lost seven killed and 25 wounded in the process. Division sent out the 2d Battalion, 5th Marines, as a relief force, since Puller had to use most of his battalion to get the casualties safely back into the perimeter. Puller then continued on with his one remaining rifle company and the 2d Battalion. The combined force reached the Matanikau on 26 September, proceeded down the east bank, then tried to cross the sandbar at the river's mouth. A Japanese company blocked the way and drove the Marines back with heavy fire. Meanwhile another enemy company moved into defensive positions on the eastern end of the single-log bridge that served as the only crossing upstream. The Marines remained ignorant of that move. That afternoon Vandegrift ordered Edson to take charge of the operation, and sent the raiders along to assist him.

Puller and Edson jointly devised a new plan that evening. In the morning the raiders would move upriver, cross at the bridge, and then come back downriver on the far bank to take the Japanese at the river mouth in the flank. To ensure that the enemy force did not retreat out of the trap, the 2d Battalion, 5th Marines, would pressure them with its own attack across the sandbar. Finally, the bulk of the 1st Battalion, 7th Marines, then in the perimeter after the casualty evacuation, would make an amphibious landing beyond Point Cruz to slam shut any possible escape route. The ambitious plan received division's blessing.

After a night of heavy rain, the 2d Battalion launched its assault at the river mouth, but made no progress against continuing strong opposition. The raiders, reinforced by Puller's lone company, advanced upriver, but soon found themselves wedged into a narrow shelf between the water and a steep ridge. The Japanese had placed a tight stopper in this bottle with infantry supported by machine guns and mortars. Bailey responded in his typical fashion and tried to lead the assault—he soon fell mortally wounded. Griffith ordered Company C up the ridge in an effort to outflank the enemy. The Japanese had this approach covered too. When the battalion commander appeared on the ridgeline to observe the action firsthand, a sniper put a bullet in his shoulder. With no outside fire support, the raiders could make no headway against the dug-in Japanese.

Poor communications made things worse. Edson misinterpreted a message from the raiders and thought they were across the river. He launched the 2d Battalion, 5th Marines, in yet another assault, this time with help from additional mortars and 37mm antitank guns, but it met the same fate as all previous attempts. Upon landing in the enemy's rear, the 1st Battalion, 7th Marines, was surrounded by a large-force enemy bivouaced in the vicinity. The unit had brought no radios ashore and consequently could not immediately inform division of its plight. Eventually the Marines used air panels to signal supporting aircraft. When that word reached Puller, he wanted the 2d Battalion to renew the assault to take pressure off his men, but Edson refused to incur further casualties in a hopeless frontal attack.

Puller eventually extricated his beleaguered force with naval gunfire and messages passed by semaphore flags. Red Mike then ordered the raiders to pull back to the river mouth to join 2d Battalion, 5th Marines, after which both units withdrew to the division perimeter. The units engaged had lost 67 dead and 125 wounded in the course of the operation. This aborted action along the Matanikau was the only defeat the Marines suffered during the Guadalcanal campaign.

Raider casualties during the all-day action had been comparatively light—two killed and 11 wounded—but that total included both senior officers in the battalion. Command now devolved upon Captain Ira J. "Jake" Irwin. The battalion was worn down by two months of steady fighting, and by the ravages of the tropics. Large numbers of men were ill with malaria and other diseases. The battalion had seen more action than any other on the island, and rumors persisted that they would soon ship out like the parachutists. One raider later recalled that "a more sickly, bedraggled, miserable bunch of Marines would have been hard to find."

The 1st Raiders had one more battle to go on Guadalcanal. In early October intelligence indicated that the Japanese were building up their forces west of the Matanikau in preparation for another offensive against the perimeter. Division headquarters decided to strike first to secure the crossings over the river. In a plan reminiscent of the beginnings of the previous operation, two battalions of the 5th Marines would move down the coast road, seize the near bank of the Matanikau, and fix the attention of the Japanese forces on the far side. Three other battalions would cross the Matanikau at the single-log bridge and attack north toward the sea. Once they cleared the far side of the river, a force would garrison Kokumbona and prevent further enemy operations in the vicinity. In addition to strengthening the assault forces, this time division provided ample fire support. All units were to move into position on 7 October in preparation for launching that attack the next morning.

When the 5th Marines deployed forward on 7 October, they ran into a Japanese company dug in on the near side of the river just inland from the sandbar. Edson's 2d Battalion managed to secure most of its assigned frontage farther upriver, but his 3d Battalion was unable to break the enemy resistance centered on a well-fortified defensive position. He committed Company L to the battle and then radioed division for reinforcements so he could reconstitute a regimental reserve. Division assigned Company A, 1st Raiders to the task and the unit marched off down the coast road to bivouac next to Red Mike's CP.

That night the Japanese on the near side of the river probed the lines of the 3d Battalion, 5th Marines, and mauled the company nearest the sandbar. Early in the morning of 8 October, Edson decided to commit the raiders of Company A to the task of reducing the Japanese pocket. He placed Major Lewis W. Walt in charge of the effort. (Walt had been Company A's commander until Edson had brought him over as operations officer for the 5th Marines.) The raiders drove in a few enemy outposts, but could make little headway against the interlocking fires of the concealed Japanese positions. Meanwhile, heavy rains during the night had continued into the day, and division delayed the move across the river for 24 hours. Vandegrift also decided to alter his original plan to a quick envelopment of the west bank and a return to the perimeter.

Based on these changed circumstances and his own observation at close range of Company A's predicament, Edson halted the attack on the strongpoint. His 3d Battalion would continue to encircle most of the enemy position, while Company A went into the defense on their right flank. The latter's position was shaped like a horseshoe, with the left linking up with the 3d Battalion and facing south toward the bunker complex, the center facing west toward the sandspit, and the right on the beach facing north toward the sea. To fill out the thin line, mortarmen and company headquarters personnel occupied the left flank positions. The raiders expected a Japanese assault across the river mouth to relieve the surrounded bridgehead, so the Marines strung barbed wire at the friendly end of the sandbar. The remainder of the raider battalion came up the coast road and went into reserve.

Just after dusk the Japanese in the strongpoint rushed from their positions in an effort to break through to their own lines. They quickly overran the surprised left flank of Company A and hit the center of the raider line from the rear. The enemy who survived the close-quarters fighting in both locations then ran headlong into the wire, where fire from the remaining Marines cut them down. The lieutenant commanding the raider company tried to recover from the confusion and establish a fresh line farther back along the coast road. In the morning there was some more fighting with a handful of Japanese who had sought refuge in Marine foxholes. Company C of the raiders moved up to occupy the abandoned enemy position and killed three more Japanese still holed-up there. They found an elaborate complex of trenches and bunkers connected by tunnels to an underground command post. The Marines counted 59 bodies stacked up against the wire or strewn about the perimeter. The battalion lost 12 dead and 22 wounded during this stint on the Matanikau.

The raiders suffered one additional casualty during the operation. When Red Mike had gone over to the 5th Marines, he had taken with him his longtime runner, Corporal Walter J. Burak. While carrying a message along the river on the afternoon of 9 October, Japanese machine-gun fire killed the former raider. He was the last member of the 1st Raiders to die in action on Guadalcanal. On 13 October a convoy delivered the Army's 164th Infantry to the island and embarked the raider battalion for transport to New Caledonia. There were barely 200 effectives left in the unit—just a quarter of the battalion's original strength.

THE LONG PATROL

Not long after the departure of the 1st Raiders, it was the turn of the 2d Raiders to fight on Guadalcanal. Carlson's outfit had been refitting in Hawaii after the Midway and Makin battles. In early September the unit boarded a transport for Espiritu Santo in the New Hebrides, the primary staging area for most reinforcements going to the southern Solomons. There they continued training until Rear Admiral Richmond Kelly Turner (Commander, Amphibious Force, South Pacific) decided to land a force at Aola Bay on the northeast coast of Guadalcanal to build another airfield. He assigned Carlson and two companies of raiders to secure the beachhead for an Army battalion, Seabees, and a Marine defense battalion. The *McKean* and *Manley* placed Companies C and E ashore on the morning of 4 November. There was no opposition, though it soon became apparent the swampy jungle was no place to put an airfield.

On 5 November Vandegrift sent a message to Carlson by airdrop. Army and Marine elements were moving east from the perimeter to mop up a large force of Japanese located near the Metapona River. This enemy unit, the *230th Infantry Regiment*, had cut its way through the jungle from the west as part of a late-October attack on Edson's Ridge by the *Sendai Division*. For various reasons, the *230th* had failed to participate in the attack, and then had completed a circumnavigation of the Marine perimeter to reach its current location in the east. The Tokyo Express had recently reinforced it with a battalion of the *228th Infantry*. Vandegrift wanted the raiders to march from Aola and harass the Japanese from the rear. Carlson set out with his force on 6 November, with a coastwatcher and several native scouts as guides. Among the islanders was Sergeant Major Jacob Vouza, already a hero in the campaign. The men initially carried four days of canned rations.

The raiders moved inland before heading west. The trails were narrow and overgrown, but the native scouts proved invaluable in leading the way. On 8 November the point ran into a small Japanese ambush near Reko. The Marines killed two Japanese; one native suffered wounds. The next day the column reached Binu, a village on the Balesuna River eight miles from the coast. There Carlson halted while his patrols made contact with Marine and Army units closing in on the main Japanese force.

On 10 November Companies B, D, and F of the 2d Raiders landed at Tasimboko and moved overland to join up with their commander. (Company D was only a platoon at this point, since Carlson had used most of its manpower to fill out the remaining companies prior to departing Espiritu Santo.) From that point on the raiders also received periodic resupplies, usually via native porters dropped on the coast by Higgins boats. Rations were generally tea, rice, raisins, and bacon—the type of portable guerrilla food Carlson thrived on—reinforced by an occasional D-ration chocolate bar.

On the nights of 9 and 10 November about 3,000 Japanese escaped from the American ring encircling them on the Metapona. They were hungry and tired, and probably dispirited now that they had orders to retrace their steps back to the western side of the perimeter. But they were still a formidable force.

On the 11th the 2d Raiders had four companies out on independent patrols while the fifth guarded the base camp at Binu. Each unit had a TBX radio. At mid-morning one outfit made contact with a patrol from 1st Battalion, 7th Marines, and learned of the enemy breakout. A few minutes later Company C ran into a large force of Japanese near Asamama on the Metapona River. The Marines had been crossing a wide grassy area. When the advance guard entered a wooded area on the opposite side it surprised the enemy in their bivouac. In the initial action, the advance guard inflicted significant casualties on the Japanese, but lost five men killed and three wounded. In short order the enemy had the remainder of the company pinned down in the open with rifle, machine gun, and mortar fire.

Carlson vectored two of his patrols in that direction to assist, and dispatched one platoon from the base camp. As it crossed the Metapona to reach the main battle, Company E tangled with another enemy group coming in the opposite direction. The more numerous Japanese initially forced the Marines to withdraw, but Major Richard T. Washburn reorganized his company and counterattacked the enemy as they attempted to cross the river. The raiders inflicted significant casualties on their opponent, but could not push through to link up with Charlie Company. In mid-afternoon, Carlson himself led Company F toward Asamama.

By the time he arrived, Company C had extricated itself under covering fire from its own 60mm mortars. Carlson called in two dive bombers on the enemy, ordered Company E to break off its independent action, and launched Company F in a flanking attack against the main Japanese force. Those raiders completed the maneuver by dusk, only to find the enemy position abandoned. The battalion assembled back at Binu that night. There Company D reported that it had run into yet another group of enemy and been pinned down for most of the afternoon. The understrength unit had lost two killed and one wounded.

On 12 November Carlson led Companies B and E back to the woods at Asamama. Throughout the day enemy messengers attempted to enter the bivouac site under the mistaken notion that it still belonged to their side; the raiders killed 25 of them. In the afternoon Carlson ordered Company C to join him there. The next day he observed enemy units moving in the vicinity, and he placed artillery and mortar fire on five separate groups. After each such mission the raiders dealt with Japanese survivors trying to make their way into the woods. On 14 November Carlson decided to pull back to Binu. That same day a Company F patrol wiped out a 15-man enemy outpost that had been reported by native scouts.

After a brief period to rest and replenish at Binu, the 2d Raiders moved their base camp to Asamama on 15 November. During two days of patrolling from that site, Carlson determined that the main enemy force had departed the area. At Vandegrift's request, the raider commander entered the perimeter on 17 November. Vandegrift directed Carlson to search for "Pistol Pete," an enemy artillery piece that regularly shelled the airfield. The battalion also was to seek out trails circling the perimeter, and any Japanese units operating to the south. The raiders moved forward to the Tenaru River over the next few days.

On 25 November Company A arrived from Espiritu Santo and joined the battalion. For the next few days the 2d Raiders divided into three combat teams of two companies apiece, with each operating from its own patrol base. Each day they moved farther into the interior of the island, in the area between the headwaters of the Tenaru and Lunga rivers. Carlson remained with the center team, from which point he could quickly reinforce either of the flank detachments.

On 30 November the battalion crossed over the steep ridgeline that divided the valleys of the Tenaru and Lunga. Discovery of a telephone wire led the raiders to a large bivouac site, which held an unattended 75mm mountain gun and a 37mm antitank gun. Marines removed key parts of the weapons and scattered them down the hillside. Farther on the advance guard entered yet another bivouac site, this one occupied by 100 Japanese. Both sides were equally surprised, but Corporal John Yancey charged into the group firing his automatic weapon and calling for his squad to follow. The more numerous enemy were at a disadvantage since their arms were stacked out of reach. The handful of raiders routed the Japanese and killed 75. Carlson called it "the most spectacular of any of our engagements." For this feat Yancey earned the first of his two Navy Crosses (the second came years later in Korea).

The next day, 1 December, a Douglas R4D Skytrain transport air-dropped badly needed rations, as well as orders for the battalion to enter the perimeter, Carlson asked for a few more days in the field and got it. On 3 December he held a "Gung Ho" meeting to motivate his exhausted men for one more effort. Then he divided the 2d Raiders in half, sending the companies with the most field time down to Marine lines. The rest he led up to the top of Mount Austen, where a raider patrol had discovered a strong but abandoned Japanese position. The force had barely reached their objective when they encountered an enemy platoon approaching from a different direction. After a two-hour fire fight and two attempts at a double envelopment, the Marines finally wiped out their opponents. The result was 25 enemy dead at a cost of four wounded Marines (one of whom died soon after). The raiders spent a tough night on the mountain, since there was no water available and their canteens were empty. The next day Carlson led the force down into the Marine perimeter, but not without one last skirmish. Seven Japanese ambushed the point and succeeded in killing four men before the raiders wiped them out.

The long patrol of the 2d Raiders was extremely successful from a tactical point of view. The battalion had killed 488 enemy soldiers at a cost of 16 dead and 18 wounded. Carlson's subsequent report praised his guerrilla tactics, which undoubtedly played an important role in the favorable exchange ratio. Far away from the Marine perimeter, the Japanese became careless and allowed themselves to be surprised on a regular basis, a phenomenon other Marine units had exploited earlier in the campaign. Since the 2d Raiders operated exclusively in the enemy rear, they reaped the benefit of their own stealthiness and this Japanese weakness.

The stated casualty figures, however, did not reflect the true cost to the Marines. During the course of the operation, the 2d Raiders had evacuated 225 men to the rear due to severe illness, primarily malaria, dysentery, and ringworm. Although sickness was common on Guadalcanal, Carlson's men became disabled at an astonishing rate due to inadequate rations and the rough conditions, factors that had diminished significantly by that point in the campaign for other American units. Since only two raider companies had spent the entire month in combat, the effect was actually worse than those numbers indicated. Companies C and F had landed at Aola Bay with 133 officers and men each. They entered the perimeter on 4 December with a combined total of 57 Marines, barely one-fifth their original strength. Things would have been worse, except for the efforts of native carriers to keep the raiders supplied. Guerrilla tactics inflicted heavy casualties on the enemy, but at an equally high cost in friendly manpower.

Nevertheless, the 2d Raiders could hold their heads high. Vandegrift cited them for "the consumate skill displayed in the conduct of operations, for the training, stamina and fortitude displayed by all members of the battalion, and for its commendable aggressive spirit and high morale."

THE RAIDER LEGACY

While the 2d Raider Regiment had been fighting on Bougainville, the raiders who had participated in the New Georgia campaign had been recuperating and training in the rear. Both the 1st and 4th Battalions enjoyed a month of leave in New Zealand, after which they returned to their base camps in New Caledonia. Just after Christmas 1943 Colonel Liversedge detached and passed command of the 1st Raider Regiment to Lieutenant Colonel Samuel D. Puller (the younger brother of "Chesty"

Puller). The regiment embarked on 21 January and arrived at Guadalcanal three days later. In short order the 2d Raider Regiment disbanded and folded into the 1st, with Shapley taking command of the combined unit and Puller becoming the executive officer.

Bougainville, however, was the last combat action for any raider unit. Events had conspired to sound the death knell of the raiders. The main factor was the unprecedented expansion of the Corps. In late 1943 there were four divisions, with another two on the drawing boards. Even though there were now nearly half a million Marines, there never seemed to be enough men to create the new battalions needed for the 5th and 6th Divisions. In addition to the usual drains like training and transients, the Corps had committed large numbers to specialty units: defense battalions, parachute battalions, raider battalions, barrage balloon detachments, and many others. Since there was no prospect of increasing the Corps beyond 500,000 men, the only way to add combat divisions was to delete other organizations.

Another factor was the changing nature of the Pacific war. In the desperate early days of 1942 there was a potential need for commando-type units that could strike deep in enemy territory and keep the Japanese off balance while the United States caught its breath. However, there had been only one such operation and it had not been a complete success. The development of the amphibian tractor and improved fire support also had removed the need for the light assault units envisioned by Holland Smith at the beginning of the war. Since then the raiders generally had performed the same missions as any infantry battalion. Sometimes this meant that their training and talent were wasted, as happened on Bougainville and Pavuvu. In other cases, the quick but lightly armed raiders suffered because they lacked the firepower of a line outfit. The failure at Bairoko could be partially traced to that fact. With many large-scale amphibious assaults to come against well-defended islands, there was no foreseeable requirement for the particular strengths of the raiders.

Finally, there was institutional opposition to the existence of an elite force within the already elite Corps. The personnel and equipment priorities given to the first two raider battalions at a time of general scarcity had further fueled enmity toward these units. Now that the war was progressing toward victory, there was less interest on the part of outsiders in meddling in the details of Marine Corps organization. Just as important, two senior officers who had keenly felt pain at the birth of the raiders—Vandegrift and Thomas—were now coming into positions where they could do something about it. On 1 January 1944 Vandegrift became Commandant of the Marine Corps and he made Thomas the Director of Plans and Policies.

In mid-December 1943 Thomas' predecessor at HQMC had already set the wheels in motion to disband the raiders and the parachutists. Among the reasons cited in his study was that such "handpicked outfits . . . are detrimental to morale of other troops." A week later, a Marine officer on the Chief of Naval Operation's staff forwarded a memorandum through the Navy chain of command noting that the Corps "feels that any operation so far carried out by raiders could have been performed equally well by a standard organization specially trained for that specific mission." The CNO concurred in the suggestion to disband the special units, and Vandegrift gladly promulgated the change on 8 January 1944. This gave Thomas everything he wanted—fresh manpower from the deleted units and their stateside training establishments, as well as simplified supply requirements due to increased uniformity.

The raiders did not entirely disappear. On 1 February the 1st Raider Regiment was redesignated the 4th Marines, thus assuming the lineage of the regiment that had garrisoned Shanghai in the interwar years and fought so gallantly on Bataan and Corrigedor. The 1st, 3d, and 4th Raider Battalions became respectively the 1st, 3d, and 2d Battalions of the 4th Marines. The 2d Raider Battalion filled out the regimental weapons company. Personnel in the Raider Training Center transferred to the newly formed 5th Marine Division. Leavened with new men, the 4th Marines went on to earn additional distinctions in the assaults on Guam and Okinawa. At the close of the war, the regiment joined the occupation forces in Japan and participated in the release from POW compounds of the remaining members of the old 4th Marines.

The commanders in the Pacific Theater may not have properly used the raiders, but the few thousand men of those elite units bequeathed a legacy of courage and competence not surpassed by any other Marine battalion. The spirit of the raiders lives on today in the Marine Corps' Special Operations Capable battalions. These infantry units, specifically trained for many of the same missions as the raiders, routinely deploy with amphibious ready groups around the globe.

Sources

"Snipers, Brothers" from *Sniper: American Single-Shot Warriors in Iraq and Afghanistan*. Gina Cavallaro, with Matt Larsen. Guilford, CT: Lyons Press, 2010.

"The Best-Laid Plans: Mission to Tehran" excerpt from *Inside Delta Force: The Story of America's Elite Counterterrorist Unit* by Eric Haney, copyright © 2002 by Eric L. Haney. Used by permission of Dell Publishing, an imprint of Random House, a division of Penguin Random House LLC. All rights reserved.

"Riding with Quantrell" from *The Story of Cole Younger, by Himself, Being an Autobiography of the Missouri Guerrilla Captain and Outlaw, His Capture and Prison Life, and the Only Authentic Account of the Northfield Raid Ever Published*. Cole Younger. Chicago: The Henneberry Company, 1903.

"Kicking Charlie's Ass" excerpt from *13 Cent Killers: The 5th Marine Snipers in Vietnam* by John Culbertson, copyright © 2003 by John J. Culbertson. Used by permission of Presidio Press, an imprint of Random House, a division of Penguin Random House LLC. All rights reserved.

"'Daring beyond the Point of Martial Prudence'" from *Gray Raiders of the Sea*. Chester G. Hearn. Camden, Maine: The McGraw-Hill Companies/International Marine, 1992.

"Jumping into North Korea" excerpt from *In the Devil's Shadow: U.N. Special Operations During the Korean War*. Michael E. Haas. Annapolis, MD: Naval Institute Press, 2000.

"The Green Faced Frogmen, An Oral History" excerpt from *Everything We Had: An Oral History of the Vietnam War* by Al Santoli, copyright © 1981 by Albert Santoli and Vietnam Veterans of America. Used by permission of Random House, an imprint and division of Penguin Random House LLC. All rights reserved.

"The Final Battle for Murphy's Ridge" from *Lone Survivor* by Marcus Luttrell with Patrick Robinson. Copyright © 2007 by Marcus Lutrell. Reprinted with the permission of Little, Brown and Company.

"The Marauders' First Mission: Walawbum" from *Merrill's Marauders*, firsthand battle report of the group's first action. First printed by the Historical Division, War Department, for the American Forces in Action series, 1945. CMH Pub 100-4.

"The First Rangers: Fighting the French and Indians" from *Ben Comee: A Tale of Rogers's Rangers*. M. J. Canavan. New York: The MacMillan Company, 1922.

"Rebel Raider: Mosby the Gray Ghost" from *Rebel Raider*. H. Beam Piper. First published in *True: The Man's Magazine*, 1950.

"The Marine Raiders of the Pacific" from *From Makin to Bougainville: Marine Raiders in the Pacific War*. Major Jon T. Hoffman. Marines in World War II Commemorative Series.